BULLY ABLE LEADER

BULLY ABLE LEADER

THE STORY OF A FIGHTER-BOMBER PILOT IN THE KOREAN WAR

LT. GEN. GEORGE G. LOVING
USAF (RET.)

STACKPOLE BOOKS

Published by
STACKPOLE BOOKS
5067 Ritter Road
Mechanicsburg, PA 17055
www.stackpolebooks.com

Printed in the United States of America

10 9 8 7 6 5 4 3 2 1

Library of Congress Cataloging-in-Publication Data

Loving, George G., 1923–
    Bully Able Leader : the story of a fighter-bomber pilot in the Korean War / George G. Loving.
        p. cm.
    Includes index.
    ISBN 978-0-8117-1026-8   4748 4257   09/11
    1. Loving, George G., 1923–   2. Korean War, 1950–1953—Personal narratives, American. 3. Korean War, 1950–1953—Aerial operations, American. 4. Fighter pilots—United States—Biography. I. Title.
    DS921.6.L784 2011
    951.904'248—dc22
    [B]
                                              2011007896

Contents

Preface

While some in recent years have taken to calling the Korean War "The Forgotten War," the memory remains strong for those of us who fought in it. As a fighter-bomber pilot, my assignment was to do battle with North Korean and Chinese soldiers and attack enemy targets on the ground—artillery pieces, tanks, trucks, trains, bridges, communications facilities, supply dumps, airfields, and antiaircraft weapons. Some of these targets were heavily defended by enemy soldiers intent on killing any fighter-bomber pilot within their reach.

Flying at high speed close to the ground—sometimes in foul weather, often in mountainous terrain, and diving repeatedly to strafe and launch rockets, napalm, and bombs, all the while being under fire by enemy soldiers—was exciting and dangerous. A World War II Soviet attack pilot who flew similar missions described the experience as "a dance with death." Although this may or may not accurately describe the challenge that faced fighter-bomber pilots in the Korean War, such a description never occurred to me during my combat tour. I'm glad that it didn't. I was there as a volunteer, and while I knew I wasn't bullet-proof, I held to the belief that I would survive, that the other guy would buy the farm, not me. And I was right.

This is the first time this story has been told. Occasionally over the years, in conversations with old comrades at squadron reunions, I have spoken briefly of some particularly amusing or unusual incident, and a description of one combat mission found its way into print some years ago, but not until now, more than half a century later, have I set forth a comprehensive account of my Korean War experiences. At a book signing in 2003, shortly after my World War II memoir* was published, an old-timer asked me, "What took you so long?" I replied that there was the small matter of earning a living that occupied my attention for the forty-four years following the war, and then after my retirement, the golf course and fishing received priority. But in my spare time, I conducted research for the World War II book and sporadically did some writing over a period of ten years. It was not an easy project. But even so, two years after that book signing, I decided to tackle my Korean War memoir. This project took "only" five years.

As exciting as my assignment was, it was rarely possible to evaluate from the air the full impact of my combat efforts. Sometimes, this was because the enemy was dug in and camouflaged, hidden by foliage and terrain, but even when the target was visible and I knew I had destroyed it, I could often only guess at the impact on the enemy. Occasionally, we would get a "well done" from a forward air controller for striking a heavy blow on an enemy formation, or we could see the results of dive-bombing a bridge, or we could count the burning North Korean or Chinese vehicles we had strafed. Nevertheless, while the number of trucks blasted or troops killed or bridges destroyed might indicate success on a given mission, the aggregate of such successes during a tour of combat service just didn't resonate with us as a yardstick of success. Instead, our measure of success was simple: survival equaled success. Although seldom the recipients of public notice or accolades, at the end of their combat tours, the fighter-bomber pilots with whom I flew had the satisfaction of knowing that they had unflinchingly done their duty and had survived. For them, that was success.

---

* *Woodbine Red Leader: A P-51 Mustang Ace in the Mediterranean Theater* (New York: Ballantine Books, 2003).

Introduction

For centuries, the great powers of northeast Asia sought to control the Korean peninsula. Located at the crossroads between powerful and expansionist-minded neighbors, Korea has suffered from repeated invasions and encroachments—in modern times by China, Japan, and Russia. For almost a thousand years prior to 1895, Korea acknowledged a particular relationship to China based on Chinese cultural influences, the superiority of the Chinese state, and China's enforced claim of suzerainty.

Korea's modern period began in 1876 with the signing of a trade treaty with Japan. Thereafter, Japanese influence in Korea increased steadily while China's influence began to wane. These two great Asian powers engaged in open armed conflict in Korea during 1894–95, when they fought for control of the strategic peninsula during the Sino-Japanese War. Japan was the unexpected victor and forced China to relinquish its tutelage over Korea and recognize the independence of Korea.

Japanese attempts to consolidate power in Korea met with considerable internal resistance because of heavy-handed efforts to reform the country. Russia was quick to take advantage of this development and became increasingly involved in Korean affairs to the detriment of

Japanese influence. This lead to the Russo-Japanese War (1904–05), in which Japan soundly defeated Russia, forcing the recognition of Japan's predominant interests in Korea.

In the years that followed the Russo-Japanese War, Japan proceeded to assume full control over Korea's economic, political, and social affairs. In 1910, Japan formally annexed Korea and thereafter ruled her as a colony until the end of World War II.

Two years before the end of World War II, in December 1943, President Franklin Roosevelt, Prime Minister Winston Churchill, and Generalissimo Chiang Kai-shek pledged in the Cairo Declaration that "the aforesaid three great powers, mindful of the enslavement of the people of Korea, are determined that in due course Korea shall be free and independent." At the Yalta Conference in early 1945, the subject of a multipower trusteeship for Korea was discussed, but no decision was made.

The Allied chiefs convened for a final wartime meeting at Potsdam, Germany, in July 1945. Among other matters, the provisions of the Cairo Declaration were reaffirmed with respect to Korea, but it was further agreed that the question of colonies and trusteeships would be referred to the foreign ministers for later discussion. The American nuclear bombing of Hiroshima occurred on August 6, followed by Nagasaki on August 9. In between, on August 8, 1945, the Soviets entered the war against Japan and invaded Korea. The Japanese surrender offer came on August 10.

The precipitous conclusion of the war found the United States unprepared for the role it was destined to play in Korea. With the end of the war in September 1945, the United States was faced with the monumental task of taking the surrender of Japanese troops all over the Pacific and in Asia as well. As a temporary measure, the United States proposed to the Soviet Union that the Soviets take the surrender of Japanese troops in Korea above the 38th parallel while the United States would take the surrender of those below, and that is what happened.

The American military authorities in Korea were faced with a massive challenge that involved, among other things, the disarmament and evacuation to Japan of 200,000 Japanese troops, the repatriation to

Korea of some 2 million Koreans from all over Asia, and the sorting out of the role Koreans would play in governing Korea. It didn't take long before what proved to be a far more serious challenge arose: the unfriendly and uncooperative attitudes on the part of the Soviets north of the 38th parallel. The Soviets cut off electricity for an area north of Seoul, and the Soviet commander declined the American commander's invitation to discuss various economic and political problems arising from the arbitrary division of Korea into two parts, with virtually all movement between the zones curtailed.

The division of Korea had serious economic implications. Two-thirds of the people and most of the food supply were located in the southern zone while the greater part of the country's mineral wealth and heavy industry was in the north. American attempts to secure Soviet cooperation in relaxing travel restrictions between the two zones and to achieve unification of the economy were to no avail. The Soviet commander indicated that matters of unification could only be resolved by the government of the occupying powers.

From December 1945 until July 1947, more than forty formal diplomatic meetings between Soviet and American diplomats were held to discuss the future of Korea. The United States wanted all political and social parties consulted in the formation of a provisional democratic Korean government. The Soviets would not agree. They insisted on excluding most of the parties so that the communist minority would remain in a position of overwhelming influence. It was obvious that further discussion would be fruitless.

In the south, elected representatives convened as a national assembly in May 1948 and adopted a constitution. Syngmann Rhee was elected President of the Republic of Korea in July, and the government of the Republic of Korea (ROK) was formally inaugurated on August 15. The American military government was terminated on the same day.

In the northern zone, the Soviets were making final preparations to formally install a communist regime, the Democratic People's Republic of Korea, a government that was proclaimed in September 1948. The Soviets announced that all of their forces would be withdrawn from Korea by the end of 1948, and the United States withdrew all except a

500-man training detachment by mid-1949. The United States continued to provide substantial economic assistance to the Republic of
Korea.

In a speech on January 12, 1950, Secretary of State Dean Acheson
spoke of an American defensive perimeter in the Pacific area. The
perimeter, he noted, "runs along the Aleutians to Japan and then goes to
the Ryukyus" and "from the Ryukyus to the Philippine Islands." He
further stated that "so far as the military security of other areas of the
Pacific is concerned, it must be clear that no person can guarantee these
areas against military attack." Should such an attack occur, "the initial
reliance must be on the people attacked to resist it and then upon the
commitments of the entire civilized world under the Charter of the
United Nations." Seven months earlier, the United States had completed
the withdrawal of its troops from Korea. Secretary Acheson now seemed
to be saying that the United States disclaimed unilateral responsibility
for the future security of Korea, leaving that job to the United Nations.

During the six months preceding Dean Acheson's statement, border
incidents, skirmishes, and firefights involving the North Korean and
Republic of Korea forces took place with such frequency that the
United Nations commission warned the General Assembly of the growing possibility of full-scale civil war. Such activities continued into 1950
as the North Koreans made final preparations for war.

PART 1

World War II P-51 Mustang Ace Goes to War in Korea

Chapter 1

Early in the morning on June 25, 1950, North Korea launched an all-out military offensive against the Republic of Korea (ROK). The United States' response was swift. That same day, it obtained a United Nations Security Council resolution condemning the attack, and President Harry S Truman ordered Gen. Douglas MacArthur, the American military commander in the region, to furnish ships and planes to assist and protect the evacuation of American dependents from Korea. The United States Seventh Fleet was placed under MacArthur's command and ordered to move northward to protect the evacuation. MacArthur was to furnish ammunition and supplies to the Republic of Korea Army (ROKA).

On the following day, as the situation worsened, President Truman ordered MacArthur to use his air and naval forces to support the ROK, but only south of the 38th parallel. Three days later, the president authorized MacArthur to extend air operations into North Korea and to dispatch U.S. Army combat and service troops to Korea to ensure the retention of ports and airfields at Pusan and Chinhae. South Korea's capital city, Seoul, fell to the North Koreans on June 28. On June 30, as the situation was rapidly deteriorating, the president authorized "full utilization of the Army-Navy-Air team."

As soon as I heard the news that the Air Force would be involved in the conflict, I knew that I would soon be heading back to the Far East to fight in yet another war.

Almost every able-bodied man in the United States entered the armed forces during World War II. I was among those who answered the call to colors, serving in the U.S. Army Air Forces as a fighter pilot. Following nineteen months of training, I joined the 31st Fighter Group in Italy in October 1943 and flew 101 combat missions in Spitfire Mark V and Mark IX aircraft. We flew on patrols to protect U.S. Army and Allied ground forces fighting near Cassino and on the Anzio beachhead from attacks by German fighters and bombers. We also provided escort for light and medium bombers on missions to attack targets in northern Italy.

After I had been in the outfit for five months, the 31st Fighter Group was assigned a different mission and a different airplane: the Air Forces' most modern fighter, the P-51 Mustang, a long-range high-performance airplane. Our new mission was to participate in the great strategic air offensive against German military, oil, manufacturing, and transportation targets across Europe. My fighter group was assigned to the Fifteenth Air Force, which was responsible for targets in southern and eastern Europe, while the Eighth Air Force, based in England, took care of targets in western Europe.

The Fifteenth Air Force employed hundreds of heavy bombers—B-17s and B-24s—to attack targets all across southern and eastern Europe, including northern Italy, southern Germany and France, Austria, Bulgaria, Czechoslovakia, Poland, Hungary, Romania, and Yugoslavia. The 31st Fighter Group, one of seven fighter groups in Italy that were each equipped with seventy-five airplanes, provided vital escort to protect the bombers against attacks by German fighter aircraft and those of Germany's allies.

During my five months as a Mustang pilot, I flew fifty combat missions that took me to targets in each of the countries mentioned

above. I participated in many air battles, witnessed a great deal of car-
nage, and was among the lucky ones who survived and achieved the
kind of success that every fighter pilot dreams about. I earned the designation "ace" by shooting down five enemy airplanes. I also damaged
two others in aerial combat. My three closest friends weren't so fortunate: they all went down—two were listed as missing in action while
the third became a prisoner of war. The two who were missing were
never found.

I flew almost all of my Mustang missions as a flight or squadron
leader, as well as some as group leader of all three squadrons, so I gained
a good bit of leadership experience. During my ten-month assignment
with the 31st Fighter Group, I advanced from second lieutenant to captain, and I had just turned twenty-one years old when I departed the
group for an assignment in the United States.

My postcombat assignment was as a P-47 Thunderbolt instructor at
Millville Army Airfield in New Jersey. Prior to arriving at Millville, I
spent a few weeks at the P-47 instructors' school at Providence, Rhode
Island. Millville was an enjoyable assignment. My job was to teach fledg-
ling P-47 pilots how to employ the airplane effectively as a weapon.
Strafing, dive- and skip-bombing, and aerial gunnery were the principal
activities. We had a first-rate bombing range near the base, with the out-
line of an aircraft carrier marked out on the ground as a bombing target,
as well as mock troops, tanks, and vehicles along roads and in the woods
for strafing practice. We conducted aerial gunnery against towed targets
over the Atlantic Ocean just off Atlantic City.

★ ★ ★

Ambler Thomasson and I (we had been high-school sweethearts in
Lynchburg, Virginia) were married five months after I returned from
overseas in January 1945. We traveled to New York City on our honey-
moon and enjoyed the sightseeing and nightlife. We stayed at Millville
Army Airfield until it was closed the month after the war ended in
September 1945. We then moved to Shaw Army Air Field at Sumter,
South Carolina.

With the war over, Shaw became a holding base—a place where personnel were congregated until it was decided what to do with them. Soon after I arrived at Shaw, the Army announced that applications for regular commissions would be accepted. This was big news: except for graduating West Point cadets, no regular commission had been granted during the war. In anticipation of this, I had obtained letters of recommendation from senior officers with whom I had flown in combat. These proved to be important. A week or two after I made application and had met a board of examining Army officers, I was elated to be among the four who were selected for a regular commission from among the many applicants at Shaw.

After nine months at Shaw, during which I was in command of a squadron of communications personnel, I received orders to proceed overseas, and in August 1946, I arrived at Itazuke Air Base, located near Fukuoka, Japan, on the main island of Kyushu. Here I would be a part of the U.S. occupation force. Since there was no family housing available, Ambler was not permitted to accompany me. But upon arriving at Itazuke, I learned that houses were under construction, financed by the Japanese as part of the reparations they were required to pay as the defeated party in World War II. After several months, I was assigned a newly constructed duplex that was fully furnished with everything from knives, forks, spoons, glasses, table cloths, and napkins to stove, refrigerator, vacuum cleaner, sheets, and pillow cases. At that point, Ambler was given authorization to proceed to Japan. She would come via ship—the USS *Hope*, a U.S. Army hospital ship—from San Francisco to Yokohama, where I would meet her. Then we would travel by rail to Fukuoka.

As I made plans to go to Yokohama, I learned that the American military governor of the Fukuoka region had at his disposal a rather fancy rail car containing sleeping compartments, a spacious lounge and dining area, and a tiny kitchen. If not otherwise being used, he had from time to time made it available to other officers. In response to my inquiry, I learned that he would permit its use for a round trip to Yokohama, but only to a field-grade officer. That's when I called the several Air Force units on Kyushu to find out if such an officer was planning a trip to Yokohama to meet the *Hope*. I was successful. The major I located was delighted to learn of the military governor's rail car, and he set about making the arrangements.

Three of us—the major and I, plus a lieutenant—boarded the rail car at Fukuoka station; it was attached as the last car to a passenger train headed to Tokyo. We brought food for several days as well as a supply of beer and booze. A Japanese cook and a waiter/porter greeted us as we came aboard, and it was immediately clear this was going to be a comfortable trip. The food, cooked over a small charcoal fire, was surprisingly good, and the scenery was interesting. At Tokyo's main station, after our car was disconnected, we were shunted over to Yokohama, where the car was parked on a siding connected to a donkey engine that provided steam and electricity.

At Yokohama's port, I wrangled my way aboard a tug that was going out to meet the USS *Hope* and was surprised and delighted to spot Ambler on deck standing against the railing. Thanks to my vigorous waving, she soon spotted me, and then it was all smiles from the two of us. To welcome our wives aboard our rail chariot, before we left for the port, we had brought aboard fresh flowers and fruit, a large celebratory cake, and a couple of bottles of champagne. We travelled like potentates all the way back to Fukuoka.

Initially, I was assigned as a staff officer in the headquarters of the 315th Air Division, which oversaw all Army Air Forces units in western Japan. My job assignment came about in a surprising way. During an interview to determine where I would be assigned, the major who headed the officer personnel section asked if I had a preference of fighter groups, the 475th at Itazuke Air Base or the 8th at Ashiya Air Base. I told him that up to this point in my career, all I had done was fly airplanes and that I would now like get some broader experience. Upon hearing this, his eyes lit up. He picked up my file, told me he would be right back, and walked out of the office. He returned a few minutes later and asked me to accompany him to the director of personnel's office. The director, Lt. Col. Elmer Hoelscher, was an old-timer who had headed a Civilian Conservation Corps camp in the 1930s during the Depression. He was highly competent, friendly, soft spoken, and supportive of his subordinates. He looked over my file and asked some questions about my background and interests. I didn't grasp where the conversation was leading until Hoescher informed me that he was assigning me to take the major's job as chief of officer personnel. He assured me that I would get some very valuable experience in the job.

The major whom I replaced departed within a few days, and I was left to shift for myself. I knew next to nothing about staff work and even less about the personnel matters for which I was now responsible. If I was going to succeed, I would have to get moving. I set about reading all of the personnel directives issued by higher headquarters. Then I went through the several hundred documents in the office filing cabinet, paper by paper. Here, documented in detail, were all of the personnel actions taken over the past three years. This was my guide for the future. It would serve me well.

One of the most interesting projects I worked on was "The Purge." That was not the official title, just my label for a project initiated in Washington to rid the officer corps of marginal performers. We were directed to establish a board of officers at each base to review the records of all assigned officers with the objective of identifying those with marginal potential. I was in charge of organizing and managing that effort.

At the peak of World War II, the Army Air Forces (AAF) contained 243 combat groups and 2,282,000 personnel in uniform. Following the pell-mell demobilization which followed the war, the number of combat groups shrunk to 52, and by May 1947, the AAF had only 303,600 military personnel remaining. The ranks were decimated as more than eight out of ten uniformed personnel went home. There was still plenty of equipment left, but few men to repair it. However, we did not feel the full impact of demobilization in Japan because priority was given to manning the overseas combat groups at full strength. But not all of the personnel were of top quality.

The boards established at each base did their job, and we received from them lists containing the names of the lowest-performing 10 percent of their assigned officers. After staff review and a few adjustments, the 315th Air Division's commander approved the list and forwarded it to our higher headquarters, the Fifth Air Force. A few weeks later, those on the list received orders transferring them to the States for discharge. I felt sorry for them, but I knew this was a step the AAF had to take in order to be a first-class fighting force. Closely related to this action was the Air Force's seemingly cautious program of granting regular commissions. Only a handful had been granted up to 1947. Clearly, this was considered so important that it was not to be rushed. Evidently, the few regular commissions handed out in the year following the end of the war went to individuals with outstanding war records—officers the AAF did not want to lose.

In my assignment as a staff officer, I gained valuable experience in the workings of a higher headquarters and in conducting staff work. During this period, I was attached for flying to a fighter squadron where I flew a P-51 Mustang every week to keep my hand in.

✯ ✯ ✯

The last year of my two-and-a-half-year assignment in Japan was the most satisfying. I was assigned to command the 433rd Fighter Squadron, 475th Fighter Group, a P-51 Mustang outfit, and I was elated. Normally, a lieutenant colonel commanded a fighter squadron, but there was none available, and even though I was only a captain, I received the command.

I had flown a few hours each month with squadron to keep proficient in the P-51, so I knew most of the twenty-five pilots. About a quarter of them were combat-experienced.

There were four standouts in the squadron. Capt. Frank O. Lux had flown combat missions in Europe during World War II and went by the nickname Soapy (based on Lux, a popular brand of soap). Capt. Ras B. Cypert, the squadron operations officer, was very likeable, a smooth talker from Texas who wore a Clark Gable mustache and was particular about his appearance; an outdoorsman, he was especially proud of his fine English shotgun, engraved with pheasants on the wing, and his custom-made golf clubs. Capt. Clark Manning, a World War II combat veteran from Pennsylvania, had flown P-40s and P-51s in China from August 1944 until the war ended. He was credited with destroying one

Japanese fighter in the air and another on the ground. A friendly, unassuming fellow who had something of a studious air about him, he served as squadron adjutant.

No one was likely to forget 1st Lt. Claire "Pat" Chennault, a laid-back good old boy from Louisiana. His father was Lt. Gen. Claire L. Chennault of Flying Tiger fame. During World War II, even though Pat had a short leg and wore an elevated shoe, he was given a given a waiver and accepted for pilot training. Afterwards, he flew combat missions in Europe, primarily escorting bombers, and was credited with destroying two enemy aircraft. Friendly and outgoing, he had frank opinions on many subjects. Should we go to war, I would depend on these four stalwarts to provide leadership on combat missions.

Each pilot flew a minimum of twenty-five hours a month, and we adhered to a training syllabus that included formation, night, and instrument flying; cross-country navigation; dive-bombing; strafing; rocketry; and aerial gunnery. This resulted in a high degree of proficiency. We were a spirited bunch, confident in our ability to take on anything that came our way.

Much was going on in our part of the world that led us to believe that the peace that followed the end of World War II would not last forever. Several hundred miles away, the Communist Chinese were beating down our ally, the Chinese Nationalists, and just across the Korea Strait, the Soviets, who occupied the northern portion of Korea, were demonstrating some very hostile behavior. The Cold War was underway, and we viewed the Soviet Union as an enemy.

In June 1948, the Cold War heated up when, in an effort secure full control of Berlin, the Soviets blocked all roads and railroads leading to the French, British, and American sectors of the city. This unexpected move led to a major U.S. operation known as the Berlin Airlift, in which supplies were flown into the city for almost a year. For us, this meant that we had to remain alert. Our fighter group kept two Mustangs on strip alert during daylight hours, ready to scramble should radar pick up unidentified aircraft.

On a quiet Sunday morning shortly after the start of the Berlin Airlift, I was on strip alert as the pilot of one of the two Mustangs parked at the end of the runway. We were ready to scramble at a moment's notice should unidentified aircraft enter our sector. We had been on duty for over an hour, sitting in the cockpit, ready to go, but did not expect any action on a Sunday morning. In every instance to date, the unidentified aircraft had turned out to be friendly, and if scrambled, we expected that we would again discover friendly aircraft. Then we heard the jangle of the field telephone. Scramble! Once we were airborne, I contacted the controller and learned that we were not being sent to intercept unidentified aircraft, but to search for an unidentified submarine. That was a first for me and probably for every pilot in the group. The controller vectored us out to the area of the Korea Strait where a submarine had supposedly been sighted. Our task was to attempt to determine its nationality. We searched for thirty minutes but spotted nothing afloat, not even a fishing boat. Shades of the Cold War, I decided. We did spot a massive waterspout—a menacing phenomenon. We stayed well clear of it.

There has always been friendly rivalry between fighter groups. Someone in our squadron proposed that we should mount a mass "attack" on the 35th Fighter Group located on Johnson Air Base near Tokyo. If we caught them by surprise, we would demonstrate that we were the dominant unit. This would be a morale booster for us and good training as well. I talked with the group commander, Lt. Col. Woodrow Ramsey, about the proposal, doubtful that he would approve it. I believed he was likely to be skittish about any activities out of the ordinary, but to my surprise, he liked the idea and gave his approval.

We flew at low altitude to evade the radar in the Tokyo area, located some 600 miles from Itazuke. We achieved complete surprise and "beat up" the airdrome, all sixteen Mustangs racing across at very low altitude—masters of the sky. (This squadron would be one of the first to enter combat in the Korean War. Some of the pilots from my time with the squadron would be among the first to fight. Almost all of the others would eventually return to participate in the war.)

Six months after I assumed command of the 433rd Fighter Squadron, a lieutenant colonel took my job, and I was reassigned as the 475th Fighter Group operations officer, the next best position in the group for an officer of my grade.

We did little traveling while in Japan. As a result of the war, the economy was in shambles, and the Japanese had little to offer a traveler. However, there was one notable landmark within a day's round trip of from Itazuke: Mount Aso, an active volcano with the world's largest caldera. It was less than three hours away by jeep, our sole means of road transportation, but this posed a problem because my dear wife, Ambler, was pregnant, and our military physicians had decreed that pregnant women must not ride in jeeps because a number of miscarriages were thought to have been triggered by riding in jeeps—all with firm suspension systems—over the mostly unpaved, bumpy roads in our area.

Our solution was to go by train—a seventy-five-minute ride to Kumamoto, where we met our friends Capt. Billy Bob Zellers (his given name, but he preferred to be called Bill) and his wife, Peg. Bill had a reserved, professorial demeanor but flashed a ready smile. He wore a burr haircut, smoked a pipe, and collected stamps. Peg, who had been an elementary school teacher, was attractive and sociable. They had driven from Itazuke in a well-used jeep Bill had purchased for a few hundred dollars at a U.S. Army surplus sale.

From Kumamoto, we drove to the base of Mount Aso, which rose to an elevation of 5,223 feet. The road to the summit was unpaved, which made for slow going. About halfway up, we entered the clouds. Near the 4,000-foot mark, we encountered a Japanese man who signaled that we should not proceed any farther. We didn't understand why and certainly didn't want to abandon our planned trip to the top, so we continued our ascent. As we neared 5,000 feet, the clouds broke, giving us a clear view of the road ahead and the summit just above us. That is when we came upon a crude sign with Japanese characters beneath a depiction of a skull and crossbones—clearly a warning of some kind, but what exactly did it mean? We were within yelling distance of the volcano and decided to take a cautious look. As soon as we reached the rim, we heard a low rumbling. Suddenly, a barrage of stones, some as large as basketballs, came hurtling up, shooting more than fifty feet into the air. There were hundreds of similar stones scattered all around the rim, not far from where we were standing. Equally ominous, there were gaping holes in the roof of a nearby shed that were obviously created by falling stones. We had seen all that we needed to see and quickly retreated back down the mountain. Later, we learned that poisonous volcanic gases could pose a greater danger than the material ejected by the volcano.

Upon arriving back at the Komomoto train station, we learned that we had just missed the train, so we returned to Fukuoka via jeep over eighty miles of bumpy road. Ambler was given the front seat, rather than a rear seat over the springs. Later in the week, Ambler's doctor asked her if she had been riding in jeeps. "Oh, no," she responded. Afterwards, we kept our fingers crossed, hoping that the baby would be all right. As it turned out, the baby survived the visit to Mount Aso and the jeep ride back to Itazuke. Our daughter, Cary Ambler Loving, was born in Fukuoka on December 17, 1946.

My tour of duty in Japan was one of the most enjoyable in my career. In addition to some great flying, we had an active social life—bridge, poker, and many parties, as well as golf and duck hunting. A strict rule decreed no fraternization with the Japanese population, so we lived our lives on base and made many friends there.

Chapter 2

We returned to the United States in January 1949, and I was assigned to the Reserve Officers Training Center at Byrd Field in Richmond, Virginia, with responsibility for the training program. It didn't take me long to get into trouble. At my initial meeting with 100 or so reservists, I said that as a native of Virginia, I was really pleased to be back among fellow Virginians, but I would have to admit that it was something of a comedown to find myself flying training planes again after years of flying Thunderbolts and Mustangs. That innocent comment soon came back to haunt me.

Several weeks later, I received a message instructing me to report to Lt. Gen. Patrick Timberlake, commander of the Ninth Air Force, at his Langley Air Force Base headquarters. I couldn't image why he wanted to see me. After I saluted, he played me a recording of a telephone conversation he had had with Lt. Gen. Elwood R. "Pete" Quesada, who was responsible for Air Force Reserve training nationwide and known for his aggressive nature. General Quesada said he had been informed that there was a newly assigned disgruntled captain by the name of Loving who was in charge of training at Richmond and he wanted him out of there.

General Timberlake asked me what I had to say. I told him exactly what I had said at the meeting of reservists and noted that I was not in any way disgruntled, that I was quite happy to be back in Virginia, my home state, and that I had done a first-class job in organizing and supervising two two-week annual training sessions for reservists, each with 100 in attendance. Then I said to him that I would like to have the opportunity to face my accuser. According to my understanding, I added, that was the way the American system of justice worked. General Timberlake did not signal his agreement or disagreement; he simply terminated the interview. I knew then that I wouldn't be given the opportunity to face my accuser and would never learn who made the spurious charges against me.

A week later, I was reassigned to Headquarters, Ninth Air Force, at Langley Air Force Base and put behind a desk in the personnel section. But other than that, no permanent damage was done since I got off without a black mark on my record. Evidently, General Timberlake didn't believe I had done anything seriously wrong but found it easier to acquiesce to General Quesada's demand than to argue my side of the situation.

I viewed my assignment in the personnel section as akin to purgatory. It wouldn't last forever, I knew, but I had no notion how long I would have to endure. On the bright side, Langley was a great place to be stationed. We lived in fine quarters across the street from the headquarters building where I worked, many different cultural and recreational opportunities were available, and our families were only a few hours away in Lynchburg. Since there was nothing I could do to change the situation, I did the best job I could and bided my time while enjoying life in on the Peninsula (as the locals called the area). It was not until more than a year had passed that my time came.

From the moment I heard of the North Korean invasion of South Korea on June 25, 1950, news of the conflict held my rapt attention. Knowing that my former fighter pilot comrades in Japan would likely be the very first sent to engage the North Korean forces, I was absorbed with every detail of the rapidly changing situation. The first thing I did every morning upon arriving in my office was read the cables that had come into the headquarters overnight. Six days after President Truman's decision to involve our armed forces fully in the conflict, a top-secret cable got my full attention: the commander of Far East Air Forces requested the immediate shipment to Japan of 150 F-51* Mustangs, 75 Mustang pilots, and a whole flock of armorers and Mustang mechanics. The message, passed down from the Pentagon, asked that volunteer pilots be sought—a request that felt as if it was directed at me. I was an experienced Mustang pilot and knew the area. Moreover, this would be a way out of my year-long purgatory, and there was sure to be adventure involved. As a fighter pilot, I felt a strong urge to get involved in the fighting. I took the folder into my boss's office and showed him the message. When he finished reading it, I told him I was a volunteer. Without hesitation, he agreed to release me and wished me well.

My family had grown since its arrival at Langley. Our daughter Betty Page Loving was born on September 26, 1949. That meant that I would be leaving Ambler with two young children. That was a very hard thing to do, heartbreaking for both of us. But my wife was a real trooper—a strong person who understood and accepted that when war came, I would have to go where I was needed. We decided that she would go to Lynchburg, our hometown, to await my return. There was one small problem: although we had just bought a brand-new car, she did not know how to drive. Ambler contacted the salesman of the new Buick and told him that he would have to teach her. He agreed.

As soon as my boss agreed to release me, I began to make hurried preparations for my departure. I wanted to get current in a Mustang before I left so that I would be ready to get right into the fray in Korea without being held up for a formal flight check. Since I hadn't flown one in a long time, such a flight check would have required a written examination and a blindfolded cockpit test before I could fly. The 1st Fighter Group at Langley had switched to jet fighter aircraft, but still possessed an F-51—the last one remaining at Langley—which was used to tow aerial targets. In response to my query, the operations officer said, "Sure, come down at 0800 hours, and we'll have the Mustang ready for you to fly." When I arrived, there was no mention of a written exam or

---

*The designation of the P-51 had been changed to F-51 in 1948. "P" for "Pursuit" was changed to "F" for "Fighter."

blindfolded test, so I just went out and cranked up the bird and went flying for an hour. That made me current in the F-51.

Five days later, I boarded a C-47 twin-engine transport bound for California. It would be a long, tiring trip, ambling along at 150 miles per hour while covering more than 2,600 miles. Passengers in a C-47 are seated in two rows of metal bucket seats installed along the length of the plane, with a single aisle in between. The noise level discouraged conversation, so there was time to think. I wondered just what kind of war I would find in Korea. I was confident that U.S. Air Force fighter pilots would have eliminated the North Korean air force well before I arrived, so unless North Korea's Communist mentor, the Soviet Union, replaced the lost aircraft or entered the war, we wouldn't encounter enemy air opposition. If that was the case, I was likely to be assigned as a fighter-bomber pilot. But would the war end before I arrived? That question troubled me more than any other. I could imagine being stuck for a year or more at some dusty outpost or another unwelcome assignment.

We made a number of stops along the way to pick up Mustang pilots, mechanics, and armorers before we arrived in San Francisco. At the same time, dozens of others were flying in from bases across the United States, and scores of F-51 Mustangs, taken from Air National Guard squadrons, were being flown to San Francisco. Only eight days after I volunteered, we boarded the USS *Boxer*, a Navy aircraft carrier. One hundred forty-five F-51 Mustangs, with their noses cocooned in plastic wrapping to protect the engines against saltwater corrosion, were parked all over the flight deck and hangar decks. The pace of activity was brisk.

For reasons I never learned, I was designated adjutant of the Air Force contingent. I had no idea what this would entail, but the job came with the privilege of boarding the vessel as part of the advance party and having a choice of cabins. It turned out that my duties involved little more than maintaining a roster of the Air Force people aboard and answering an occasional question. I was surprised that I knew only one of the seventy-five Air Force pilots in the contingent: Capt. Frank O. Lux, who had been a member of the 433rd Fighter Squadron when I was in command a couple of years earlier at Itazuke Air Base in Japan.

When I spotted him, I called out, "Soapy, good to see you."

"Good to see you, too, George." Then with a smile, he asked, "What are you doing here?"

I took the bait. "Soapy, fighter pilots exist to fight—you know that. That's why I'm here. And I'm assuming that's why you and the other seventy or so Mustang pilots who volunteered for this excursion are here."

"You're right," he replied. "And I'm ready to give it a go. My only concern is that it'll be over before we get there."

"Could be, Frank, but I hope not. It would be a big disappointment to come halfway around the world for naught."

"Yes, I agree."

We set sail on July 14 and proceeded at high speed, making a record-breaking 8.5-day crossing from San Francisco to Yokohama. Several times each day during the voyage, we listened intently to news broadcasts about developments in Korea. The news was not good. The North Korean People's Army (NKPA) advances continued day by day. Would South Korea fall before we reached Japan? What would happen then? Where would I be assigned?

Just before I departed Langley, I had seen an order-of-battle document that was circulated by our intelligence section. It gave no reason for optimism given South Korea's deficit in tanks, artillery, and combat aircraft. On the day the North Koreans invaded the south, this was the estimated order of battle:

	North Korea	South Korea
Combat Troops	112,000	98,000
Constabulary/Police	41,600	45,000 unarmed & untrained for tactical use
Tanks	150	0
Artillery	NK outgunned ROK 3 to 1	Artillery/mortar ammo stocks limited to a few days
Fighter Aircraft	70	0
Attack Aircraft	62	0
Transport Aircraft	23	0
Liaison Aircraft		13
Training Aircraft	8	3

It is readily apparent from these numbers that the South Koreans—with no tanks, limited artillery ammunition, and no fighter or attack aircraft—were very much the underdogs, ill equipped to deal with the invading North Koreans.

We staged at Johnson Air Base, just outside Tokyo. Here we awaited the unloading, and preparation of the F-51s. This was an involved process. Each had to be hoisted from the carrier's deck onto a lighter and transported to the maintenance depot at nearby Kisarazu Air Base, where the coverings and preservatives were removed. When all of the mechanical work was completed, each had to be flight-tested. The process took several days, during which we kept close watch on what was going on in Korea. There was no good news, only reports that the North Korean advances were continuing. Following the fall of Seoul on June 28, the NKPA continued to advance southward: Taejon fell on July 20, Kwangju on July 23, and the port city of Mokpo on July 24. This positioned the North Koreans to move eastward toward Pusan.

While we were waiting for the F-51s to be made ready, we attended a number of lectures, evidently intended to prepare us for our role in the war. Headquarters, Far East Air Forces, had directed that these talks be provided, and they had been hurriedly put together. From my perspective, they were a waste of time since I heard nothing I didn't already know. I felt sorry for the lecturers who had been thrust into an ill-conceived program.

It wasn't until July 30, a week after we arrived in Japan, that the first four Mustangs were ready to go. I had flight-tested one of the airplanes that morning and was pleased to be selected to take that airplane and, as the leader of the four, head off to Korea. Our destination was the airstrip at Taegu, in southeast Korea. No one could tell me to whom I was to report at Taegu, but I was told that a unit of the 18th Fighter-Bomber Group had moved from Clark Air Force Base in the Philippines to Taegu and was flying Mustangs from the airstrip. "You'll just have to play it by ear," I was advised.

As we prepared to depart, I wasn't at all sure that Taegu would still be in American hands by the time we arrived. That's just how bad the latest intelligence reports had been. Consulting with the operations officer, I decided that it would be prudent to have enough fuel aboard when we arrived over the airstrip to make it back to Japan if the situation at Taegu had gone sour. The direct route from Johnson Air Base to Taegu was about 635 miles, making it an inappropriate choice because of the distance, most of which was over the Sea of Japan. The best route, I decided, was via Ashiya Air Base on the north coast of Kyushu, some 550 miles away. We could refuel there before continuing to Taegu.

The four of us departed Johnson late in the morning and arrived at Ashiya in time to grab a late lunch while our planes were being refueled. Afterwards, I hightailed over to the operations office to check on any news about Taegu. The latest information they had received, I was told, was that the airstrip was still in American hands.

It was late afternoon when we launched off for Taegu, some 180 miles away. Our route took us across the Korea Strait to the tip of the island of Tsushima, then over the port of Pusan, where we angled toward Taegu, 60 miles to the north.

No one had been able to tell me much of anything about the situation at Taegu, so I was mentally prepared for just about anything. Nevertheless, surprises awaited.

Chapter 3

Taegu* is situated in a broad valley with mountains to the north and south that rise to over 3,000 feet. Aside from Taegu—a small, compact city—the valley was a patchwork of rice paddies, orchards, and small villages. Everything was green except the mountains. They had a dull brown color, having been denuded of trees, which had been chopped down to provide building materials and charcoal. The mountain ridges crowd uncomfortably close to the airstrip, which is located some four miles to the north of town. (Some months after I arrived at Taegu, a friend with whom I had flown during World War II slammed into the mountains as he attempted an instrument approach during bad weather.)

As we flew across the airstrip, I could see a great deal of activity along the length of the runway—trucks, piles of materials, and a swarm of workers. I would have to keep a sharp eye to be certain that the runway remained clear as I made my approach. There were two C-47 transports on the parking ramp, a small cluster of Mustangs, and a good bit of vehicular traffic. The runway, to my surprise, was a short dirt strip

---

* Because alternate place names appeared on different maps and some place names could easily be confused with others, Far East Air Forces assigned a "K-site" designation to each airfield in Korea. The airfield at Taegu was designated K-2.

23

only 3,800 feet in length. On the final approach for landing, I could see that that the hundreds of workers were busily installing a second runway adjacent to the active one, using pierced-steel planking.

After turning off the runway, I taxied toward the Mustangs and was shocked to see that there were only four parked on the ramp—and they all looked worn and tired. A short distance from the Mustangs was a row of pyramidal tents and a small adobe-like building in a line beside the ramp. These housed the various squadron activities—operations, intelligence, maintenance, and so forth. Another group of pyramidal tents was located on a hill sloping up from the flight line. There was a small hangar a couple of hundred yards in the distance, as well as what appeared to be an old operations building.

I parked next to one of the Mustangs, and my three companions pulled in beside me. As soon as I shut down the engine, the first person to approach me was a fellow wearing captain's insignia who introduced himself as Harry Moreland.

"Boy, am I glad to see you," he said. "We were down to seven airplanes, and your four increases our strength by over 50 percent."

He said he was commander of the 12th Fighter-Bomber Squadron and told me to find an empty cot in one of the tents up on the hill, leave my gear on it (I had only a small canvas bag; the rest was to be sent to me from Johnson Air Base), and then come back to the operations tent to meet the other pilots and get an update on the situation.

I received a friendly welcome from the squadron's pilots and quickly discovered that many had nicknames, the origins of which weren't readily apparent in most instances. In addition to Stoop, there was Spud, Scrappy, Mo, Bud, Sandy, Wild Bill, and Chappie. The last was attached to 1st Lt. Daniel James, who stood six feet, four inches, and later became the Air Force's first black four-star general. All of the pilots were volunteers, and their spirits were high. I sensed right away that I would be comfortable with this bunch.

The squadron operations officer, Capt. Jerry Mau, was busy when I got back to the flight line, so it was 1st Lt. Duane "Bud" Bitteman, the squadron intelligence officer, who took me in hand. He was a humorous guy with lots of energy who unhurriedly got me up to speed on the situation. I learned from him that three days after President Truman, on June 30, authorized "full utilization of the Army-Navy-Air team" in Korea, a call was made at a meeting of the pilots of the 18th Fighter-Bomber Group at Clark Air Base in the Philippines for volunteers to go to Korea to fly F-51 Mustangs. Some months earlier, all of the fighter groups in the Pacific area had turned in their Mustangs and been reequipped with the more modern F-80 Shooting Star, a jet aircraft. Now, however, because the available airfields in Korea had short, unim-. proved runways unsuitable for jet fighters, there was an urgent need for Mustangs. Thirty of the group's approximately seventy-five pilots volunteered. They were formed into an organization named the Dallas Provisional Squadron, and, after obtaining tents, a field kitchen, and other supplies and equipment, they began arriving at Taegu on July 12. At that point, they had no airplanes.

Earlier, on the day the war started, the Republic of Korea's president, Syngman Rhee, had asked Truman for a "fleet of airplanes" to counter the North Korean invasion, and Truman had authorized the transfer of ten F-51 Mustangs to the Republic of Korea Air Force. The only Mustangs available were the handful being used by the various fighter groups to tow targets, and these were not in first-class condition. Ten Mustangs were flown to Taegu on July 2 and turned over to the ROK Air Force, which at this point had about fifty pilots, but only four light liaison airplanes and seven advanced training planes, having lost almost half of its force fighting valiantly during the opening days of the war. The U.S. Air Force sent along a training detachment of 10 pilots, 4 maintenance and supply officers, and 100 airman to help train the Koreans to fly and maintain the Mustangs. Things didn't go well. It was too much to ask of the Korean pilots, trained in light aircraft, to quickly start flying combat missions in Mustangs from the clay-and-gravel runway at Taegu.

Eleven days later, after the Koreans had lost one Mustang, it was clear that they were in over their heads. The remaining birds were turned over to Dallas Squadron, which was soon redesignated as the 12th Fighter-Bomber Squadron. Three days later, with thirty pilots and nine Mustangs, the 12th began combat operations. By the time I arrived, the outfit was down to seven Mustangs. One pilot, Billy Crabtree, had been shot down over enemy territory, and Harry Moreland, after taking some hits from North Korean antiaircraft guns, had to crash-land in the Naktong River.

The war had progressed from a seemingly hopeless beginning to a critical juncture as the defending ROK army units and reinforcing U.S. Army troops were squeezed into the southeast corner of the Korean peninsula, an area that came to be known as the Pusan Perimeter. At the end of the first week, the situation was dire. Seoul, the Republic of Korea's capital, had fallen after only four days of fighting, and many of the retreating South Korean soldiers had been trapped when the bridges over the Han River were prematurely destroyed in an effort to hinder the advance of the North Korean People's Army. Of the 98,000 ROK troops at the start, only 54,000 reached the south bank of the Han. In just a few days, the ROK Army had lost almost half its fighting force and 70 percent of its weapons.

The North Koreans continued to advance for the next month, but at a declining pace. By week five, four U.S. Army divisions had been deployed to Korea from Japan. They had been garrison troops, not well trained, understrength, and lacking in some weaponry and ammunition. The ROK army had been reorganized into five divisions, though it was still a weak force. In addition, a well-trained and -equipped U.S. Marine brigade had been brought in. On July 13, Lt. Gen. Walton H. Walker established Headquarters, U.S. Eighth Army Korea (EUSAK), at Taegu. Walker was given command of all United Nations ground forces in Korea. At about the same time, the commander of the Fifth Air Force, Lt. Gen. Earle E. Partridge, who led all United Nations air force elements in Korea, began to move his headquarters to Taegu. Things were beginning to look somewhat better, but the crunch was fast approaching.

The U.S. Air Force had been involved from the beginning, first in evacuating 851 American nationals and foreign diplomats and then in the fighting. Within a few days, American pilots had essentially wiped out the North Korean Air Force, the first North Korean airplane having been downed by an F-82 interceptor pilot. Air Force B-26 light bombers, B-29 heavy bombers, and F-80 fighter-bombers flying from bases in Japan were engaged in relentless attacks on NKPA forces; U.S. Navy planes flying from a carrier were involved as well.

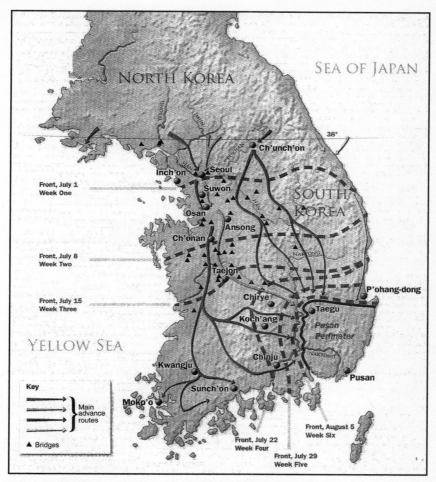

The situation as it unfolded during the first five weeks of the war.
AIR FORCE MAGAZINE

In addition to Harry Moreland's F-51 Mustangs at Taegu, there were two squadrons of the 35th Fighter Group operating F-51s from Pohang, a hastily constructed airstrip on the coast east of Taegu. The F-51s at Taegu and Pohang were the only fighter aircraft based within the Pusan Perimeter. They provided close air support to Army forces only minutes away from their bases.

USAF pilots had had a significant impact on the NKPA and were primarily responsible for the slowed rate of advance. They had destroyed more than 100 NKPA tanks (leaving the North Koreans with only 40) and dozens of highway and railroad bridges, and it would be learned later that they had killed 58,000 North Korean troops. This had slowed the NKPA advance from seventeen miles a day during week two down to two miles a day by week six.

But the NKPA was still on the move, and the Pusan Perimeter was being squeezed day by day. In the face of this, and with only a handful of airplanes, Moreland was sending his Mustangs off in pairs with bombs, rockets, and six fully loaded machine guns—rather than the usual practice of dispatching four-ship flights. As soon as a pair landed, the F-51s would be quickly refueled, rearmed, and launched on another mission to provide support for nearby U.S. and ROK ground units. Two planes were the minimum needed for mutual protection against other fighters and for support in the event that one airplane went down.

With thirty-four pilots and only eleven airplanes in the squadron, I had to wait a couple of days before being scheduled to fly my first combat mission. While waiting, I got a good look at what was going on around me. Hundreds of Korean laborers, under the direction of Air Force engineers, were feverishly at work to complete installation of the new pierced-steel-planking runway while others were erecting a mess hall, several small operation buildings, some barracks, and other essential facilities. They had started work only two weeks earlier and were making remarkably fast progress. Work on the runway was nearing completion, and as soon as this occurred, work would begin on a second runway. Parallel to the first, this runway would be used as a taxiway because the areas adjacent to the runways were unpaved and the packed clay soil had soft spots that deteriorated under constant use by heavily loaded airplanes. At this point, none of the Korean airfields remaining in U.S. hands had a jet-capable runway, so completion of these runways was vitally important.

The pierced-steel planking that was being used to construct the runway adjacent to the existing clay-and-gravel runway had first been used during World War II. It was considered by some historians to have been one of America's secret weapons given its versatility and ease of construction. Stamped out of steel, with closely spaced holes, each plank weighed 66.2 pounds and measured 10 feet long by 15 inches wide. When locked together, 60,000 were required to construct a runway 5,000 feet long and 150 feet wide.

The 12th Fighter-Bomber Squadron setup wasn't much different from what I had experienced on field exercises and during World War II. Here I lived in a pyramidal tent bare of everything except six canvas cots, ate from a mess kit, and hung out after hours in what was laughingly called the pilots' lounge—a tent with boxes for seats and a packing-case bar. The bathing facilities were primitive—a couple of fifty-five-gallon drums crudely mounted eight or so feet into the air, filled with water from a nearby creek (no doubt heavily polluted) and fitted with a simple shower head. But no one complained about the austere arrangements. We were there to fight a war and personal comfort would have to take a back seat.

Chapter 4

By the time I prepared to fly my first combat mission on August 2, North Korean forces had advanced to within fourteen miles of our airbase (K-2), and the situation in the Taegu area was approaching a critical state. The map in the squadron intelligence tent showed six NKPA divisions deployed in a semicircle to the north and west of Taegu. Five were infantry divisions, and the sixth was an armored division. Their obvious objective was Taegu. The numerical strength of the enemy force totaled around 50,000 soldiers. We didn't know the exact number since they had suffered numerous losses, but the number wasn't what was important. It was the fact the North Koreans had advanced relentlessly to this point and had to be stopped now—or we Americans and our ROK allies would be pushed into the sea or worse.

In conversations with the pilots who had been flying combat missions starting two weeks earlier, I learned that there had been a significant change in the movements and actions undertaken by the NKPA. In the beginning, the North Koreans openly moved forward against our troops during the daylight hours, seemingly oblivious to the toll American pilots were inflicting on their troops, tanks, and trucks. Then, having suffered horrific losses from air attacks all across South Korea, they basically ceased daylight movement and started to hide out during the day in favor of making troop and vehicle movements under the cover of darkness. As their forces neared the Naktong River, our pilots had to search diligently for them, looking under trees and inside the buildings of each village. The North Koreans rammed their tanks through the walls of buildings in a village, drove their trucks and tanks inside, then camouflaged the openings with net or straw so that they would not be easily detected from the air. If there were no villages nearby, they parked under a clump of trees and spread camouflage netting and branches over their equipment. To find them, it was necessary to search out the targets at tree-top level or look for tank tracks that might lead to targets. This made the role of airborne controllers highly important in spotting targets. Flying T-6 aircraft, a relatively fast two-seated training plane with a pilot and an observer, airborne controllers could remain in an area for an extended period searching for suitable targets at low altitude. They were not often fired upon since the North Koreans had learned from experience that such action on their part could invite an air strike by American fighter-bombers. I would learn firsthand about the important role of airborne controllers on my initial combat mission.

Capt. Jerry Mau, the operations officer, informed me the night before that I would be flying as his wingman on the third mission, with takeoff scheduled for dawn. At this point, I guessed that Mau had flown a couple dozen missions.

The intelligence briefer didn't have much to say. He noted the position of the bomb line (a line located beyond the line of contact between friendly and enemy forces, beyond which we could attack targets without being under the direction of a forward air controller), called attention to the areas of reported heavy antiaircraft fire, and told us that we would get our assignment from Mellow (the Joint Air Operation Center) once we were airborne.

Mau's briefing was short and to the point. He noted that the airfield at Pohang (located about fifty miles to the east) was the best bet should we be unable to use K-2, and he reviewed hand signals to be used in the event of radio failure. He then told me, "As soon as we are both cranked up, give me a call on Channel B for a radio check. Our call sign is Tamerlane Green. I'll be on C when we taxi and will contact Mellow on Channel A as soon as we get airborne to get our assignment." That was it. From early conversations, Jerry knew I was an experienced Mustang pilot, so he apparently didn't see the need to talk about strafing and dive-bombing procedures. That was okay with me: I knew all of the basics and had gotten up to speed on the local situation while hanging around operations and the intelligence debriefing tent.

Before we left the operations tent, I was surprised and puzzled to be handed a black-and-white aeronautical chart, which I had never seen before. The usual charts were in color, enabling the user to differentiate quickly between land and water and discern at a glance the terrain elevation at various points on the chart. Shortly after the war started, it had been discovered that the supply of aeronautical charts of Korea was quite limited. Until more could be printed, some of us would have to make do with the black-and-white version—photographic prints of the original.

There was another oddity about this mission. I would be flying a Mustang with ROK markings: a roundel containing a red field at the top with a curving white line separating it from a blue field at the bottom—a yin-yang symbol. This was one of the birds the squadron had gotten from the ROK Air Force but hadn't had time to repaint. That led to a thought: how would NKPA troops react if I went down in North Korean–held territory and was discovered to be the pilot of an ROK Mustang? I decided that even though this would be a surprise to the North Koreans and might initially cause some excitement, it wasn't likely to make much difference in the way I would be treated. Harsh treatment was to be expected. World War II provided many examples of the brutal treatment of POWs by Japanese and Chinese captors. It was unlikely that the North Koreans would be different.

I did a walk-around inspection of the airplane, checked the wings, fuselage, tail section, and propeller to be sure that they were undamaged. I noted that the gust locks had been removed and confirmed that the tires were properly inflated, the pitot tube (airspeed sensor) cover had been removed, and there were no leaking fluids. In addition to a flying suit and boots, I had around my waist a pistol belt with a holster containing a .45-caliber pistol, and I was wearing a Mae West life jacket. At this point, I took a look at the Form 1A to check the status of the airplane to determine if it was mechanically ready to fly and if it had been fully serviced with fuel and oxygen.

After climbing onto the left wing, I pulled on a backpack parachute and tightened the heavy straps. Upon entering the cockpit, I sat down on the dinghy (one-man life raft) that had been placed in the seat-well by the crew chief. The dinghy was a compact package—vital in the event of an over-water bailout or a ditching on the sea—but it was almost as hard as a rock and decidedly uncomfortable. Now came the tricky task of fastening the life raft to the parachute harness. This took some doing given that I had very little space in which to get the dinghy's heavy snap fasteners attached to the rings sewn into the parachute harness.

The next steps were to position the shoulder harness and fasten the lap belt, don my helmet, plug in the radio cord, and attach the oxygen hose. Then came the cockpit check, starting with the armament switches. With six .50-caliber machine guns in the wings, each with several hundred rounds of ammunition (1,880 total), six 5-inch high-velocity rockets (HVARs) installed under each wing, and a 500-pound demolition bomb slung under each wing, it was a must to check that none of the armament switches had been inadvertently left in the "on" position. An overlooked "on" switch could lead to an accidental firing of the machine guns or rockets or to the premature release of the bombs—all potentially disastrous events.

The rest of the cockpit check consisted of noting the position of switches and circuit breakers, adjusting the trim tabs, checking the fuel and oxygen gauges, turning the fuel selector tank valve to "fuselage tank," and adjusting the altimeter to the local barometric pressure. Then I waited for a signal from Mau. When he nodded, I started the engine, switched on the radio, and punched the "B" channel button. With the engine running smoothly and the engine instruments in the green, I called Mau for a radio check. He responded, "Read you loud and clear. Going to C."

The Mustang is a tail-wheel airplane, which means the pilot can't see over the nose when taxiing and has to continually S-turn the airplane to see what is ahead, first a few degrees in one direction and then in the other. The unpaved ramp had an uneven surface and a number of soft spots. So we had to use care when taxiing, given our heavy load. Mau was churning up dust as he proceeded toward the runway, so I lagged behind to escape as much of it as I could. At the runway, the armament crews rushed out to pull the safety pins from the rockets and bombs. When they had moved clear, we made our engine run-up checks. Once Mau had finished his engine check, he taxied onto the runway, and I followed him and moved to the upwind side of the runway. I held my position until he was about halfway down the runway and the dust had drifted off enough for me to see clearly. I then released the brakes and advanced the throttle. The Mustang lumbered for a distance because of the heavy load and clay runway surface, but it soon picked up speed, and I was airborne well before the end of the strip. I turned as soon as the gear was up to get the airplane's nose inside of Mau and shortly moved into position on his left wing.

I switched to Channel A just as Mau was contacting Mellow Control. Mellow acknowledged Mau's call and directed us to proceed to the vicinity of Waegwan, about fifteen miles northwest of Taegu, and to contact Mosquito Baker. Mosquito Baker was an airborne controller in a T-6 aircraft. Airborne controllers were assigned the call sign Mosquito plus an additional word that identified the particular controller. They were usually accompanied by an Army sergeant in the rear seat. The sergeant acted as an observer and assisted in identifying friendly and enemy troop positions. Mosquito Baker responded immediately to Mau's call and asked our armament load, altitude, and position. Mau told him we were at 5,000 feet just north of Taegu with a full load of 500-pound bombs, rockets, and .50-caliber machine-gun ammo. The controller said that elements of the 1st Calvary Division were engaged in a firefight and needed some support, but first he had a bombing target. He directed us to maintain 5,000 feet and rendezvous along the main road thirty miles east-northeast of Waegwan.

A short time later, as we approached the rendezvous point, Mosquito Baker called that he had spotted us and that he was at 2,500 feet, two o'clock (just to the right) to us. When we had sighted him, he directed our attention a bit farther down the main road to a secondary road and then to an orchard off that road, which he said contained a number of Soviet-made T-34 tanks and trucks hidden beneath the trees and camouflage nets. This is where we should place our bombs, he said. I couldn't see the tanks or trucks from 5,000 feet, but there were some hints in the form of squared-off shapes. I could see that what should have been a narrow dirt trail leading into the orchard was scarred, rutted, and much wider than it should have been—an indication of heavy vehicular activity.

After acknowledging the targets' location, we climbed to 8,000 feet to get in position for a dive-bomb attack. I armed the bombs by lifting the switch guard and moving the bomb switch to the armed position. Now all I needed to do to release the bombs was to punch the red button on the top of the control stick.

As Mau began his overhead approach to the target, I dropped back to get some spacing. My plan was to enter my dive-bomb run just as Mau's bombs exploded. The explosion of his bombs would divert the attention of any gunners and hopefully leave me unscathed on my bomb run.

I watched as Mau made a sharp wingover and entered a forty-five-degree dive from 8,000 feet. As he plunged downward, I spotted some muzzle flashes at the edge of the orchard, which I assumed came from small-caliber weapons. When Mau's two bombs struck in the orchard, near one edge, they emitted bright flashes and churned up debris and dust.

When the target passed under the leading edge of my Mustang's wing, I made a wingover and entered a forty-five-degree dive, maneuvering the airplane so that the target was just above the airplane's nose. At this point, it was essential to maintain steady, coordinated flight—no skidding or slipping—until I released the bombs at 4,000 feet and began a 4G pullout at about 3,000, safely above the bomb blast. I didn't observe any fire being directed at me during my brief dive-bomb run or as I pulled sharply up to 5,000 feet to observe where my bombs hit. Mine were closer to the center of the orchard than Mau's, but I had no idea how much damage we had caused. At this point, if we hadn't had more pressing business, we would have backed off a few miles and then made a low-level high-speed run across the orchard to get a closer look at the aftermath. But our controller had a higher-priority task. "Well done, fellows," he said. "Now let's get back down the road and give hand to the Army."

We retraced our route about ten miles to the east toward Kumchon. This was mountainous terrain without many prominent landmarks, but Mosquito Baker, by patiently describing various terrain features, set about pinpointing for us the exact location of the 1st Cavalry Division's troops and those of the enemy. This was important because we would be attacking NKPA forces that were in close proximity to friendly forces and it was vital to avoid friendly casualties. Once we were confident that we had the picture, Baker instructed us to observe as he fired a smoke rocket toward the NKPA position. The rocket's impact point then served as the spot from which the controller subsequently directed where we

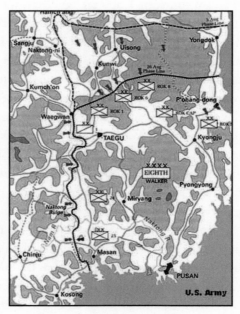

The Pusan Perimeter, August 1950

were to place our firepower. For starters, he asked Mau to place his rockets fifty yards to the north of the smoke, and having observed where they landed, he asked me to move mine fifty yards farther to the north.

The 5-inch HVARs we employed required that we approach the target in a thirty-degree dive and fire at about 1,500 feet from the target. Firing from a shallower approach angle was dangerous because the pilot could then find himself flying through the debris from the exploding rockets, and the airplane could sustain damage, possibly fatal.

After we fired our rockets, the controller asked that we concentrate our initial strafing attacks on an area farther to the north of our rocket attacks and, on subsequent passes, keep moving to the north. Strafing with .50-caliber machine guns could be highly accurate. An approach angle of twenty to forty degrees was most often used, but terrain features and the exact location of the target sometimes required a much steeper dive angle. In this instance, I approached the target in a thirty-degree dive and began to fire at 1,500 feet. As Mau was pulling off the target after his first strafing attack, I noted muzzle flashes from the area he was attacking, so I took spacing that would allow me to begin my attack just as he was pulling off the target on his second run. In this way, I hoped to minimize the fire we were receiving. As a further defensive tactic, we approached on a slightly different heading each time and pulled up sharply. In all, we each made half a dozen strafing attacks before our ammunition supply was exhausted. I don't know how many rounds of ammunition the North Koreans fired at us, but I saw numerous gun flashes aimed in our direction. Luckily, we emerged untouched. At this point, Mau bid adieu to the controller, and we turned toward K-2, which was only minutes away.

After hanging around the operations tent for all of the next day, hoping for a mission assignment that didn't materialize, I decided to call it quits when the last scheduled flight launched as the sun was settling in the western sky. I hadn't gone more than 100 yards when the operations officer ran out of the tent and shouted at me to come back and get ready to go. He had just gotten instructions from the Joint Operations Center to get two airborne as soon as possible.

I don't remember who the flight leader was, but our orders were to proceed north to the vicinity of Andong. We were given a forward air controller's (FAC) call sign and the coordinates of his location. Before heading out, we quickly located Andong on the aeronautical chart and found it to be on the east branch of the main road some forty miles north-northeast of K-2. The FAC was assigned to the ROK 8th Division. Our two Mustangs were armed with rockets and machine guns.

By the time we lifted off, the sun was low in the sky, and there wasn't much daylight left. Our call sign was Tamerlane Orange. When contacted, the FAC asked our altitude, location, and armament load. We were twenty miles to the south at 5,000 feet, and he asked that we fly directly over the main road that approached Andong. He spotted us shortly and directed that we make a ninety-degree right turn so he could confirm our identity. Then he advised us of his location, which was marked by a white cloth panel. When we had spotted it, he asked us to watch for the smoke from a white phosphorus mortar shell. The FAC used the white smoke from the shell to orient us precisely on the desired target. He stated that they were under heavy pressure and in the process of relocating to other positions. "Stay with us as long as possible," he asked. He instructed that we place our fire along and just below the ridge line to the east and west of the white phosphorus smoke.

We went to work, first with our rockets. Then we strafed. After each attack, the FAC gave an assessment—"Right on the mark" or "That was where I wanted it"—as well as instructions for the next attack. After three passes, as darkness was creeping and daylight was fast disappearing, the situation on the ground became increasingly visible, delineated by artillery flashes and widespread rifle and machine-gun fire, much of which was aimed at us. There was a fierce firefight in progress, and the North Korean 8th Division was applying aggressive pressure on the ROK 8th. The FAC asked that we alternate firing passes with dry passes in order to extend our stay. The dry passes were intended to cause the enemy troops to hunker down and cease activity. We were in mountainous terrain, and at this point, with darkness enveloping us, our depth perception was severely degraded. I had to rely on my altimeter to know the heights at which to initiate and terminate a pass. We continued our attacks until we were in black darkness and reluctantly left the scene when we were out of ammunition.

On our return to K-2, we found the runway area lit up like Broadway on a Saturday night; work on the pierced-steel-planking runway was proceeding around the clock. Back on the ground after an hour and a half of flying, an hour of which we logged as night flying, I told the crew chief (mechanic) that I may have taken a hit or two and he should take a look at the wings, tail section, and fuselage. I had heard and felt what I thought was a hit at about the halfway point of our mission. My senses were correct: there was a nice round hole in the horizontal stabilizer. The damage wasn't serious and could be repaired with a bit of sheet metal.

So ended my second day of combat flying in Korea.

★ ★ ★

There were many things going on that I didn't know about. On August 1, the day before I flew my first combat mission, the Eighth Army had issued an operational directive to all United Nations ground forces to withdraw behind the Naktong River. By nightfall of August 3, all units were across the Naktong except a rearguard that held a blocking position on the Songju Road southwest of the Waegwan bridges. The eastern bank of the Naktong River provided the last good defensive barrier available to the Eighth Army in South Korea. Clearly, the withdrawal across the Naktong signaled that the North Korean advance had not been blunted. It was equally clear that the objective of the North Koreans was Taegu.

The gravity of the situation was underscored by the increase in air-transport activities at K-2. On August 2 and 3, a stream of transport planes flew in from Japan, each loaded with high-priority supplies and equipment for Army units. I later learned that in a twenty-four-hour period, more than 300,000 pounds of equipment and supplies had been airlifted from Japan to Korea, most of it to K-2.

As unlikely as it may seem, the Eighth Army's commander, Lt. Gen. Walton H. Walker, did not inform Lt. Gen. Earle E. Partridge, the Fifth

Air Force's commander, of his decision to withdraw behind the Nak-tong, and it wasn't until two days later that the Air Force learned of it. This was not the way to fight a war. In fact, it was just plain stupid. Despite the critical role the Air Force was performing, neither the Eighth Army's commander nor his staff seemed willing to recognize the Air Force as an important partner. On August 4, General Partridge wrote to Walker about the situation, highlighting the need for better cooperation between the Eighth Army and Fifth Air Force and under-scoring the importance of Taegu. The letter did the trick.[*]

☆ ☆ ☆

During July, the North Koreans had made no serious offensive oper-ation in the mountains of the east coast, where ROK troops managed to contain the NKPA 5th Division. Early in August, however, the enemy began to mass north of Yongdok, as North Korean guerrillas units formed in the mountains inland from Pohang. These action could threaten the airfield at Pohang on the coast just to the east of Taegu. This was the situation as I readied for my third mission, this one in support of the ROK Capital Division, which was located south of Yongdok.

I led this mission, which, like all of the other Mustang missions, involved only two aircraft. We were scheduled to be the first pair to get airborne at dawn (0530 hours). This meant waking around 0400 in order to have time to dress, shave, and get some breakfast before we headed to the operations tent. Stumbling around in the dark is not a good way to start a day. Breakfast was marginal, maybe nourishing, but entirely lacking in visual and taste appeal. Virtually all of our food came out of cans, was warmed, and then served. But this morning, the coffee was okay and pro-vided a welcome bit of stimulation to help me get going.

After a briefing by the intelligence officer, we conducted our air-craft preflight checks, and at first light, just as soon as I could see well enough to taxi safely, we started engines and made our way out to the

---

[*] Robert F. Futrell, *The United States Air Force in Korea, 1950–1953* (Washington, DC: Office of Air Force History), 1983.

runway. We got airborne before the sun was visible and contacted Mellow Control for instructions.

Mellow directed us to proceed northward along the road to Yongdok, which is located to the northeast on the coast, and contact an FAC serving with the ROK Capital Division. The flight took about ten minutes, and I was able to contact and then locate the FAC's position without difficulty. Like all of the FACs, this one was a USAF fighter pilot who had flown at least twenty combat missions and had been detailed to serve as a controller for twenty-one days. If given a choice, no one would have wanted to be assigned to an ROK army unit because the ROK army had not performed well in the opening days of the war and because there was the problem of communications. None of the FACs spoke Korean, and few Koreans spoke English. But the assignment was an essential one since the ROK army was entirely dependent on the United States for air support and it was the FACs who provided the vital link among ROK army elements, the JOC, and the fighter-bomber pilots.

An NKPA 5th Division facility on a mountaintop was our initial target—a radio station with a machine-gun emplacement, troops, and several vehicles. We took it out with one pass, firing our full load of rockets. The FAC then had us strafe along a ridge line in close proximity to the friendlies. The entire area appeared quiet except for a few artillery shells lobbed by the ROK forces. My guess was that the North Koreans were keeping their heads down while we were in the area, not wanting to invite an attack. We conducted half a dozen strafing passes before we exhausted our ammunition and returned to K-2.

The massing of NKPA units in the north signaled the beginning of an all-out assault to complete their conquest of South Korea, only a remnant of which remained unoccupied by the invaders. At this point, the Americans and their ROK allies had been steadily pushed back into a relatively small enclave and had their backs to the sea. In the face of unrelenting pressure by the NKPA, the Eighth Army had withdrawn all of its forces to the east side of the Naktong River and destroyed the bridges by early August 4 in preparation for making a last–ditch stand. Although supplies and reinforcements were pouring in through Pusan and the Fifth Air Force had established air supremacy over the Pusan Perimeter (which meant that allied forces could move openly without any fear of enemy air attack), few within the perimeter were optimistic about the outcome of present and future battles. What was certain was that the North Koreans would undertake crossings of the Naktong without delay. Kim Il Sung, the North Korean premier, had set August 15 as the date for final victory and the liberation of all of Korea.

The first enemy crossings of the Naktong River came on August 5 at three places. Two took place north of Waegwan, and this was the area to which I was directed on a mission in support of the 1st ROK Division, whose troops were in defensive positions on the east side of the Naktong, ready to oppose crossings by the North Korean 3rd Division.

From our base just north of Taegu, it took only a few minutes to reach the target area. When my wingman and I arrived on the scene shortly after first light, the airborne controller was ready with initial targeting instructions. He had selected an area where he believed the enemy was massing troops, artillery, and equipment for river crossings. Following his directions, we dive-bombed that area, after which I observed a number of explosions. Evidently, we had hit an ammunition dump, and it was gratifying to observe the resulting fireworks. After this, we spent almost two hours in the area attacking and searching with the controller for promising targets. We fired our rockets at one target and mounted repeated strafing attacks against others. In return, we received a good amount of defensive fire, and my wingman's airplane was struck by a small-caliber round that penetrated the left wing near the tip. This might have raised his adrenaline level a bit, but it didn't adversely affect his airplane or our mission performance, and we completed our attack without any further difficulties.

Because the North Koreans rarely showed themselves during daylight hours, we knew the bombing and strafing by the Fifth Air Force's fighter-bombers was having a significant impact. This was further confirmed by the contents of a captured field order issued by the commander of the NKPA 25th Rifle Regiment who was involved in the Naktong River crossing. He was so concerned about the potential impact of attacking fighter-bombers that he directed that half of his infantry firepower be diverted to antiaircraft defense, even while attempting a river crossing. Up to this point in the war, the Air Force had flown some 5,000 close air support sorties—an average of 125 a day.

On Sunday, August 6, I flew my fifth close air support sortie. Earlier, two of our pilots had sighted ten barges ferrying troops across the Naktong north of Taegu in the ROK 6th Division's area. The pilots, who were returning from a mission, were out of ammunition and unable to mount an attack, but they notified Mellow, who was heard diverting other flights to attack the barges.

When I got airborne, Mellow sent me south to contact an airborne FAC in the U.S. 24th Infantry Division's area. A few hours earlier, at midnight, flares had burst over the Naktong, and 800 North Koreans began to cross in shoulder-deep water at the Ohang ferry site. They waded across, some using makeshift rafts to float their weapons, clothing, and other equipment. Others held their gear over their heads. Their objective was Yongsan. By the time I arrived on the scene, hours later, the NKPA soldiers had moved into the hills on the river's east bank, but thousands more NKPA soldiers hid on the west side of the river awaiting the opportune time to cross. The task assigned to my flight by the controller was to prevent the North Koreans from making any further crossings in the 24th Division's area.

My wingman and I patrolled the area for more than two hours, searching, with the help of the controller, the west bank and the area beyond for enemy targets. We attacked all of the camouflaged troops, vehicles, and equipment that we sighted. During my time on station, the enemy made no attempt to cross the river.

Upon arriving back at K-2, I parked the airplane, filled out the airplane forms, and started to walk toward the operation tent to debrief. Then I noticed that tents were coming down all over the place and packing crates were being filled. The intelligence tent was gone, and the operations tent was empty of all equipment except a telephone sitting on a packing box. Jerry Mau gave me the startling news that the squadron had been ordered to evacuate back to Japan as soon as possible, leaving behind only a handful of personnel and some equipment to service a refueling and rearming operation. The Fifth Air Force's commander had decided that it was too risky to leave the squadron at K-2 in the face of North Korean advances.

That wasn't the only startling news. The 12th Fighter-Bomber Squadron's commander, Captain Moreland, informed me that I would be staying at K-2 as a part of the small cadre that would keep the base operating to service planes operating from bases in Japan. The news stunned me. I had volunteered to come halfway around the world to fight in this war as an F-51 Mustang pilot in response to an urgent appeal by the Air Force, and now, with only five missions under my belt, I was being sidelined. Thoughts raced through my mind: this wasn't right, this was unjust, how could this be happening to me? But it *was* happening, and there was nothing I could do about it. Even if I could get in touch with higher authority (which I couldn't at this point), it would be highly imprudent of me to complain about my predicament. Any senior officer to whom I might complain would likely view my problem as quite petty, considering that North Korean soldiers were already crossing the Naktong River and the most critical point of the war was at hand. Suck it up and do the best job you can, I decided. I felt certain that I would find my way back into the cockpit in due course.

Chapter 5

Within twenty-four hours of the time the order was received to evacuate to a base in Japan, all of the Mustang squadron's planes, equipment, and people had departed K-2, except for two fuel trucks, some munitions-handling equipment, a couple of jeeps, and officers and airmen to conduct a refueling and rearming operation and keep the base open to traffic. The plan was to refuel and rearm Mustangs from Japan after they had completed a combat mission and then send them off on a second, and perhaps a third, combat mission before they returned to Japan. This arrangement would enable Mustang pilots to respond more quickly to urgent calls for close air support, remain longer in the combat area, get in another combat mission without making the hour-and-a-half round trip to Japan, and reduce pilot fatigue. First Lt. Harry E. Dugan was the officer left behind to head the operation. Thirty-eight enlisted men were assigned to assist him.

My assignment was related, but I had broader duties. The 6149th Air Base Unit, commanded by Col. Aaron "Pete" Tyer, had been established that day with overall responsibility for K-2. Tyer told me that I would be the base operations officer. He didn't give me any specific instructions, and since I didn't have access to any Air Force regulations or manuals that might fill me in on the duties and responsibilities of a base operations officer, I knew I would have to rely on the general understanding I had acquired over the years. What the job involved, as I perceived it, was responsibility for the flying portion of the base—runways and aircraft parking areas—and oversight of various supporting activities such as the control tower, weather office, crash rescue, refueling and servicing transient aircraft, and control of any assigned support airplanes.

Harry Dugan and I became friends almost immediately. Both of us had flown Mustangs in combat during World War II, and we both had flown on a "shuttle mission," escorting heavy bombers to bases in the Soviet Union—high adventure for both of us. He had been assigned to the 4th Fighter Group based in England while I was with the 31st Fighter Group in Italy. We had much to talk about, and since few officers remained at K-2 and our duties overlapped, we were together often. He was sociable, upbeat, and confident and, from the first day, proved to be highly competent in the way he organized and managed his refueling/rearming operation. We enjoyed each other's company for the weeks he remained at K-2. It was not until years later that I learned why he was selected to stay behind at K-2 when his squadron withdrew to Japan.

At the start of the Korean War, Dugan had been based at Clark Field in the Philippines. When the call went out for volunteers to go to Korea to fly Mustangs, he was one of the first to sign up. Given his World War II experience, he was accepted. But after about six missions as a fighter-bomber pilot—a much different kind of combat from what he had experienced during World War II—he threw in the towel. It was more than he could stomach, and he felt that he would be endangering other pilots if he continued. He told Harry Moreland, the 12th Fighter Squadron's commander, of his desire to be removed from combat flying and offered to perform any duties that Moreland might specify. That is why he was designated to remain at K-2. Dugan never gave any inkling of this to me, but it wouldn't have made any difference if he had. I perceived him to be a fine fellow and a friend, and word that he had run into a wall on his second tour of combat wouldn't have lessened my high opinion of him.

Why I was tagged to stay at K-2, I don't know, but it is highly likely that Moreland selected me, the newcomer, in deference to the other pilots, all of whom were members of the Philippines gang to whom he owed loyalty. Another factor may have been that I had been a captain for six years, which meant that I had a good deal of seniority. I didn't know the date of rank of the other captains in the squadron, but if I was senior to them, Moreland would have been faced with some job shuffling, something he wouldn't have wanted to do. So the easy way out was to throw me overboard. Although I was unhappy with his decision at the time, as it turned out later, he did me a big favor.

The day after the Mustang squadron departed was my twenty-seventh birthday, but there was no celebration, only a cold shower and warm chow served in a mess kit. And there was more bad news: the aviation engineers who had worked around the clock for weeks to construct the new 5,000-foot pierced-steel-planking runway were ordered to evacuate to Pusan after completing only 4,700 feet. They had planned to begin work on a second runway, longer and jet-capable, within a few days, but now that work would be delayed indefinitely.

The Mustang squadron's evacuation to Japan didn't interrupt its combat operations. F-51s were in the sky over Korea the next morning, and four of them arrived at K-2 following their first mission to obtain fuel, munitions, and an intelligence briefing before launching off on another mission. The number increased substantially the next day, and by day ten, upwards of 150 Mustangs refueled and rearmed each day. F-51s from every group in the theater used K-2, including those of the Royal Australian Air Force. Clearly, this was an important operation.

Base operations was located in one the few buildings on K-2 and had just enough space to accommodate the operations office in the front and a small weather office in the rear. There was one other small room, not much larger than a broom closet; this is where I decided to make my home. I didn't have an assistant authorized to sign flight clearances, so I needed to be close at hand around the clock. An open-air platform had been hastily constructed on top of the building from which a tower operator could control air traffic. Assigned to assist me was a tech sergeant with extensive operations experience, a couple of airmen who were operations specialists, five airmen assigned to the crash crew, six assigned to transient aircraft maintenance, and three control tower operators. The weather office was manned by a first lieutenant weather officer and two enlisted weather observers; they made hourly observations of the weather and passed them on to weather central in Tokyo.

One of the first actions I took after being assigned to my new job was to get into a jeep and explore the network of roads, trails, and paths that surrounded the base out to a radius of several miles. There was a high probability that aircraft crashes would occur in the vicinity, so I wanted to know how to reach the scene by the most direct route. Rice paddies, orchards, and small villages made up most of the countryside, all connected by a labyrinth of narrow roads and even narrower trails that squeezed into paths. What struck me quite forcefully right from the beginning of my tour was the scarcity of people. I saw a few along the main road but none on the byways. As I drove around, I discovered that all of the villages and scattered houses were deserted—a big surprise to me. I knew that hordes of refugees from the north had passed through the Taegu area, but I hadn't given a thought to locals fleeing even farther to the south. Now I saw that they had departed in mass. There was no sign of panic or disorder; instead, it appeared as if the inhabitants had simply locked their front doors and departed for the afternoon. It was strange to stand in the middle of what was obviously a prosperous village and see not a living soul. But that is the way it was throughout the area. Adding to the eeriness was the sight of apple orchards with the trees heavily weighed down with ripening fruit and no one to harvest it. Even before I completed my exploration, it had become clear that circuitous routing would be required to reach all but a few crash sites. That made my survey even more important, and by the time I had finished, I had a pretty good idea about how to get where I needed to go without wasting much time.

Before I returned to the base, I filled up the back of the jeep with bushels of Stark Delicious apples, a variety I knew well since it was grown back home in Virginia. My thought was that the owner of the orchard, who had fled south with thousands of other refugees, wouldn't be coming back anytime soon and it was better that airmen who were fighting for his freedom consume the apples rather than have them rot on the ground. Back on the base, I set out boxes of apples for everyone to enjoy.

Another precautionary measure I took involved runway lights. We had a single gasoline-powered generator that provided electricity to the string of lights on either side of the runway. I fretted for a while over what I could do if the generator failed or the lights were taken out by an aircraft crash. The solution I came up was as rudimentary as one could devise. I asked the cooks to save fifty empty one-gallon food cans, which we filled with a bottom layer of rocks topped with coarse sand. I stored these behind the base operations building together with a couple of cans of gasoline. In the event the runway lights failed, I could gather up a crew of GIs to place the cans filled with gasoline at intervals along both sides of the runway, lighting the fuel in each can before proceeding to the next spot. This scheme worked well during practice sessions, but thankfully, we never had to use it in an emergency.

The only flying unit remaining on the base was a squadron of T-6 Mosquito aircraft flown by airborne controllers. It was essential that they be based as close to the scene of action as possible so that they could be on station from dawn to dusk. Aside from this squadron, the number of airmen on the base totaled about ninety, including the thirty in Dugan's refueling/rearming gang—an austere number given all of the functions involved.

None of the news we received—some via rumor, others from our direct phone connection with the JOC—was encouraging. Although the allies were holding in many areas, the North Koreans were continuing to advance in the northeast sector and were exerting heavy pressure to the west of Taegu. On August 16, ninety-eight Air Force B-29s made a "carpet-bombing" attack on suspected NKPA positions in the Waegwan area. Acting on information from Korea that an estimated 40,000 NKPA troops were massed there, poised for an assault on Taegu, Gen. Douglas MacArthur had ordered the Air Force to mount this all-out B-29 raid. Bombings of this kind against large areas of real estate had not been especially successful in the past, so the Air Force brass weren't pleased with the order. In this instance, the Eighth Army had designated a target area three and a half miles wide and seven and a half miles long—much too large to be covered effectively by the 3,084 500-pound and 150 1,000-pound bombs dropped by the B-29s. Afterwards, despite extensive reconnaissance, it was never determined just what damage was done and whether it was worth the costly effort involved. Air Force leaders didn't think so. Nevertheless, the Eighth Army's commander, Gen. Walton H. Walker, stated that it must have had a negative effect on North Korean morale and he knew it had a positive effect on his troops. The airmen at K-2 were pleased to see this massive effort, and we hoped it would have a decisive impact on the North Koreans.

A few days later, I was surprised to see Generals Partridge and Walker arrive on K-2 without any fanfare and climb into a T-6—Partridge in the front and Walker as a passenger in the rear. They flew off toward the northeast on what I learned later was a reconnaissance mission and were gone about an hour. I was impressed by the fact that had struck out on their own—without a bunch of aides or any fighter cover—to make a firsthand assessment of the situation.

Eighteen days later, on September 4, as the situation in the Taegu area continued to deteriorate, the headquarters of the Eighth Army evacuated everyone except a skeleton crew from Taegu to Pusan. Two days after that, the rest of the headquarters left for Pusan. That same day, the Mosquito outfit was ordered to evacuate to the Pusan area along with all the personnel at K-2, except the refueling/rearming gang and eight others, including me. The question now on the minds of those of us who remained was the same one we had had for more than a month: will the NKPA advance be halted in time to save K-2? The pullout of Headquarters, Eighth Army; the Mosquito squadron; and almost half of our base's meager population provided a rather clear answer: don't count on it!

Up to this point, we at K-2 had believed that if the base was ever in imminent danger of falling into NKPA hands, we would be evacuated in a timely manner, probably by air. Now, however, that seemed to be an iffy assumption. Should the North Koreas make a sudden breakthrough, especially if it occurred at night, an organized evacuation might not be feasible. To deal with this worst-case scenario, my plan was to depart K-2 in a jeep, along with my sergeant and the two other airmen remaining in operations, followed by a truck carrying the other airmen for whom I was responsible, each of us equipped with a carbine, plus a good supply of ammunition, water, and C rations. We would also have a reliable map in hand. The others for whom I was responsible were to follow in other jeeps. If travel by jeep wasn't possible, we would hoof it.

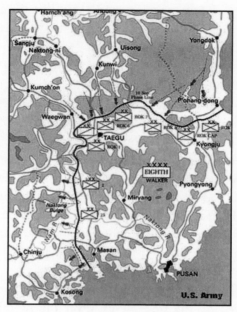

Defense of the Naktong, September 1950

I took one other step to guard against the unexpected. K-2 was located within the 1st Calvary Division's area of responsibility, so I drove over to the division command post in Taegu and talked with the chief operations officer, the G-3. I explained to him what was going on out at K-2 and that forty-six Air Force people were out there performing a vital mission in support of his operations. I asked his assurance that we would not be overlooked and abandoned should the division withdraw from Taegu. He told me that he would get word to us in a timely manner, either by phone or messenger, should a withdrawal be contemplated.

Beginning shortly after dawn each day, there was a constant stream of airplanes into and out of K-2—scores of Mustangs and dozens of transport aircraft engaged in evacuating the wounded and bringing in vital supplies and passengers. Because it was the air base closest to the scene of combat, K-2 was a magnet for aircraft in trouble. Some were simply short of fuel, but others were shot up to various degrees. One T-6, heavily damaged by ground fire, staggered in and crashed on the runway, interrupting takeoffs and landings for a brief period until we got the wreckage off the runway. Luckily, the Mosquito pilot and Army observer were uninjured. The next day, a Mustang pilot crashed his badly shot-up F-51 just short of the runway. The plane was a total loss, but the pilot, who had been wounded in his right leg, seemed okay otherwise. I took him to the U.S. Army field hospital in Taegu for treatment.

Rumors were always floating around, many without much foundation. One of the encouraging ones concerned a couple of F-51 Mustang pilots who had accidentally strayed into Chinese airspace and strafed an airstrip near Antung after mistaking it for a North Korean airstrip at Sinuiju. That was the good news, but the downside was that the Chinese were exploiting the incident for propaganda purposes. I hoped this didn't result in much trouble for the pilots.

One of my assigned responsibilities was to meet and welcome all VIPs who arrived on the base by air. Over the months, I welcomed many visiting generals, diplomats, and politicians, including all of the top brass in the theater, and a covey of congressman who looked very much out of place in their business suits, dress shirts, ties, and fedora hats.

Some visitors to K-2 weren't there by choice. Occasionally, small groups of captured NKPA soldiers were herded onto the base to await transportation to a prisoner of war camp in the south. Many were ill-clothed, and uniformly, they were without expression, seemingly resigned to their fate. They were not by any measure an imposing group of soldiers. I wondered if they were representative of the army that had pushed us back into a small corner of Korea. If so, given the growing strength of the Eighth Army, maybe there should be reason for optimism. But I was not at all optimistic, considering what had occurred up to this point. What happened next didn't change that.

It was after midnight when I was awakened by the sound of explosions. Throwing on some clothes, I raced up to the platform on top of the operations building to see what was going on. The base was quiet, and I didn't observe any smoke or fire. What was happening? Then there were two more explosions just off base, maybe a quarter of a mile to the east. We were under artillery attack! In all, I counted twelve explosions before the attack ceased, but I couldn't tell where the attacks were coming from. We asked the JOC to have a Mosquito pilot search the area between seven and ten miles north of K-2, but nothing suspicious was found. Later in the day, four U.S. Army Sherman tanks rumbled onto the base, made their way to the dry river bed on the northern perimeter, dug in facing to the north with front ends angled upward thirty degrees, and began firing their 76-millimeter guns at possible NKPA artillery locations.

The next night, another artillery attack took place, during which one shell struck the runway overrun but caused no significant damage. This time, I was equipped with binoculars and spotted flashes coming from the mountain area to the north. I plotted the location of the flashes on a map and relayed it to the JOC. Early the next morning, we watched as four Mustangs carried out a napalm attack on the location. That ended the artillery attacks, but with the NKPA now so close, there was good reason to remain pessimistic about the future of the base. But there was another development that raised the spirits of everyone at K-2: each day for three straight days, more than 100 Mustang attack sorties, many within sight of the base, were directed against NKPA forces to the north of K-2.

As if we didn't have enough problems with the North Koreans, Typhoon Kezia entered the picture on September 13. It slammed into southern Japan, hampered USAF operations, and forced many aircraft to be moved out of its path. Many aircraft evacuated to K-2, which put a strain on our limited servicing capability.

At first, the news was vague—something about an amphibious landing by U.S. Marines at Inchon, not far from Seoul. The date was September 15, the beginning of a major turning point in the war. General MacArthur had developed a plan to land an invasion force made up of the 1st Marine Division and the U.S. Army's 7th Infantry Division at Inchon, far to the rear of the North Korean divisions deployed around the Pusan Perimeter. Few agreed with this plan, deeming it too risky given the nature of the tides at Inchon. But MacArthur prevailed, asserting, "The history of war proves that nine out of ten times an army has been destroyed because its supply lines have been cut off. We shall land at Inchon, and I shall crush them."

MacArthur did as promised. An early objective of the 1st Marine Division, after securing the beachhead, was Kimpo Airfield, sixteen road miles northeast of Inchon. Then the Marines were to cross the Han River and mount a drive on Seoul. But the Han River bridges had been destroyed back in June during the withdrawal of the ROK Army from Seoul. To facilitate the crossing of the Han River by the Marines, seventy Air Force C-119 transport flights airlifted a pontoon bridge from Japan to the Seoul area to span the Han River. Things went well. By the fourth day, Kimpo Airfield had been captured, giving the Air Force access to its 6,000-foot-long, 150-foot-wide hard-surfaced runway.

Meanwhile, in a coordinated operation, the Eighth Army broke out of the Pusan Perimeter and pushed toward Seoul. But it was slow going. The repair of the railroad and highway bridges presented a challenge; earlier in the war, Fifth Air Force fighter-bombers and light bombers had destroyed 140 bridges between Seoul and the front line and made many others unusable. But the North Koreans were on the run. By the time Seoul had been seized, UN forces had captured more than 140,000 North Korean soldiers.

I got back into combat at this point in an F-51 Mustang that had been left at K-2 for repair of some battle damage. I had noticed two Mustangs parked on the ramp for several days and learned from Harry Dugan that they were awaiting pickup by pilots from one of the outfits in Japan. I told Dugan that I'd like to take them on a mission. "Sure, go ahead," he said. That's when I got moving. I rounded up a Mustang pilot who was stranded at K-2 while his F-51 was being repaired, and the two of us got an intelligence briefing on the location of friends and foes and received instructions from the JOC to conduct an armed reconnaissance mission along the 150-mile stretch of road to Seoul. Armed with rockets and machine guns, our task was to report what we observed along the route and to attack any and all enemy elements that we sighted.

The North Korean withdrawal was in an early stage, so I didn't really know what to expect. Would there be a pell-mell exodus in progress or just a trickle? I got the answer as soon as we started up the road toward Seoul: it seemed to be deserted. The North Koreans had learned early on that if they were visible from the air, they would likely come under air attack. But we were flying low, almost down on the treetops, where we could see what was under trees along the edges of the road and in adjacent areas. We hadn't gone more than fifteen miles before I spotted a convoy of trucks under a tree line. We gave them a working over with machine-gun fire. Scores of troops scrambled for safety, but many didn't make it. Farther up the road, we saw a truck turning off the highway into what we discovered was a badly camouflaged truck park. That is where we placed our rockets. During the course of our two-hour mission, we attacked a dozen different targets—mostly vehicles and personnel—and we didn't take any hits.

Thirteen days after the Marines first came ashore, they seized Seoul. The next day, General MacArthur and South Korean president Syngman Rhee entered the city together, and as they proceeded to the National Assembly Hall, they were greeted by enthusiastic crowds of Koreans of all ages gathered along the street. The hall was filled with South Korean officials, citizens, and representatives of the combat units involved in freeing Seoul. In a brief ceremony, General MacArthur noted that the United Nations had liberated "this ancient capital city of Korea," and then turning to the president, he said that on behalf of the United Nations Command, "I am happy to restore to you, Mr. President, the seat of your government that from it you may better fulfill your constitutional responsibilities."*

---

* MacArthur commanded both the U.S. Far East Command and the United Nations Command, which in time included forces of twenty-one nations. Five of these nations provided air support in Korea: Australia, Greece, the Republic of Korea, South Africa, and the United States.

Fifth Air Force aircraft had played a significant role in defeating the North Koreans who were attacking the perimeter. During August, airmen flew 7,397 close-support sorties, an average of 238 each day. This tempo was sustained in September, with 6,440 sorties flown in support of the ground troops, an average of 215 per day. Such activity brought lavish praise from many of the ground commanders fighting in the perimeter. On September 2, the day after Fifth Air Force planes helped repel a heavy enemy assault on the 25th Infantry Division's lines, the division commander, Maj. Gen. William B. Kean, told reporters, "The close air support strikes rendered by the Fifth Air Force again saved this division, as they have many times before." General Walker was equally laudatory about the Fifth's efforts during the Eighth Army's defense of the Pusan Perimeter: "I am willing to state that no commander ever had better air support than has been furnished the Eighth Army by the Fifth Air Force. I will gladly lay my cards right on the table and state that if it had not been for the air support that we received from the Fifth Air Force, we would not have been able to stay in Korea."

There were a number of sure signs that North Korean resistance was crumbling all along the Pusan Perimeter. I learned of one from a friend assigned to the Mosquito squadron at K-2. Lt. George W. Nelson, one of the squadron's Mosquito aircraft pilots, had dropped a note to 200 enemy troops northeast of Kunsan demanding their surrender. They complied, moving to a designated hill to be captured by nearby UN ground troops. I don't know if this was a wartime first, but it was surely one for the books.

Another development was the return to the Taegu area of thousands of Korean residents who had fled to the south months earlier as the NKPA closed in on Taegu. Within two weeks of the Inchon landing, smoke began to curl out of chimneys in villages around K-2, and the movement of Koreans increased markedly along local roads. Life was beginning to return to normal for the local inhabitants.

✩ ✩ ✩

The invasion at Inchon set in motion a whole host of events at K-2. Two days after the Marines went ashore, everyone from K-2 who had retreated to Pusan was back on base, and with them came the aviation engineers, who resumed round-the-clock work on the runways, barracks, and mess hall. One day while that work was going on, President Syngman Rhee arrived at the base with scant notice. A guard at the front gate called to report that he was on the way to base operations, and I quickly informed Colonel Tyer. President Rhee was riding in back seat of an ancient black Chrysler and was accompanied by a couple of aides and a jeepful of guards. As soon as the car stopped, he quickly exited, and with a smile and some friendly words, he extended his hand to Colonel Tyer and then to me. I was struck by his seemingly affable nature as well as by his diminutive stature and heavily lined face. He said he wanted to thank the Air Force for fighting so bravely in support of his country and that he would like to look around the base. As a starting point, Tyer instructed me to take President Rhee out to look at the runway work. With me in the driver's seat of a jeep, Rhee beside me and two guards in the rear, I drove out to the new runway, where hundreds of Korean workers were installing pierced-steel planking. The president was all smiles, obviously immensely pleased to be able to greet so many of his countrymen who were hard at work on a vital project. As we drove along, he did a good bit of waving, and he asked me to stop several times so he could have a closer look and talk with the workers. After a brief tour of the base and a leisurely cup of coffee, he thanked us and departed.

Within ten days after they had arrived back at K-2, the aviation engineers finished installation of the last 300 feet of pierced-steel planking on the 5,000-foot runway and completed construction of a new 5,700-foot jet-capable runway. Concurrently, they completed the mess hall and dozens of simple buildings to be used as barracks. The day after the new runway was completed, the 49th Fighter-Bomber Group began moving to K-2 from its base in Japan. The group's seventy-five F-80 Shooting Star fighter-bombers were the first jet aircraft to operate from a Korean base. This move added hundreds of additional personnel to the base almost overnight. Still more were added when a photo-reconnaissance squadron moved in a few days later.*

The war continued to go well. Fifteen days after the Marine landed at Inchon, ROK forces crossed the 38th parallel, and eighteen days later, on October 19, UN forces captured Pyongyang, North Korea's capital city. Then, on October 24, as the UN vanguard crossed the Ch'ongch'on River, General MacArthur issued an order to his ground commanders to remove earlier restrictions on the employment of UN ground forces in the border regions adjoining China and the Soviet Union. He instructed them to press forward to the northern limits of Korea, utilizing all their forces. Somehow, earlier concerns that the Chinese might enter the war had evaporated in Washington and at MacArthur's Tokyo headquarters. Optimism was in the air. A few days earlier, MacArthur had predicted that "the war is very definitely coming to an end shortly." At K-2 and everywhere else in Korea, the rapid advance of UN forces created a great deal of talk about being home by Christmas. But for me it was just talk. While the war might end soon, it seemed highly unlikely that anyone at K-2 would be heading home anytime soon. World War II had ended six years earlier, but we still had forces in Japan and Germany. Would Korea be any different? I didn't think so.

One of the first Air Force outfits to move forward was the 614th Tactical Control Squadron with its T-6s and airborne controllers. They

---

* While conducting research for this book in the archives at Maxwell Air Force Base, I came across two pages in the 6149th Air Base Unit history that I had written in October 1950 detailing the activities of base operations from August 6 to October 1, 1950. I noted that all of the men assigned to me—crash crew, control tower, weather section, transient maintenance, operations—worked seven days a week, with many sleeping at or near their place of duty. How busy were we? The number of aircraft arrivals and departure during the fifty-five-day period of the report gives some indication: 38,000 aircraft, with a daily peak of 635 on August 26.

needed to be as close to the front lines as possible in order to provide timely air support to the Army. The squadron first moved to Kimpo on the outskirts of Seoul, but two weeks later, it received orders to move to nearby Seoul Municipal Airfield to make room for a fighter outfit. Radio repairman William H. Hayward remembered an interesting aspect of the move: "When we moved from Kimpo over to Seoul Municipal, about fourteen miles, we had two T-6's that had damage, and we could not fly them, so one of the mech's [mechanics] decided, 'We'll just taxi them down the highway.' And that is what we did. About half way there, we came upon a column of British armor, Centurion tanks to be exact. When the Limey's saw us, they just pulled off the road and were all sitting on their tanks when we went by. I could almost read their mind. 'What are these bloody Yanks going to do next?'"

As soon as the Pyongyang area was secure, the Fifth Air Force began moving units into the three nearby airfields. A flight of the 3rd Rescue Squadron equipped with H-19 helicopters, the 6147th Tactical Control Squadron with its T-6 Mosquito aircraft, and the 18th Fighter-Bomber Wing with seventy-five F-51 Mustangs deployed to K-24 (Pyongyang East) and began operations from its sod runway. At about the same time, an F-51 Mustang wing was deployed to nearby K-27 (Yonpo) and another Mustang wing to K-23 (Pyongyang). The deployment of these units from southern Korea to the north placed them much closer to the Army units they were supporting and enabled them to have shorter response times and to remain on station longer. Shortly afterwards, the 502nd Tactical Control Group, equipped with the radars needed to control and direct air interceptions and other air operations, was sent to Sinanju, some forty miles north of Pyongyang at the Ch'ongch'on River.

Now that the North Koreans were on the run and the war was going well, I had some time to do something about my clothing. When I departed Johnson Air Base for Korea in that Mustang, I was able to carry with me only a musette bag—a small canvas bag about the size of a bread box. That is all of the luggage that could be squeezed into the Mustang. The bag contained underwear, socks, and my toilet kit. All of my other possessions, including my uniforms, were packed in a roomy canvas B-4 bag that was to be sent to me. But the bag never showed up,

which meant that someone wasn't doing his job. It also meant that for
weeks I had been wearing the same flying suit. I had been unable to
have it washed because I had nothing else to wear during the washing.
When I heard that the supply sergeant had obtained a small batch of
clothing, I hustled over to the small hangar where several bundles of
clothing were laid out on the floor: fatigue jackets, hats, trousers, and a
stack of winter underwear. The sergeant said that I could take whatever
I wanted, no charge. Great! Now I would have a change of clothes. I
gathered up one of each item—long johns, fatigue jacket, trousers, and
hat. The next morning, dressed in rumpled fatigues, I looked more like
the proverbial "Sad Sack" than a commissioned U.S. Air Force officer.
Except for my captain's insignia, I was indistinguishable from an Army
private who had slept for a week in his fatigues. But I wasn't in the least
self-conscious. I was wearing clean clothes, and that is all that mattered
to me.

At this point, my job as base operations officer underwent a welcome change. As an additional responsibility, I became a transport pilot.
There were now more than 125 planes based at K-2, with many others
coming and going each day, and a population of more than 2,000 airmen. Given the scale of operations, the Fifth Air Force redesignated the
unit to which I was assigned as the 49th Fighter-Bomber Wing. That
change brought with it the assignment of a C-47 transport plane to be
used for hauling people and freight in support of the operations taking
place on the base. As base operations officer, I had responsibility for the
plane and for scheduling its flights. I saw to it that I got my share of the
flights.

The C-47 was developed as a military transport from the Douglas
DC-3 airliner and was used extensively during World War II for the
transport of troops, cargo, and casualties. More than 10,000 C-47s were
produced. With two engines, the plane cruised at 160 miles per hour
and had a range of 1,600 miles. The C-47 wasn't a stranger to me; I had
logged many hours as a passenger over the years and a few hours as a

co-pilot the previous year. So, after learning that there wasn't a C-47 instructor pilot on K-2 to check me out as a pilot, I just jumped in and went flying along with a fellow I drafted as co-pilot. Stable in flight and without any quirks, the C-47 was an easy airplane to fly. It wasn't what a fighter pilot would choose to fly, but it was all I had available, so I made the most of it. I made fifteen or so flights a month, most of them hauling cargo and people to and from Itazuke Air Base near Fukuoka on Kyushu, Japan's westernmost main island. I also made trips to air bases near Tokyo and in northern Honshu.

My first trip to Itazuke Air Base, like all of the others to Japan, was an overnight visit. This provided an opportunity to enjoy a hot shower, clean sheets, and a steak at the officers' club. More important than these pleasurable activities, I hoped to get some money. My wallet was getting mighty thin, and I wanted to replace my lost uniforms. As soon as I had parked the airplane, I went into the operations building and asked for a jeep ride to the finance office. The finance officer listened to my story about how I was sent to Korea in July and had been there ever since, hadn't been paid for three months, had lost my uniforms, and was down to my last ten bucks. He asked if I had a copy of the orders assigning me to the 49th Fighter-Bomber Wing. Fortunately, I had brought a copy of the orders with me, and with these and my identification card in hand, he made some phone calls to try to locate my pay records. He didn't succeed but told me that they would turn up eventually, and meanwhile, he would give me an "emergency payment" of $250 to see me through. My next stop was the base exchange, where I purchased a new uniform, along with a belt, shirts, socks, hat, and shoes.

That night at the officers club, I was delighted to find three old friends I hadn't seen for years, all fighter pilots who had just arrived from the States. We had a great time talking about times past and about what the future might hold for us.

While the air traffic at K-2 was heavy during daylight hours, it dropped off considerably at night. A few transport aircraft came and went, and there were usually upwards of a dozen flights by RB-26s on night reconnaissance missions. Also, a night-fighter aircraft or two might drop in. While a number of aircraft crashes had taken place on and around the base during daylight hours, I didn't think the chances were high for night occurrences. I was wrong. The first one came when an RB-26 blew a tire on takeoff, veered off the runway, and slammed into a batch of F-80 fighter-bombers. This caused a huge commotion, and since it occurred during darkness, it took a while to determine that no one was injured. Four F-80s had been destroyed. Luckily, they were not loaded with bombs and rockets, as were others nearby.

A week later, also in the middle of the night, a C-46 transport plane owned by Civil Air Transport swerved off the runway during takeoff when its landing gear collapsed. It skidded into some of the F-80s that had narrowly escaped destruction by the errant RB-26. I heard the crash and hurried to the scene. With no illumination except jeep and truck headlights, it was difficult to assess the damage. Upon arriving at the crash, I found myself wading in jet fuel almost ankle-deep. Had this been gasoline, it is likely that scores of airplanes would have been destroyed by fire. But jet fuel is not as volatile as gasoline, so we were spared what could have been a very bad situation. The jet fuel I waded through came from six ruptured F-80 wingtip tanks, each of which had contained 265 gallons of fuel. This time, the damage to the F-80s was minimal, limited to ruptured tip tanks and damaged wingtips. But the big problem was how to move the C-46, now resting on its belly, with its nose intruding into the fighter-bomber area and its tail blocking the adjacent taxiway. If further damage to the transport was to be avoided, this was going to require more than just brute horsepower against a C-46 that weighed twenty tons and had a wingspan of 108 feet. The solution arrived the next afternoon, flown in from a base near Tokyo: large inflatable rubber bladders. These were placed beneath each of the C-46's wings and inflated with compressed air until the airplane was raised far enough above the ground to provide space to lower the landing gear. At that point the airplane was towed to a maintenance area.

That wasn't the end of the night crashes. A few nights later, an RB-26 crashed north of the base shortly after takeoff, slamming into a

mountain. I didn't know the cause of the crash but surmised that whatever it was, the plane was too low for crew members to bail out. All four
of them were killed.

Then, on one cold and blustery day, an F-80 pilot returning from a
mission to North Korea didn't make it to the runway. His supply of fuel
gave out twenty-five miles from K-2. For a while, he thought he could
glide to safety. The control tower alerted me that they had received a
mayday call from an F-80 out of fuel and dead-sticking toward the base.
I sighted the plane as it neared to about three miles to the northwest. I
could tell by its location and altitude that it wouldn't reach the base.

At this point, the pilot should have bailed out, but he stayed with
the airplane. He came down a mile to the west in wooded area I had
surveyed in anticipation of the need to rescue downed airmen, and I
found him in relatively short order. The pilot was sitting on a downed
tree, head in hand, not far from his mangled airplane. He didn't look up
when I approached and replied in a low voice to my query about his
condition. I could see no blood or other obvious signs of injury, but I
figured that either he was in shock or his head had forcefully struck the
gunsight during the crash and he was suffering from a concussion. I
asked him if he could walk. He nodded yes and trudged to my jeep,
which was parked a quarter of a mile away. I probably set a speed record
driving him to the Army field hospital in Taegu.

There was always something interesting going on at K-2. Two
young F-80 pilots who had been sent on an armed reconnaissance mission over northeast North Korea were more than thirty minutes over-
due when they finally arrived back at K-2 with little more than fumes
left in their fuel tanks. They had an exciting story to tell about how they
had come across a North Korean airfield loaded with fighter aircraft and
had given it a working over, making repeated strafing attacks and
destroying a number of enemy airplanes. The intelligence officer who
debriefed them had no knowledge of any serviceable airfields in that
part of Korea, and their report surprised him. He asked them to point
out the exact location of the airfield on an aeronautical chart, but the
pilots could point only to a broad area where they thought the airfield
was located. The weather had been marginal, they said, and they were

uncertain about the exact location. Further investigation by Fifth Air
Force intelligence officers failed to reconcile the report with the information they had in their files. Two weeks later, the mystery was solved
when the Fifth Air Force learned that the Soviets had made a formal
protest to the U.S. State Department, citing an attack on the day in
question by two American jet fighter planes on one of their airfields
some forty miles from Vladivostok.

Following orders from above, General Partridge relieved the 49th
Fighter-Bomber Group's commander and directed that the two pilots,
both lieutenants, be court-martialed. The question of how to deal fairly
with errant combatants seems to arise in every war. The pilots of the
49th Fighter Group were highly displeased when the two pilots were
brought before a court-martial. They believed that it would be a breach
of justice to harshly punish the two pilots, who in marginal weather and
hundreds of miles from base had innocently strayed across the border
and mounted an attack against what is normally a very dangerous target.
Not surprisingly, neither was convicted. Afterwards, General Partridge,
mindful of the fog of war and the loyalty he owed to his subordinates,
assigned one of the pilots to be aide-de-camp to the commanding general of the 314th Air Division in Japan, and the other was sent to an
F-80 squadron in Japan. He brought the ousted 49th Fighter-Bomber
Group commander to his headquarters to be director of combat operations. I never learned what happened to the Soviet commander who
failed to mount a defense of his airfield.

As reports came in that UN forces were north of Pyongyang and
advancing toward the Yalu River, which separates North Korea from
China, morale soared at K-2. It now appeared certain that war would
soon end. To communicate a surrender ultimatum from General
MacArthur, Air Force aircraft dropped more than four million leaflets
over parts of North Korea not yet in UN hands.

In addition to that good news, word was circulated that Bob Hope
was coming to entertain the troops in the Taegu area. Many of us from

K-2 drove over the "Taegu Bowl"—a hillside area not far from the town—to join an appreciative crowd of more than 4,000 GIs gathered to witness an outstanding show featuring Bob, Hollywood star Marilyn Maxwell, and Les Brown and his Band of Renown. In addition to performing for the troops, Bob and Marilyn visited all sections of K-2, including the hospital. That impressed me even more than the wonderful show they had staged. All of us greatly admired Hope for organizing and providing entertainment for U.S. servicemen overseas. For us, it was tangible evidence that we had not been simply shoved off overseas and forgotten.

Then, suddenly and unexpectedly, came another major turning point in the war. The first such point, at Inchon, had surprised the North Koreans. This one would stun the Americans and their UN allies. China had entered the war. Just as a united, noncommunist Korea seemed within reach, more than 180,000 Chinese Communist Forces (CCF) troops slipped over the Yalu River into North Korea. We would *not* be home for Christmas.

The first word of Chinese involvement came from ROK I Corps and II Corps units of the Eighth Army which were approaching the Yalu River. They were ambushed by what they thought were NKPA units and had suffered heavy losses, as did a regiment of the 1st Cavalry Division when it came forward to cover the withdrawal of the heaviest hit ROK division. Much to the surprise of the ROK commanders, Chinese soldiers were found among the captives taken on October 25.

A friend of mine in the Army, 2nd Lt. George M. Johnson, from Milwaukee, Wisconsin, was assigned to the 8th Cavalry Regiment, the unit that got chewed up. It experienced the brunt of the CCF attack beginning on November 2. Ordered to withdraw southward to Ipsok, the regiment was trapped by CCF roadblocks south of Unsan, located north of the Chongsong River above Anju. Within hours, the ROK 15th Regiment, on the 8th Cavalry's right flank, collapsed, and the 1st and 2nd Battalions of the 8th Cavalry fell back in disarray into the city of Unsan. By morning, as their positions were being overrun, the men of the 8th Cavalry tried to withdraw, but a Chinese roadblock to their rear forced them to abandon their artillery and take to the hills in small groups. Only scattered survivors made it back to tell their story. Of the 900 men assigned to the 3rd Battalion, 8th Regiment, only 245 survived; of the battalion's 40 officers, only 2 made it out safely. George Johnson was one of the them. During his trek to safety, he was joined by a machine-gun sergeant who had a leg wound that made it impossible for him to walk without assistance and a young lieutenant who had been hit on the head with a rifle butt by a Chinese soldier. Along the way, Johnson commandeered a huge ox to transport the wounded sergeant, and the small band finally trudged to safety with the ox's unhappy owner following to protect his animal.

A week later, there was another report of a Chinese attack on U.S. Army units. Initially, the reports of the Chinese presence were doubted by intelligence officials. Then it was thought that there were only a few Chinese "volunteers" mixed in with regular NKPA units. Then came a month-long pause in Chinese attacks, which confused American officials. Unnoticed by the UN command, an estimated 325,000 Chinese soldiers had deployed into North Korea and were poised for a massive attack. UN forces were not prepared for what came next. They were thinly spread and poorly positioned to withstand a major assault, and they were split into two commands: the Eighth Army in the west and the X Corps on the east coast. Almost everyone still believed that victory was close at hand.

Ignoring the reports of Chinese involvement and earlier warnings from China's leaders, General MacArthur ordered the resumption of the drive to the Yalu and the seizure of all of Korea. On November 24, a month after the initial reports of Chinese involvement, the Eighth Army resumed its advance toward the Yalu. On the very next night, the Chinese launched a massive offensive. Strong CCF units hit the Eighth Army's IX Corps and the ROK II Corps, collapsing the ROK II Corps on the Eighth Army's right flank. Two days later, in the east, attacks engulfed the leftmost forces of the X Corps at the Chosin Reservoir, and by the next day, the UN position in North Korea began to crumble.

Almost immediately, the Eighth Army began to withdraw. Soon it was in full retreat, no longer a fighting force, destroying vast quantities of equipment and supplies. The retreat would cover 120 miles in ten days, the longest in U.S. history. Hardest hit during the retreat was the 2nd Infantry Division, whose casualties for the last half of November numbered 4,940—90 percent of which had been incurred since November 25. This represented one-third of the division's actual strength of 15,000 on November 15. Losses in equipment were likewise heavy: hundreds of trucks and trailers, sixty-four artillery pieces, almost all of the 2nd Engineer Combat Battalion's equipment, and 20 to 40 percent of the signal equipment carried by the various division units.

The three F-51 Mustang wings deployed on bases around Pyongyang were withdrawn to bases in South Korea without any loss of personnel or equipment. But with only a few hour's notice and no rail transportation available, the 502nd Tactical Control Group (recently deployed to Sinanju, some forty miles north of Pyongyang) was forced to abandon its radars and other heavy gear—a great loss.

On the east coast, as the X Corps began a withdrawal to the port city of Hungnam, the center and rightmost units experienced little difficulty. But the 1st Marine Division and the remnants of a 7th Infantry Division task force in the mountains around the Chosin Reservoir faced seven Chinese divisions—and temperatures as low as forty degrees below zero. Although surrounded by Chinese force, the Marines, buoyed by tremendous courage, broke out of the trap set by the Chinese and carried out a successful withdrawal. Savage fighting occurred all along the route as they made a fighting retreat toward the sea. An estimated 40,000 Chinese were killed and as many as 20,000 wounded. By the time the withdrawal ended on December 10,454 Marines had been killed and 2,844 wounded, 94 died of wounds, and 174 were missing in action—a total of 3,572—and there were thousands of nonbattle injuries, mostly frostbite. Upon reaching Pusan, the Marines once again joined the Eighth Army and soon took up the fight in the west.

News of the Chinese intervention and the Eighth Army's subsequent bloody and disorderly retreat swept through the K-2 like a tidal wave. "Bug-out" was the term widely used to describe this terrible development. What did this mean to us? Would American forces again be pushed back into the southeast corner of Korea or even into the sea? There were no answers. Meanwhile, pilots of the fighter-bombers based at K-2 provided support to both the Eighth Army and the forces withdrawing from the Chosin Reservoir.

Air Force support was critical to the UN's retreat back to the south. At K-2, the intensity of operations by the F-80s of the 49th Fighter-Bomber Group increased. They were joined in mid-December by seventy-five F-84 Thunderstreaks of the 27th Fighter-Escort Group, just deployed to K-2 from the United States. The F-84s would be employed as fighter-bombers. The arrival of the 27th just about doubled the base's population and brought to nearly 200 the number of airplanes parked on the ramp. In anticipation of this expansion, Air Force engineers had erected some 100 buildings of wood and stucco on concrete floors.

The word circulated at the speed of light among pilots throughout the Fifth Air Force: an enemy swept-wing jet fighter, identified by intelligence officials as a MiG-15, had flashed by a Mustang pilot near the Yalu River on the afternoon of November 1. This was big news because the MiG-15's performance outclassed that of every allied aircraft in the theater. A week later, the first jet-versus-jet combat took place. Lt. Russell J. Brown, flying an F-80, shot down a MiG-15. The MiG-15 had a 100-mile-per-hour speed advantage over the F-80, so Brown's victory pointed up the inexperience of the MiG pilots.

The MiGs operated from a newly constructed 6,000-foot all-weather runway at Antung, just across the Yalu River in China, together with a newly operational early-warning radar that had a 150-mile reach. The Chinese Air Force was thus poised to seriously challenge UN air operations in North Korea and potentially farther south. At this point, our intelligence estimated that the Chinese Air Force operated 650 combat aircraft, including 250 conventional and jet fighters, 175 ground-attack aircraft, 150 conventional twin-engine bombers, and 75 transports.

To confront the threat posed by the MiG-15s, the U.S. Air Force moved quickly to deploy F-86s to the theater. These swept-wing fighters offered performance believed to be comparable to the MiGs. The first F-86s, based at Kimpo Air Base at Seoul, went into action on December 17 and scored the kill of a MiG-15. That was the beginning of an intensified campaign to contain the Chinese Air Force.

The question on everyone's lips at K-2 was, Where would the Eight Army make a stand? First, we heard that it would be made at Pyongyang, but that didn't happen. After that, there was daily speculation as we watched the retreating line of contact on the situation map. When the CCF crossed the 38th parallel on Christmas Day, Air Force people wondered how this could have happened. We had complete control of the air over the Eighth Army, thus providing it the freedom to move and operate without fear of enemy air attack. We had much higher firepower in the form of artillery and tanks and almost unlimited support by Air Force fighter-bombers. We had trucks to move troops and supplies. On the other side, the CCF had no air support and modest artillery support and had to walk into battle and move supplies using humans and animals. But still the Chinese kept moving south.

Two days before the CCF crossed the 38th parallel, the Eighth Army's commander, Gen. Walton H. Walker, was killed in a jeep accident. Three days later, Gen. Matthew B. Ridgway arrived from Washington and assumed command of the Eighth Army. He had served with distinction as a division commander in Europe during World War II.

As massive numbers of Chinese troops crossed the frozen Han River east and west of Seoul, the Eighth Army began to evacuate the South Korean capital. At the same time, USAF units burned nearly 500,000 gallons of fuel and 23,000 gallons of napalm at Kimpo Air Base in preparation for abandoning the base to the advancing enemy.

On January 4, Seoul changed hands for the third time when CCF troops moved into the city. Prior to the entry of the CCF troops, some 600,000 of Seoul's citizens, about half the population, fled to the south, and most of the remainder moved to nearby villages. Upon learning of the fall of Seoul, my thought was, "Are we going to be pushed back into the Pusan Perimeter once again?" I knew the situation was bad, but it was even worse than I thought. What I didn't know was that the very next day, the commander of the Fifth Air Force approved a plan to withdraw the entire Air Force contingent to Japan if the situation continued to worsen and our bases were threatened.

A few days before Seoul fell to the CCF, I asked Colonel Tyer to release me from my assignment as base operations officer and secure me an assignment to a fighter squadron. I hadn't asked him earlier because of the tenuous situation we had faced at K-2 and the shortage of personnel. During that period, the last thing he would have wanted to hear was a request for anyone to leave. But now that I had served at K-2 for five months and there was no longer a shortage of personnel, I felt he would likely agree to my request. I told him that back in July, at Langley Air Force Base, I had responded to an Air Force call for volunteers to fly F-51 Mustangs, and I had flown six missions before being side-tracked to become part of the small group at K-2 operating the vital refuel/rearm operation. As disappointing as that was, I said, I had done my job to the very best of my ability, and now that the situation was under control, I would like to get back to being a fighter pilot. Any Mustang outfit would be fine with me, I told him, and as an indication of just how desperate I was, I told him that even an assignment to the F-51 photo-reconnaissance squadron on K-2 would suit me if a fighter slot wasn't in the cards.

Other than a nod, the colonel had no visible reaction to my request, leaving me to wonder if I had bombed out. But this was his usual way of dealing with subordinates, and since he hadn't said no, I was hopeful. A few days later, I got a huge surprise when I was handed orders assigning me to the 49th Fighter-Bomber Group, which was equipped with F-80 jet aircraft and located on K-2, just 100 yards away from base operations.

PART 2

Shooting Stars—
Fast and Deadly

Chapter 6

With transfer orders in hand, I wasted no time in making my way over to the headquarters of the 49th Fighter-Bomber Group (49th FBG), where I told the adjutant that I wanted to speak with the commanding officer.

"What's your business?" he wanted to know.

"I'm checking in," I said. "Newly assigned."

The adjutant disappeared into the adjacent office, then returned after a brief delay. "Colonel Murphy will see you now."

Lt. Col. John R. Murphy was exceptionally well qualified for his job—a World War II fighter pilot who commanded a fighter group and flew P-47s on 139 combat missions over Europe. In 1949, he commanded the 49th Group for six months before being transferred to Fifth Air Force headquarters as assistant director of operations and then director. In that position, at the start of the Korean War, he served as the first director of the Joint Operations Center and helped organize the tactical air control system. After some months in that job, he flew missions in F-51s with the 18th Fighter-Bomber Group. Now he was back in command of the 49th. I was impressed by his record.

After saluting, I told Colonel Murphy that I was reporting for duty. He asked me to tell him about my background. This was an invitation I had anticipated. Looking to the future, I had prepared a little speech that I hoped would cause him to remember me favorably when a squadron commander slot came open. For starters, I told him I had stepped forward at the beginning of the war in response to the Air Force's call for volunteer F-51 pilots, but after only six missions had gotten side-tracked. I then recited a brief synopsis of my World War II experience, subsequent assignments as a P-47 instructor, and my recent experience as a Mustang squadron commander and fighter group operations officer at Itazuke Air Base, Japan. Finally, I told him that I was pleased to be assigned to the 49th and excited by the prospect of flying the F-80.

"Welcome to the 49th," he said. "I'm assigning you to the 9th Squadron. Go see Squire Williams. He's the commander."

The 9th was the 9th Fighter-Bomber Squadron (FBS), and Lt. Col. Charles H. "Squire" Williams was the heaviest fighter pilot I had ever met. He stood six feet and weighed 240 pounds. Outgoing, jovial, and friendly, he enjoyed nothing more than a gathering of fellow fighter pilots at which jokes and friendly insults kept everyone entertained. Asked by a reporter if he had any difficulty getting into the cockpit of an F-80, he responded saying that he had no trouble at all since he used a "greased shoe horn." But once in the cockpit, he said, "I can't take sitting-up exercises while I'm in there, that's all." In contrast, his deputy, Maj. Clyde Good, weighed a scant 140 pounds and stood only five feet, four inches—the minimum height for an Air Force pilot. And then there was Capt. Robert L. Eckman, squadron engineering officer, who stood six feet, three inches, and wore size thirteen shoes. But Squire Williams and Eckman weren't the only tall ones in the squadron; nearly half of the pilots stood six feet or more in height. Certainly, no one arranged this; it just turned out that way.

The 9th Fighter-Bomber Squadron was one of three assigned to the 49th FBG, each with twenty-five F-80s. There were thirty-three pilots assigned to the squadron, more than the authorized twenty-five, the overage having been created by an influx of new pilots in anticipation of eight who would complete their tours of combat duty and transfer out before month's end. The pilots were housed in two recently constructed one-story stucco buildings built on concrete floors with open interiors wide enough for two rows of metal cots placed perpendicular to the side walls and long enough for each row to contain a dozen cots, each equipped with a mosquito net. Three pot-bellied stoves, one near either end of the building and one in the center, sat in the aisle that ran down the middle of the building, separating the two rows of cots. Squire told me to take any empty cot that I desired, and I selected one near the door. This would be austere living—even less personal space than the broom closet I had occupied for the last five months—but certainly drier and more comfortable than a tent.

As it turned out, the twenty occupants were all congenial and got along without any friction. Things got a little noisy at times, but at lights out—2200 hours—all went quiet. There was one problem with the seemingly well-constructed building: the Korean contractor had cheated on the concrete by using far less cement than called for. As a consequence, the floor emitted sand. Regardless of how often it was swept, it was never free of sand. Every morning, the Korean houseboy sprinkled water on the floor before he swept in an effort to keep the dust down, but sand still came to the surface.

The houseboy's most important function was to prevent theft of our possessions. We hired him to be in our barracks whenever we were absent. This was because pilfering was quite prevalent, and nothing was safe if left unguarded. This was probably a legacy of the forty years of Japanese rule during which many Koreans endured hardship and poverty. Stories always went around of thefts of various sorts. The best one I heard involved a fighter-bomber squadron commander from an outfit in Japan who had spent the night in a tent for visitors at K-2. He had laid his clothing on a chair beside the bed, but when he woke the next morning, everything was gone except the long winter underwear he had on and his shoes. He flew back to Japan in his winter underwear, which must have been quite a sight for his squadron mates.

The latrine was the one place on base where you could be assured of getting a laugh when a new boy walked in. Located across a dirt alley just a few steps from my barracks was a long, low building that contained a communal shower, a row of sinks, and a six-holer—the centerpiece of the latrine—constructed of rough lumber. To carry away waste, the engineers employed an ingenious contraption. A fifty-five-gallon drum was installed above a trough which ran beneath the six-holes. Water, brought up from below by a small gasoline-powered pump, slowly filled the drum, which was mounted in such a way that when nearly full, it would tip over with a thunderous clang and send all of its contents flooding with a mighty rush through the trough below the six holes. For new arrivals, especially those seated on one of the six holes, the sudden, totally unexpected metallic clang and the mighty rush of water, was a startling event. For old hands, it was a signal that they had better quickly rise up to avoid being washed by the rushing water. We got some good laughs observing the reaction of the new boys.

Maj. James E. "Jim" Anderson was the 9th Squadron's operations officer, the man in charge of flying activities. When I checked in with him, he said, "We'll get you checked out in the F-80 just as soon as possible. I've assigned Bud Evans to oversee the process. He'll get you going right away." First Lt. Nervin "Bud" Evans was an affable fellow, an old hand in the squadron who had racked up numerous missions, and I could sense from our initial conversation that he would be easy to work with. As he handed me a copy of the F-80 flight operating instructions, he said, "George, you know the drill. Study this. When you are ready, you'll have to complete a closed-book, 50-question written exam. Then you'll need to spend some time in an F-80 cockpit to get ready for a blindfold check. After that, we'll go flying."

The F-80C Shooting Star, manufactured by Lockheed Corporation, was the first U.S. Air Force jet airplane to be employed in combat. It had a wingspan of 38 feet, 10.5 inches; was 34 feet, 6 inches long; and stood 11 feet, 4 inches high. Powered by an Allison J33 engine, its maximum speed was 580 miles per hour, and its service ceiling was 46,800 feet. It was armed with six .50-caliber machine guns, could carry 5-inch rockets, and two napalm tanks, two 500-pound bombs, or two 1,000-pound bombs. With a 265-gallon droppable fuel tank attached to each wingtip, the F-80's combat radius was more than 350 miles, varying according to the type of combat mission and armament load. The cost to the U.S. government was $93,456. While the wingspan, length, and height of the F-80C weren't much different from the F-51 Mustang's, its operating performance was a world apart in terms of speed.

The airplanes of each group bore distinctive markings. Those of the 49th FBG had a six-inch band of color painted horizontally near the top of the tail of each airplane. In addition, the same color was applied to the nose of the airplane, starting at the cockpit and sweeping along either side of the black antiglare paint on top of the nose and continuing around tip and bottom of the nose. Red paint was used for the markings on the 9th FBS airplanes, yellow for the 8th FBS, and blue for the 7th FBS.

★ ★ ★

I studied the flight operating instructions for the better part of the day, committing to memory what I judged to be the most important parts, with particular attention given to those sections dealing the basics of operating the airplane and the section on emergency operating procedures. I passed the written examination without any difficulty, after which Bud Evans and I had a conversation focused on the important differences between flying the F-51 Mustang and the F-80C. Aside from tricycle landing gear, higher speed, and no propeller to create torque, there was one aspect of the F-80C that merited special attention, he said. "It's important for you to keep in mind that the engine in the F-80C is slow in developing thrust when advancing the throttle from the idle position. What this means is that on the landing approach you should not retard the throttle to the idle position until certain you're going to land the airplane. Otherwise, if the throttle is in the idle position, and you decide to make a go-around, the engine acceleration may be so slow that you don't have enough engine thrust to keep the airplane from settling onto the surface, and then you may find yourself running out of runway or otherwise getting into difficulty."

During the blindfold test, Evans called out one at a time the names of three dozen or so controls, gauges, and switches: landing-gear lever, landing-light switch, landing-gear position lights, oxygen-cylinder pressure, pitot-heat switch, and so forth. I pointed to each location or touched it. The test went well, and that same afternoon, I made my initial flight. No T-33 (two-place version of the F-80) was available, so I flew an F-80C with Bud Evans tagging along in a second bird in case I encountered any difficulty and needed expert advice. During the thirty-minute flight, I first made some turns to get a feel for the airplane, then some stalls, a chandelle or two, a couple of barrel rolls, a high-speed dive followed by a high-G recovery, and then some slow flying with the landing gear and flaps down. It was a responsive, honest airplane with no bad characteristics. The most striking features were its speed and its freedom from the vibration encountered in propeller-driven airplanes. It seemed to slide effortlessly through the air like a porpoise in the sea. In addition to all of this, its tricycle landing gear allowed unobstructed views while on the ground. I loved the F-80 from the moment I first lifted off.

Following that initial flight, Jim Anderson, the ops officer, informed me that he would begin scheduling me for combat flying as soon as I had logged ten hours in the airplane. Over the course of five days, I made seven flights and logged ten hours and thirty-five minutes, all uneventful. When I informed Anderson that I had accumulated the prescribed ten hours, he scheduled me for a combat mission the next day, January 17, 1951. By month's end, I would fly twenty missions.

The standard combat formation flown in the 49th was a four-plane flight made up of the flight leader and his wingman plus an element leader and his wingman—the same as in World War II. The 9th FBS radio call sign was Bully. The first flight of the day would be Bully Able, the second Bully Baker, the third Bully Charlie, and so on through the armed forces phonetic alphabet.

On my initial combat mission, Anderson scheduled me as element leader in a flight he was leading that was tagged Bully Baker. We were directed to proceed northeast to the Yongdok, which is located on the east coast only fifty-two miles from K-2, and contact a forward air controller with the ROK marine regiment that was attached to the U.S. 1st Marine Division. This location was so far south of the 38th parallel that

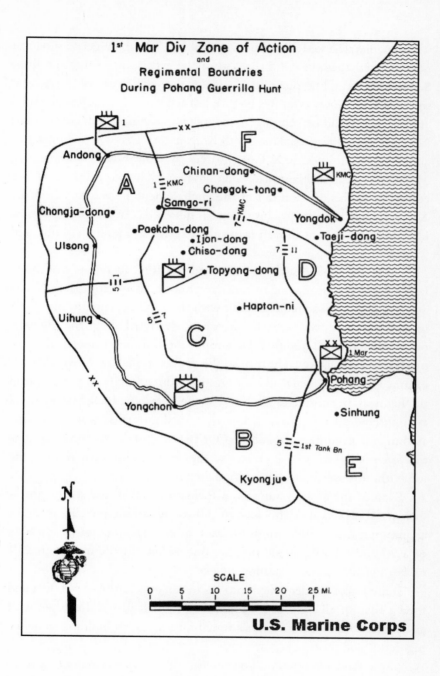

1st Mar Div Zone of Action
and
Regimental Boundries
During Pohang Guerrilla Hunt

U.S. Marine Corps

SCALE
0   5   10   15   20   25 Mi.

Andong
Chinan-dong
Chaegok-tong
Chongja-dong
Samgo-ri
Yongdok
Ulsong
Paekcha-dong
Ijon-dong
Taeji-dong
Chiso-dong
Topyong-dong
Uihung
Hapton-ni
Yongchon
Pohang
Sinhung
Kyongju

A B C D E F

we immediately asked what this was all about. The intelligence situation map showed that the CCF had advanced sixty miles southeast from Seoul to Wonju, but our target area on the east coast was far to the south of that. How could this be? We learned from the intelligence officer that we would be supporting an operation being conducted against North Korean guerrillas. The North Korean 10th Division had been just about encircled by U.S. X Corps forces, and the NKPA commander, Maj. Gen. Lee Ban Nam, had been advised by his superior that if he could not get his division out of the encirclement, he was to stay in the X Corps rear and employ his troops as guerrillas. At this point, the 1st Marine Division was moved forward to conduct a guerrilla hunt, and we would support that mission.

Once airborne, Anderson contacted the JOC to report that Bully Baker flight was in the air, en route to Yondok. As we approached Yondok, Anderson made radio contact with the FAC attached to the ROK marine regiment, who asked that we fly westward along the highway out of Yondok at 2,500 feet. He soon sighted us and directed that we make a ninety-degree right turn so that he could make positive identification. He then directed us to a group of three buildings not far from the highway. In conducting a sweep of their area, the ROK marines had encountered a large group of heavily armed guerrillas who were situated in and around the buildings. Our task was to attack and neutralize this force or at least weaken it so that the ROK marines could finish the job without suffering too many casualties.

Each of the four aircraft in our formation was armed with eight 5-inch aerial rockets and a full load of .50-caliber armor-piercing incendiary ammunition—300 rounds for each of six machine guns, for a total of 1,800 rounds. We would first fire our rockets, then employ our .50-caliber machine guns in strafing attacks.

Bully Baker Leader rolled into his rocket attack from 3,500 feet and fired a salvo of all eight of his rockets on his first pass at the target with good effect. All of his rockets slammed into the main building, generating debris and dust.

Just as Anderson was pulling off the target, his wingman began his attack run. As was the case with the leader's attack, number two scored direct hits on one of the other buildings. These direct hits provided a challenge to me and my wingman. One building remained untouched, the smallest of the three, and therefore would be the most difficult to strike squarely. My rockets struck the left half of the building, and Baker 4 finished the job, pretty much demolishing the structure.

We began our strafing attacks from 3,500 feet at a dive angle of about twenty-five degrees. Strafing, the bread-and-butter mission of fighter-bomber pilots, is highly accurate and, with the ammunition being used, deadly against many types of targets. We each executed half a dozen attacks to cover the entire area designated by the FAC. Then we bid the FAC good luck and turned to the southwest to head back to K-2. His response: "Thanks, excellent job. Well done."

We learned much later that the 1st Marine Division had difficulty locating guerrillas but not in subduing them once they were located. A captured North Korean 10th Division officer explained that the division commander, General Lee, was suffering from melancholia and was brooding constantly over his division's situation. He was providing no direction to his troops, leaving them with no options except take flight or hide. After nearly three weeks of searching the area, General Smith, the 1st Marine Division's commander, notified General Ridgway that his forces had scattered the remnants of the ROK 10th Division and that Lee's forces were not then capable of any kind of major effort. Therefore, the situation was sufficiently in hand to permit the assignment of a new mission to the 1st Marine Division.

That night, following my first combat mission, Bud Evans told me about his initial mission a few days after the war began. It was the very first mission flown by 49th Fighter-Bomber Group pilots, and it was a hairy one. The air evacuation from Seoul of U.S. embassy personnel, their families, and others was underway, but it was threatened by periodic attacks by North Korean fighter aircraft. Evans and three others were launched from Itazuke Air Base in Japan to provide protection for the transport aircraft on the ground at Kimpo Air Base at Seoul. The weather was awful, with base of clouds 175 feet and visibility of a quarter of a mile in heavy rain—well below the minimums prescribed by the Air Force, and it was forecasted to get worse. They had no aeronautical charts, the radio aids at Kimpo had been shut down, and clouds covered Seoul. In Evans's mind, there was a real question about whether they would be able to carry out their mission and land safely back at Itazuke or anywhere else. But despite the challenges, they did successfully complete their mission and somehow got safely back into Itazuke despite a dwindling fuel supply and terrible weather. Lucky fellows!

Chapter 7

Up to this point, all of my flying in Korea had been in the south, but now combat missions in the F-80 would be taking me into the north as well. A look at an aeronautical chart shows that Korea is a land of mountains and narrow valleys dotted with rice paddies and edged with mud flats. Rugged mountain peaks reach 9,000 feet in the north; farther south, two mountain ranges rise to 5,000 to 6,000 feet, with spurs from these ranges extending to the west and southwest to cover nearly all of Korea. As I had discovered on combat missions in the F-51, there is little to distinguish one mountain ridge or valley from another, and this made target identification extremely difficult at times.

It was January, and although I was wearing lots of clothes when outside, I couldn't seem to get warm. All winter, a chilling wind sweeps down out of Siberia and the mean temperature at Taegu hovers around thirty-two degrees. Up in North Korea, where I would be flying frequently, winters are bitterly cold. Fierce northern and northwestern winds bring, on average, thirty-seven days of snowfall. Deep snows accumulate in the mountainous regions, and the weather is particularly harsh. The daily average low and high temperatures for Pyongyang in January are eight and twenty-six degrees. Areas farther to the north are even colder.

This meant that whenever I prepared to launch off on a combat mission, I dressed in layers of clothing and, in addition, carried what seemed like a ton of escape-and-evasion gear. Certainly, I would not be travelling lightly. In addition to long underwear and heavy shirt and trousers, I wore a winter flying suit, over which I donned a vest containing escape-and-evasion items: nylon map, blood chit offering a reward to any Korean that assisted a downed airman, Korean money, gold coins, knife, first-aid kit, water container, water-purification tablets, high-energy bars, compass, and spare ammunition for the .45-caliber pistol carried in a shoulder holster. In addition to all of this, I carried two pairs of heavy wool socks to be used in case my feet got wet or cold. Potentially, the most important item was the bulky portable radio, about three-quarters the size of a cigar box, to be used to contact rescue forces (covering fighters and a rescue helicopter). Other items, including a rubber dinghy, were contained in the seat pack of the parachute. A heavy flying jacket was worn over the vest, and "chaps"—a G suit—were slipped on over the pant legs and abdomen and then laced tight. Once in the cockpit, I pushed my arms through the parachute harness and fastened the straps around my thighs and chest.

The G suit was designed to minimize the effect of high-G forces on a pilot by preventing or delaying a gray-out (deterioration of vision) or black-out (total loss of vision) due to the blood pooling in the lower part of the body when the aircraft is turned sharply—such as when pulling out of a steep dive—thus depriving the brain of blood containing oxygen. While tolerance level varies, many pilots will experience a gray-out beginning at four Gs and a blackout before reaching five Gs. The G suit was in the form of tightly fitting trousers worn over the flying suit and fitted with inflatable bladders which, when pressurized through a G-sensitive valve in the aircraft, squeeze firmly on the abdomen and legs, thus restricting the draining of blood away from the brain during periods of high acceleration. The bladders inflate automatically in response to G forces and subside as the forces decrease.

Back in November, when the full extent of Chinese intervention became known, there was much consternation in Washington and at General MacArthur's headquarters. Some in Washington believed that the Soviets were behind the intervention, that this was the beginning of World War III, and that Korea was not the position to fight such a war. MacArthur was extremely pessimistic about the chances of the U.S. and its allies to be able to avoid being pushed out of Korea. He called on the Joint Chiefs of Staff to provide reinforcements—four divisions—but no additional ground forces were available to send to Korea. In addition, MacArthur wanted to widen the war: blockade Chinese ports, launch air attacks on Chinese industry, and send Chinese Nationalist troops from Taiwan to Korea as reinforcements. President Truman and his advisors didn't agree. Moreover, they knew that our allies would strenuously disapprove of MacArthur's proposals, and public support would be lacking as well. At this point, MacArthur's pessimism seemed to infect Washington, where there was agreement that MacArthur should concentrate his forces into beachheads, hold as long as possible, and meanwhile plan for a withdrawal to Japan should he be unable to hold on. Fortunately, the dire outlook of American leadership did not leak out, and their pessimism was not embraced by the American fighting men in Korea.

In the case of the 49th Fighter-Bomber Group, morale was uniformly high, even as CCF forces continued to move southward. In our view, given the growing strength and effectiveness of the Fifth Air Force, the CCF could be defeated. What we didn't know was that the Fifth Air Force's commander had a plan to withdraw all jet fighter-bomber units to Japan should the CCF's advances continue. But even when the first indication of this plan emerged—my squadron was ordered to ship all nonessential equipment to Japan without delay—we weren't alarmed. Rather, we saw it as a prudent, just-in-case move, given that the CCF, after seizing Seoul, had continued its advance southward and had fought its way to Wonju, some 110 miles from Taegu.

It was at this point, in mid-January 1951, that Washington's attitude began to change, as did the Eighth Army's basic orientation. The former resulted from a trip to Korea by Army chief of staff Gen. J. Lawton Collins and Air Force chief of staff Gen. Hoyt S. Vandenberg. They first

conferred with MacArthur and then traveled to Korea to speak with
General Ridgway and visit Army and Air Force units. Ridgway was
upbeat, repeating what he had said in a letter to Collins on January 8:
the Eighth Army was "opposed by an enemy whose only advantage is
sheer numbers, whose armament is far inferior quantitatively and quali-
tatively, who has no air support whatever, meager telecommunications
and negligible armor." Ridgway also noted that while the Eighth Army
had the capability to handle the enemy, most of his subordinates did not
share his confidence. He must change this attitude, he said, and cause his
commanders to adopt an offensive orientation. Collins and Vandenberg
were impressed by what they heard from Ridgway and what they
observed on their visits to various units and said so in their report to
Washington. Thereafter, the attitude in Washington changed from pessimism to hopefulness. In the Eighth Army, the attitude and outlook
would change for the better.

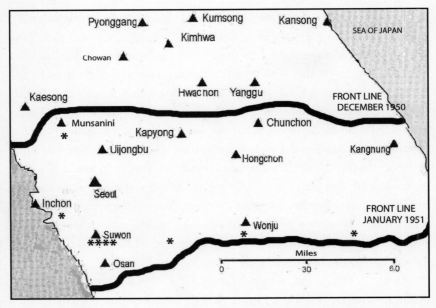

*The front lines at the end of December and three weeks later on January 24,
when the lines stabilized. During this period, I flew nine missions in support
of the Army's operations, the general locations of which are marked by asterisks.*

The change prescribed by Ridgway began to take root after the CCF's offensive had run its course in the vicinity of Wonju, an important location at which five roads came together, along with a railroad line that ran from Seoul to Pusan via Taegu. Clearly, this was where the CCF had to be stopped. Fortunately, the CCF stalled because it had run low on ammunition and supplies and had suffered many crippling casualties. Unrelenting attacks by American fighter-bombers and light bombers all along the CCF's supply line, which now extended some 260 miles from North Korea's border with China, had had a significant impact on the CCF, as did the direct support provided to the Eighth Army by Air Force and Navy fighter-bombers.

Chapter 8

To help rebuild the Eighth Army's morale, General Ridgway ordered his I Corps commander, Maj. Gen. Frank W. Milburn, to plan a major reconnaissance-in-force in his sector to determine the extent of Chinese resistance. It was known as Operation Wolfhound and was set in motion on January 19.

The day before Wolfhound began, I flew on an armed reconnaissance mission along a route from Osan to Inchon in search of enemy forces. The enemy was well hidden. We sighted a group of Chinese soldiers five miles south of Inchon and carried out repeated strafing attacks against these troops and the building into which they had retreated, killing an unknown number of CCF troops. These were the only targets we saw.

During the two-day Operation Wolfhound, I led two missions to provide close air support to I Corps elements engaged in a firefight with CCF forces near Suwon. Our controllers reported "good results," and at the end of the operation, General Milburn estimated that 1,380 casualties had been inflicted on the enemy—1,180 by air strikes, 5 captured, and 195 killed by ground troops. The I Corps' losses were 3 killed and 7 wounded.

Following Operation Wolfhound, two other reconnaissance-in-force operations were launched, one by the I Corps and the other by the IX

Corps. These were small operations but important as a prelude to a return to offensive operations by the Eighth Army. The I Corps' operation was carried out by the 1st Cavalry Division with the objective of punishing the enemy along the road toward Inchon without becoming heavily engaged. On my sixth combat mission, my flight provided air support for this operation, but received no information from the controller about results. Later, our intelligence officer informed me that the 1st Cavalry Division had suffered two killed and five wounded, while enemy casualties were estimated at fifteen killed by ground troops and fifty by air strikes.

At dawn the next morning, my flight was sent on an armed reconnaissance mission along the Seoul–Munsan-ni Highway. We had instructions to report all enemy activity observed and to attack any enemy forces we discovered. The only evidence of enemy activity we came across was a well-camouflaged truck park near Munsan-ni, which we strafed.

My eighth mission involved a first for me. The JOC had directed that the 49th launch a flight loaded with napalm, and I was designated to lead the flight. While I was familiar with napalm and knew how to attack a target using it, I had had no experience in doing so. That didn't concern me because the tactics involved were straightforward and easy to implement, but I was curious to see firsthand what it was all about. Napalm, a jellied gasoline, was perhaps the most feared and most effective antipersonnel and antitank weapon used during the war. The name is an acronym derived from the naphthenic and palmitic acids whose salts are used in its manufacture. This formidable compound was highly effective against both armor and personnel. It sticks to everything with which it comes in contact and is capable both of covering a large area and of penetrating small openings, generating flames that, burning at more than a 1,832 degrees, could destroy tanks and trucks as well as bunkers and small buildings. When burning napalm covered an enemy concentration or a group of soldiers in dug-in positions, the soldiers suffocated when all available oxygen was consumed by the burning gel or when the concentration of carbon monoxide reached high enough levels, or they were burned to death by the intense heat from its rapid combustion. These were certainly not pleasant ways to die, but in war, there are many hellish ways to meet one's end. This one just happened to be one of the more spectacular.

The call sign of my napalm flight was Bully Fox, and once in the air, I contacted the JOC and was directed to proceed to Jangjang-ni, twenty-five miles east of Suwon, to contact Burner 14, a forward air controller. Each of our four F-80s was loaded with two ninety-gallon thin-walled napalm tanks, each of which had an external white phosphorus igniter and an internal igniter that would insure instant combustion when the tanks struck the ground.

The distance from K-2 to Jangjang-ni was 130 miles—about twenty-two minutes at 360 miles per hour. Five minutes before our planned arrival time, I contacted Burner 14, who asked our position and ordnance load. He spotted us as we approached and directed that we make a ninety-degree turn to the right to verify that he had us in sight. The target, he said, was a sizable number of enemy troops dug in on the reverse side of a hilltop that he pointed out. He asked us to watch for the smoke from a white phosphorus mortar shell. Once the shell had been launched, he provided detailed instructions on where he wanted me to place my napalm in relation to the mortar shell's impact point.

This was when I flicked a switch that armed the napalm tanks and then dropped down to 3,500 feet to begin my approach to the target. At the release point, 300 feet from the target, I planned to be at 50 feet moving at 450 miles per hour. On the run-in to the target, speed was our defense against enemy ground fire. We would be moving at 660 feet per second—not an easy target for infantrymen. After we dropped our load, we would further reduce our vulnerability to ground fire by simultaneously climbing and turning.

I punched the bomb-release button 300 feet short of the target and felt the airplane lift slightly as the napalm tanks dropped away. I immediately began a climbing turn to the left, eager to see the results of my attack. It was a stunning sight—a wide swath of billowing flames, obviously white hot, that extended for over 100 yards. The controller radioed, "Great. Right on the money. Bully 2, place your napalm on the same line, starting where the leader's ended." Bully 2 did as directed, as did Bully 3 and 4. We then set to work strafing in adjacent areas pointed out by the controller. During our attacks, we observed a good number of muzzle flashes, evidently rifle fire aimed at us, but we sustained no hits. When we had expended all of our ammunition, I informed Burner 14 that we had finished our job and were heading for base. He gave us a well done. Like so many missions I would fly, I knew we had scored well, but I didn't have any hard numbers to report.

The Eighth Army's reconnaissance-in-force operations ended in success. For the first time since the Chinese intervention, it was in position to launch a counteroffensive, and my fellow fighter-bomber pilots and I would participate in that attack.

In addition to providing close air support for the ground forces, the Fifth Air Force had from the beginning of the war conducted a campaign aimed at hindering the movement and resupply of the enemy's army. Called air interdiction, the campaign targeted supply and fuel dumps, bridges, railroads, locomotives, railcars, personnel along supply routes, trucks, and all other means of moving supplies, including boats and ox carts. Tanks and artillery pieces were also targets. The objective of the campaign was to limit the capability of the enemy to conduct major operations, and this effort by the Fifth was a major reason why the CCF's offensive had been halted.

My first air interdiction strike was unforgettable. It took place on January 25. Our mission was to take out a railroad bridge on the Biryu-gang River near Songchon, northeast of Pyongyang. After completing that task, we would conduct an armed reconnaissance of a seventy-five-mile road segment, attacking any and all military elements we sighted. Our ordnance included two 1,000-pound general-purpose bombs, eight 5-inch high-velocity aerial rockets, and a full load of .50-caliber machine-gun ammunition.

On all missions, the F–80s carried a huge load of fuel, more than 950 gallons of JP-4, a low-grade kerosene, more than half of which was contained in two 265-gallon droppable tanks hung from the wingtips, plus 1,800 rounds of ammunition for the six .50-caliber machine guns. To this was added, according the requirements of the mission, either two 500- or 1,000-pound bombs, or napalm and rockets. On this mission, my plane was loaded with two 1,000-pound bombs and rockets.

The plane wallowed and lurched like an overweight drunk as I taxied slowly along the uneven surface of the unpaved ramp toward the taxiway. I was well aware that if I wasn't careful, one of the low-hanging fuel tanks could strike the ground and burst open.

On the runway, I waited for the armament crew to pull the safety pins from the bombs and the control tower to clear me for takeoff. When I was cleared, I ran the engine up to full power, holding my feet firmly on the brakes as the plane strained to move ahead. This was my first heavy-weight takeoff in the F–80. When I released the brakes, the plane started forward, not like a race horse bounding out of the gate at Churchill Downs but at a lumbering pace, slowed by the heavy load and the deeply dimpled surface of the pierced-steel-planking runway. At this point, I activated the fluid-injection system, sending a spray of water-alcohol mixture, fifty gallons in all, into the engine to increase the thrust. Gradually, the plane gained speed. With the end of the runway approaching, it finally lifted off and began a shallow climb as I raised the landing gear. It was at this point that I became aware of The Hill.

Although I had been at K–2 for five months and had made dozens of takeoffs in F–51s and C–47s as well as a number in the F–80 on training and combat missions, I had not, up until now, taken serious notice of The Hill, a low rise at the far edge of the dry river bed at the northwestern end of the 5,700-foot runway. But now it was posing a threat, looming ever larger as I flew toward it. Was I going to clear the summit? It seemed to be a touch-and-go situation. I knew that no aircraft had struck the hill during the six months we had been operating from K–2, but that didn't ease my anxiety. An F–80 with an engine that wasn't developing full power might just slam into that hilltop. I was getting closer and closer, still in a languid climb that wasn't taking me up fast enough. This is going to be close. And then the hilltop flashed below me, maybe 100 feet away, but too close for comfort.

With the hill behind me, I turned to allow the other members of my flight to join in formation before setting course for the target. This brief, anxiety-generating event, experienced many times each day by 49th Group pilots, made an indelible impression. No pilot who made heavy-weight takeoffs in F-80s from K-2 will ever forget The Hill.

As we climbed to 22,000 feet, our route took us on a northwesterly course from K-2. Some 130 miles up the road, we crossed the front lines, easy to delineate because the vehicular traffic, heavy on the United Nations' side, was completely absent on the Communist side. An artillery duel, silent to us, was in progress. It was marked by flashing explosions and smoke.

Seoul was one of our checkpoints. It had been ravaged by the North Korean Army during the opening stage of the war, then mauled by U.S. forces during the city's recapture. It was now in the hands of the Chinese Army. From our altitude, it was a scene of desolation—large areas of the city had been wiped away by bombs and artillery shells, and in others, only walls of buildings were standing. No vehicles were in sight, and we did not observe any movement. It was as if the city had been deserted.

★ ★ ★

In the hands of a skillful pilot, the F-80 was an excellent dive-bombing platform—easy to fly and highly stable in flight. This isn't to say that we could drop bombs into a pickle barrel, but we were much more accurate than the bombers who dropped bombs in level flight from higher altitudes. Usually, an F-80 pilot could deliver the goods, but not always. Given that we had to estimate three critical factors—dive angle, wind speed, and wind direction—we had our share of near misses. Accurate bomb delivery required smooth handling of the flight controls plus a knowledge of wind direction and speed. The challenge was to establish and maintain the right dive angle and airspeed while keeping the aiming pipper on the target adjusted for wind direction and speed and release the bombs at the proper altitude. If all of these conditions were met, there was a good chance that the bombs would be on target. Unless there was some smoke in sight in the target area that we could use to estimate the wind's direction and speed, we used the wind information received at the mission briefing. Neither source was likely to be highly accurate.

About 220 miles from base, I began to descend to 8,000 feet and started looking for landmarks that would lead me to the target, still about forty-five miles ahead. As we leveled off, I picked up the railroad line that ran south out of Songchon. This led me to the river and then the bridge. It was a single-track steel structure, perhaps 100 feet long. Narrow in width, it would be a difficult target to destroy.

Over the years, I had racked up scores of practice dive-bombing sessions and had flown on several in combat. Capt. Richard G. Croskrey, flying as element leader in the number-three slot, was an experienced fighter pilot with more than thirty recent combat missions under his belt, some as a flight leader. While the other two pilots in the flight were relatively new to combat flying, they were well trained and had perhaps half a dozen missions each to their credit. One of them, flying as Croskrey's wingman, was Capt. Ray O. Roberts, who would become a lifelong friend. He was smart, even-tempered—an experienced fighter pilot and, like me, a southerner.

Croskrey had been on two earlier missions to attack the bridge, but none of the bombs hit the target. At the preflight briefing, he said he was determined to hit the target this time. Intelligence had been vague about enemy defenses, but we expected antiaircraft fire from almost any target worthy of attack. Surprise, a high attack airspeed, and a steep angle of approach, together with our brief time over the target, would provide good odds for us to survive any enemy fire.

There wasn't a cloud in the sky, and smoke from a fire on the ground provided the clues we needed to judge wind velocity and direction. My gunsight was on, and the bomb-selector control switch pointed to both. As the target slid toward the leading edge of my left wing, I flicked another switch to arm both bombs.

When the target reached the wing's leading edge, I did a wing-over into a forty-five-degree dive, adjusted the throttle setting, opened the speed brakes, and maneuvered to place the gunsight's pipper on the upwind side of the target. At this point, smooth, coordinated flight was essential. I punched the bomb-release button at 4,000 feet and began my pullout to stay above the blast of my bombs. The inflating bladders in the G-suit squeezed tightly around my calves and abdomen as the pointer on the G-meter moved swiftly to the four-G mark.

Both of my bombs struck the bridge's abutment on the south bank of the river, and moments later, my wingman's bombs scored a near miss adjacent to the bridge's center section, creating two giant geysers as they struck the water and exploded.

We did not observe any antiaircraft fire during our attacks, so there wouldn't be that distraction for the last two pilots on target. As I leveled off at 6,000 feet, Croskrey was well into his bomb run, and his wingman was approaching his dive entry point. Although everything looked just fine, a catastrophic event was about to occur.

Croskrey had observed where our bombs struck and, like any red-blooded fighter pilot, would do his best to do better than we had done by placing his bombs squarely on the target. Competition has always played a strong role in fighter squadrons. In honing gunnery, rocketry, and bombing skills, careful count was kept during training sessions of the score of every pilot. One's status among fellow pilots depended on scoring well.

Down he came. I watched as he reached 3,000 feet and then 2,500 feet. No bombs. "Oh, no," I muttered. "He's going too low." Then I saw the bombs release and Croskrey start to pull up. A second or two later, the bombs struck the center of the bridge and the twin explosions emitted ugly yellow flames and powerful shock waves. For a brief instant, I thought Croskrey would be all right—a close call, but okay. Then I saw flames spewing from his aircraft like a Fourth of July rocket. Instantly, I radioed, "Bully Easy 3. Eject. You're on fire." He must have been incapacitated at that point, a victim of his own bomb blasts. The crippled aircraft slammed into a nearby hill, still streaming flames. It was a terrible sight: a comrade meeting a sudden, violent end.

The usual cause of such incidents is target fixation, a term used to describe a situation in which the pilot concentrates on the target to the exclusion of everything else, including a rapidly unwinding altimeter. It was a sad ending for an excellent pilot, a man well respected by his squadron mates.

We made a couple of circuits of the crash site, looking closely at the still smoking wreckage, and thinking as we did, "What a rotten way to die." Then I set course for the next phase of our mission. There was nothing more we could do for Croskrey beyond filing a report detailing the circumstances of his tragic demise. He was twenty-eight years old, just two months older than I, and came from Riverside, California. He was listed as missing in action and later as "presumed dead."

We had been directed to conduct an armed reconnaissance of a main CCF supply route following the bridge bombing. It didn't take long to locate the beginning point of our assigned road segment. Upon sighting it, I eased down to 50 feet and set my throttle to maintain 350 miles per hour. The other two leveled off at 1,500 feet, trailing me by a quarter of a mile, one on either side. Given our vulnerability to small-arms fire at low altitude, our usual tactic was to make a single pass on the target and not turn back unless it was something special.

United Nations Command had put out the word to the CCF that anybody and anything on the roads, waterways, or railroads would be considered a military target, subject to attack. Regular fighter sweeps of transportation arteries during daylight hours were aimed at inhibiting enemy movement to the maximum. As a result, the enemy was forced to rely increasingly on night movement and to use great care when on the roads during daylight hours. Targets were usually camouflaged and diffi-cult to spot; sometimes, they were concealed beneath foliage or other-wise hidden from view.

By flying low, I could spot targets that couldn't be seen from higher altitude, but I was flying too low and fast to attack them, so I acted as a spotter, calling out targets to be attacked by the other two.

Out ahead, I sighted about six vehicles parked beneath roadside trees at a slight curve in the road. As I flashed over them, I radioed, "Easy 2, six vehicles under tree line, left of road. Here." Easy 2 eased into a shallow dive, placed his gunsight pipper on the target area, and opened fire even before he could see the vehicles. The first of his .50-caliber bullets tore at the road some seventy-five feet short of the vehicles. Then the stream lunged forward, ripping the line of trucks from bumper to bumper.

Farther along, I spotted a group of soldiers, perhaps thirty in number, and radioed, "Easy 3, troops, right side of road heading for the ditch. Here." He laced the area with .50-caliber projectiles. As he flashed overhead at fifty feet, he could see the cringing soldiers sprawled out face-down in the ditch.

Although we were moving fast, almost six miles a minute, we made six attacks along the seventy-five mile route. Trucks, sedans, a couple of motorcyclists, small bands of troops, and a train of pack horses experienced the shock and surprise of our sudden and deadly out-of-nowhere attacks.

That mission, aimed at curtailing the flow of enemy men, equipment, and supplies, was the first of many air interdiction missions that I would fly, most of them deep inside North Korea. Some were dive-bombing missions aimed at bridges, but most were armed reconnaissance missions along main supply routes.

Not long after the successful bridge bombing and the tragic loss of Croskrey, I was assigned another bridge target. This one was near Pyongyang, about 270 miles from base. Four of us dropped 1,000-pound bombs amid a heavy barrage of antiaircraft fire, scoring some near misses and a couple that we thought were on target. But since the defenses forced us to depart the scene rather hurriedly, we didn't have the opportunity to take a good look at the aftermath. At the mission debriefing, we reported "results unknown."

A few days later, at Sunchon, about thirty miles northeast of Pyongyang, I led another bridge-bombing mission, this one against a narrow steel structure. We had near misses but no direct hits—a disappointment after all of the effort we exerted and the risks we faced from the ack-ack thrown our way.

The next day, January 31, I led an armed reconnaissance mission along the main road leading north out of Pyongyang. This road was a segment of the main supply route from Manchuria. We came across a string of eleven boxcars, undoubtedly left there by a locomotive in a hurry to make it to the safety of a tunnel, and inflicted a great deal of damage on them as we made strafing run after strafing run. We left three cars in flames. We then turned our guns on twenty adjoining buildings—probably ware-houses—which we basically destroyed.

Chapter 9

With the huge quantity of munitions stored on K-2—bombs, rockets, napalm, and machine-gun ammunition—and the nev-erending amounts being transported and loaded on airplanes preparing for missions, it is a wonder that so few accidents involving munitions took place. One accident that got the attention of everyone on the flight line involved a 5-inch HVAR that launched from a parked F-80.

I had just returned from a mission and was climbing out of the cockpit when I heard a shrieking sound followed instantly by a loud thump and a thud. The rocket had slammed into and destroyed a trailer truck and then penetrated the front wall of our operations building, passed through the briefing room, and left a hole in the rear wall where it exited.

First Lt. Walter "Jack" Doerty, who was in the briefing room, remembers: "A small group of pilots was briefing or just hanging around ops waiting for their takeoff times. Activities were as routine as any other day. Suddenly, there was a screeching roar, simultaneous with the entire room shaking and seeming to come apart. When I looked up, there was nobody to be seen. Everyone had vanished. A rocket had pen-etrated the front wall, sailed across the room, and went out the back of the building. Instinctively, every one of us had hit the floor as though we had trained for such an occurrence. Rushing outside, we realized that the rest of the world was still on its axis and normal except for some excitement on the flight line. It turned out that some of the aircraft were parked with the nose pointing towards the flight line buildings and in this case directly at 9th FBS ops building."

I hurried into the building, expecting to find casualties, but was relieved to discover that that the only damage was a hole in the front wall and another in the rear wall of the building. Later, the armament people determined that static electricity had built up and spontaneously fired the rocket. Miraculously, although flying debris filled the vicinity of the destroyed truck, no one was injured.

The next day, the group commander issued a SOP (standing operation procedure) that specified that all aircraft would be parked pointing away from buildings and ordered that new electrical grounding procedures be implemented.

The Fifth Air Force allowed the enemy no rest in the rear areas. Almost every day, multiple attacks were launched, not only against troops, transportation targets, and occasionally airfields, but also against basic infrastructure targets. The rocket-strafing attack I led against a power-and-transformer station in the Pyongyang region was one such target. Though the North Koreans had made an effort to obscure this important target, the camouflage was rather crude, and using the target photograph I had, I was able find it without much searching. We first rocketed the transformers, creating some spectacular electrical flashes, and then fired additional rockets into the other electrical equipment. We finished the job by strafing each of the twenty-five buildings in the complex.

Our intelligence officer advised us that interrogators had learned from captured Chinese soldiers that the CCF had organized "hunter groups" armed with heavy machine guns and other weapons to strengthen their capability to protect supply routes from fighter-bomber attacks. These group were made up of volunteers who received special privileges and were promised decorations and furloughs for shooting down three UN aircraft in a ninety-day period. We were also advised to be alert for flak traps. Reports had been received that the Reds were draping parachutes on trees and displaying dummy troops made of straw to draw fighter-bombers into a hornet's nest of flak. In some instances, derelict trucks and tanks, seemingly carelessly camouflaged, were left beside a road to lure unsuspecting pilots into a flak trap.

★ ★ ★

The most significant air support missions in February involved the 2nd Infantry Division's 23rd Regimental Combat Team, located at the small village of Chip'yong-ni. In mid-February, the CCF mounted an offensive that developed into a fierce battle at that village, and like dozens of other fighter-bomber pilots, I participated in the battle.

General MacArthur had directed that the CCF not be allowed to breach the Han River line. Chip'yong-ni, which is located twenty-two miles northwest of Wonju, was a principal strongpoint that blocked Chinese access to the Han River Valley. If Chip'yong-ni fell, the Chinese could sweep through the gap between Chip'yong-ni and Wonju and then on to the Han River, which lay just beyond.

Early in the CCF's offensive, Chip'yong-ni became an isolated outpost under siege, cut off from the rest of the Eighth Army. At this point, the 23rd Regimental Combat Team—made up of a U.S. infantry battalion, a French infantry battalion, a Ranger company, two field artillery battalions, an antiaircraft artillery automatic-weapons battery, and a company of combat engineers—would have to rely on Air Force transports to resupply it with ammunition and food and on Air Force fighter-bombers to provide much of the firepower needed to survive the Chinese onslaught.

Chip'yong-ni sits astride a stream at the end of a small valley near a low mountain formation. With Chip'yong-ni in the center, the 23rd's

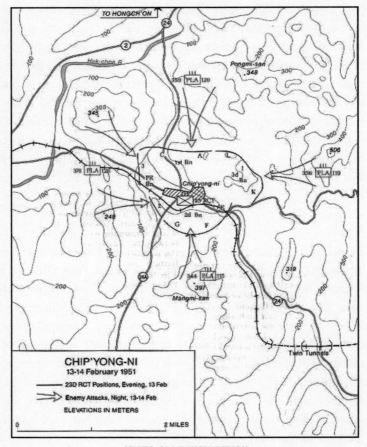

CHIP'YONG-NI
13-14 February 1951

— 23D RCT Positions, Evening, 13 Feb

⇒ Enemy Attacks, Night, 13-14 Feb

ELEVATIONS IN METERS

0   2 MILES

CENTER OF MILITARY HISTORY

defense perimeter measured about one and three-quarter miles by one and a quarter miles. The three-day battle involved almost constant fighting against a numerically superior enemy force—1,500 American and French troops versus 8,000 to 10,000 Chinese soldiers.

At the request of General Ridgway, the Fifth Air Force gave the highest priority for air support to the 23rd. Ten flights of Mosquito control airplanes were sent to the area each day in order to have constant daylight patrols aloft to direct the fighter-bombers.

I led two flights in support of the embattled force. The first was on the thirteenth, during which we were controlled by Mosquito Cottonseed. When we arrived overhead at Chip'yong-ni, I was struck by how small an area the 23rd had been squeezed into and by the ferocity of the battle then in progress. The 23rd's perimeter was under attack by Chinese forces from all four sides, and artillery pieces constantly flashed, emitting wispy clouds of drifting white smoke. Mortar rounds kicked dirt into the air, and the muzzle blasts of machine guns and rifles winked everywhere.

The heaviest pressure was apparently coming from the Chinese attackers in the east. That was the area to which Cottonseed directed our attention, specifically to a low hill just to the east of the perimeter. He asked that we drop our napalm all along the reverse side of the hill and then strafe the forward side. I set up a north-to-south flight path parallel to the ridgetop. This would ensure that we provided maximum coverage of the CCF's position but not endanger any elements of the 23rd that were only a short distance to the west. We carried out our attacks. Our four F-80s spread burning napalm along the back side of the hill and then repeatedly strafed the forward side. A good bit of rifle and machine-gun fire was being directed at us, but we took no hits. When we concluded our attacks, Cottonseed gave us a well done. Even before we departed the scene, another flight of Air Force fighter-bombers was waiting to be directed onto a target.

I returned to Chip'yong-ni two days later. The intelligence briefer reported that on some missions, ground troops reported empty .50-caliber casings dropping on their positions as aircraft fired directly overhead at enemy positions. This wasn't a complaint, just an indication of how close we were getting to our own troops in an effort to support them when in close contact with the enemy. He also warned that enemy troops were using captured identification panels, spread out on the ground, to try to mislead pilots into thinking they were friendlies.

My return mission to Chip'yong-ni involved napalm. The controller—Cottonseed again—directed that we strike enemy troops entrenched in a gap in the perimeter, and that is what we did. An account in *The Second Infantry Division in the Korean War* describes an air attack that day that probably involved the flight that followed mine:

> Napalm splashed and seared over the grimly holding enemy troops. It was too much. Burned and screaming they withdrew and "B" Company rose up, firing into the retreating forces, then advancing and regaining the lost positions. Amid the frantic battle, planeload after planeload of ammunition was dropped to the garrison which was holding on by its fingernails. Enemy mortar fire, falling into the drop zone, inflicted heavy casualties as the troops exposed themselves to regain the precious ammunition and supplies. Counter-battery fire from the RCT (Regimental Combat Team) artillery and mortar units finally silenced the pounding enemy mortars and the collection of the airdrop continued without letup.

We were pleased to have had a part in this epic battle, which, following the arrival of a relief force containing twenty-three tanks, ended with a retreat by the CCF after it had suffered massive casualties numbering almost 5,000 by some estimates. UN casualties in the fighting at Chip'yong-ni were 51 killed, 250 wounded, and 42 missing. This engagement, together with another at Wonju to the east, was a major turning point in the Korean War, marking the end of the CCF's hold on the initiative.

Later, the 49th FBG received an unexpected Republic of Korea Presidential Unit Citation issued by President Syngman Rhee. The citation cited the 49th "for extraordinary heroism and fidelity during the period 27 June 1950 to 7 February 1951." It read:

> The outstanding service rendered by the 49th Fighter–Bomber Wing while flying over 10,000 sorties in close support of United Nations in Korea is strikingly demonstrated by the huge toll it took on the aggressor forces. The aerial achievements of

this organization are resplendent with repeated acts of heroism, gallantry and high personal courage. Operating under adverse conditions on a continuous daily schedule, the officers and air-men of the 49th Fighter–Bomber Wing have manifested a performance to emulate, reflecting great credit upon themselves, their organization, the United States Air Force and the United Nations in defending Korea against aggressor forces.

Every now and then, something occurred that transported the mind away from the war and back to the home front, reminding me that the men who were fighting in Korea were not the only ones affected by the war. This time it was a copy of a letter—a most unusual letter—from the parents of a dead soldier that was circulated among the pilots. It was addressed to the Commander, Fifth Air Force, who sent a copy for us to read. It brought forth sorrow and a sense of gratitude that the parents were thinking of us at such a stressful time in their lives:

Dear Sir:

This note, in its small crude way, is written to express my gratitude to the Air Force, in behalf of our son, for the assistance given the 2nd Division in their fight in Korea.

Our son, in his letters, had only the highest praise for the support of the Air Force given the 2nd Division.

This week we received word that our son, PFC William G. Spradlin, AP 15423256, was killed in action in Korea so in this, our hour of sorrow, we wish to thank your boys for the wonderful tactical support they seem to be giving the ground forces, of which our son was a part.

Sincerely yours,
Mr. and Mrs. Ale Spadlin
Bevelo, KY

Chapter 10

Our life at K-2 didn't focus entirely on combat flying. On Saturdays nights, we gathered around the bar at the officers' club, which was situated on the high hill overlooking the flight line. It wasn't much of a club, just a room attached to the officers' mess with some tables and chairs and a bar with booze. That was just about all there was, but it didn't dampen our spirits. We didn't need a fancy place to blow off a little steam. This was where we could trade stories with pilots from other squadrons, and you might come across a friend or an old acquaintance who had stopped in for the night. Toward the end of the evening, when everyone was loosened up, a songfest might break out. Every fighter group had its own song book, some containing as many as 150 songs. Some had been written by fighter pilots, and many of these related to combat in Korea. Some focused on death while others featured humor, often black humor. Exaggerated attitudes and actions featured prominently.

The 49th FBG's Willy Williams, an outgoing fellow who loved to sing, was a prolific composer. He wrote a song called "Kuni-ri and Antung," sung to the tune of "Cigarettes and Whiskey." We sang it often.

Once I was happy and had a good deal,
Flew F–86s at old Victorville.
They asked for a volunteer, said, "I'll take you."
Then next thing I knew, I was stuck at Taegu.

Chorus:
Kuni-ri and Antung, and wild wild Pyong-yang,
They'll drive you crazy, they'll drive you insane.
Kuni-ri and Antung, and wild wild Pyong-yang,
They'll drive you crazy, they'll drive you insane.

We go down to briefing while it is still night
To lift off the runway before it is light.
We form in the gloom and we're off on our way.
We're off to the target before it is day.

We're up to the Yalu, there's cons* overhead.
We think of the wheels who are snug in their beds.
We drop our big tanks and break to the right.
Josie,** we cry with all our might.
We steer 280, we're up in the soup.
We swear that the leader is doing a loop.***
Break out in the clear and set down on K-2.
Be careful or Willy will write about you.

Another favorite focusing on death was "Korean Waterfall," adapted from the popular World War II song "Beside a Guinea Waterfall":

Beside a Korean Waterfall, one bright and sunny day,
Beside his shattered Shooting Star, a young pursuiter lay.

---

* Condensation trails left by MiG-15s.
** Shorthand for "Josephine," a code word denoting that a pilot's minimum fuel state had been reached.
***Alludes to vertigo.

His parachute hung from a nearby tree, he was not yet quite
    dead.
So listen to the very last word the young pursuiter said.
"I'm going to a better land where every thing's bright,
Where whiskey flows from telegraph poles, and poker every night.
There's not a single thing to do but sit around and sing,
And all our crews are women—Oh death where is thy sting?"
Oh, death, where is thy sting, ting-a-ling,
Oh, death, where is thy sting?
The bells of hell shall ring-a-ling-a-ling
For YOU—but not for ME!!

Songfests didn't just happen. Someone had to get things started.
When the noise level reached a dull roar, Willy Williams would call out
loudly, "All right, all together now. Hi-jig-a-jig," and he would lead the
crowd in a bawdy song or two, after which someone would yell out for
"Kuni-ri and Antung," "Korean Waterfall," or one of the many other
favorites. Songfests usually lasted for forty-five minutes but sometimes
went on for an hour.

We also had movies for a time, shown on a large outdoor screen, but
they were discontinued when the Chinese pushed down south of Seoul.
It was believed that the large illuminated screen could serve as a beacon
in the night for potential infiltrators, and the sizable group of spectators
would be an irresistible target. After the lines stabilized around the 38th
parallel and the weather permitted, movies were shown occasionally. The
only ones I remember are *Key Largo* with Humphrey Bogart and Lauren
Bacall and *It's a Wonderful Life* with Jimmy Stewart.

Gambling, a popular pastime at my World War II bases, wasn't nearly
as prevalent among officers at K-2. This may have been because there
wasn't room in the officers' club for the games favored by fighting men,
craps and poker. This probably was a good thing, given that in wartime
situations, where tomorrow is uncertain and alcohol is mixed in, gambling can get out of control and participants can lose sums they can't
afford. This invariably leads to hard feelings on the part of the losers,
and things can get tense when IOUs are involved and payment isn't

forthcoming. On Saturday nights, poker games took place around the base, as well as a variety of other card games, but there were none of the wild and wooly gambling games I had observed during World War II— Red Dog, for example.

Card games of various sorts, including cribbage, were almost always in progress in the 9th FBS's pilots' lounge as pilots awaited an assignment or socialized in the evening. Although money was involved in some cases, we didn't consider it gambling since only small stakes were at issue. I sometimes played cribbage, but found gin rummy to be much more interesting. My usual partner was 1st Lt. George "Pete" Lovas, an avid player. He and I were the only two pilots who showed any real interest in gin rummy.

Before we began our first game, Lovas and I spent some time discussing and agreeing on the rules we would follow. We would play for one-tenth of a cent per point—not much, but enough to keep things interesting. As it turned out, about $2.50 or $3.00 changed hands at the end of each session.

We were both serious players, intent on winning, and fairly evenly matched, it seemed. By the end of first session, I sensed that we each employed a different strategy. He generally waited until all of his cards were in sets or runs before he laid his hand down and declared gin. I laid down my hand the instant I had enough matched cards to qualify for a lay-down. If he held to his strategy, I felt confident that I would come out ahead over the long haul.

Pete hated to lose. When he went on a losing streak, he would ask that I change to another deck of cards. Or, as if it would alter his luck, he would get up and walk around his chair, or he would move his chair to face in another direction. I don't know if he believed these moves would change his luck or whether he was trying to break my concentration. In any case, I was amused by his antics.

We played almost every day, and our enthusiasm never flagged. Some days, he won; other days, I collected a few bucks. At the end of three months, I was $25 ahead—evidence that my strategy was working. Pete wasn't at all happy that I was ahead in winnings, but he remained ever hopeful of getting the upper hand. Besides, he was having fun, and so was I. We continued our gin rummy games right up to the week I finished my combat tour.

The officers' mess and the enlisted mess were each served by a single kitchen situated between the two. The same quality of food was served in both. Each mess was equipped with crude wooden tables with benches that would seat four on each side. The place looked more like a down-at-the-heels soup kitchen for derelicts than an Air Force eating establishment.

I had learned during World War II that food served in combat situations was not going to be anything like what was served at home. If it didn't come out of a gallon tin can, it was unlikely to be served. I'm sure the cooks did their very best to offer up palatable, varied meals, but they could do only so much with Spam, tinned Argentine beef, powered eggs, and milk, all of which turned up frequently on the menu. True, there were many ways to prepare Spam—cubed or sliced, baked, broiled, fried, sautéed, or boiled in soup—but it always tasted the same to me, as did the Argentine canned beef. As for powdered eggs, usually served scrambled, they weren't even close to the real thing, nor was milk reconstituted from a powder. So, in addition to the stresses associated with combat, we confronted marginal chow three times a day.

I had always been attracted to motorcycles, probably because they offered an experience not unlike flying an open-cockpit plane—high speed, wind in the face, leaving everyone else behind, the freedom to move easily. But there were no motorcycles around K-2, and the thought of motorcycles hadn't entered my mind until I spotted a GI on the flight line puttering along on a motorbike. It was really a motorized bicycle powered by a gasoline engine. It looked sturdy—and fun. Right away, I felt an urge to get one. I certainly didn't need one, given the compact orbit in which I moved—barracks to latrine to mess hall to flight line and back—but I just had to have one.

I talked with the fellow who had replaced me as base operations officer, and he agreed to pick one up for me the next time he was in Japan. I don't recall the price, but it was probably around $100. When it arrived, blue in color, I started motoring up and down the flight line and around the base. My squadron mates were impressed, and in time, half a dozen of them acquired motorized bikes. After flying had ended for the day and we had had a drink or two, several of us might mount our motorized steeds and try to outrace each other or attempt to outdo others in maneuvering through a quickly built obstacle course. We had great fun, but it is a wonder that we didn't break our necks somewhere along the way.

Chapter 11

Navigation could be a challenge in Korea's mountainous terrain and changing weather. We used two methods that had been employed for centuries: dead reckoning and pilotage. In making dead reckoning calculations, which required an aeronautical chart, we drew a course line from base to the target, determined the compass heading, corrected it for magnetic variation and wind direction and velocity, measured the distance, and calculated the time to the target. Once in the target area, we relied on pilotage to locate the target. This involved matching objects we could see on the ground with symbols on the aeronautical chart, such as a bridge, a lake, a prominent curve in a road, or the intersection of a road and a railroad. Once we made a match, we knew our precise location and could then proceed to the target using pilotage.

To avoid having to calculate course heading, distance, and time for every mission, I put together a folder of aeronautical charts on which I drew four course lines extending from our home base into various parts of North Korea with a magnetic heading and reciprocal heading indicated for each line. In addition, I drew on the chart arcs at fifty-mile intervals from home base. Using this arrangement, if I knew my location at any point on the chart, I could tell at glance the compass heading and distance to home base. Based on an airspeed of 360 miles per hour,

I could then quickly make a mental calculation to determine the estimated time to base.

When returning above a cloud layer or in the clouds, we needed a
way to descend safely to below the clouds and proceed to K-2. Initially,
a 280-watt radio direction-finding (D/F) station installed at K-2 provided the necessary support. A pilot would radio the station and, upon
making contact, would provide a count: "Bully Able, one, two, three . . .
ten, Bully Able." This transmission enabled the D/F station operators to
zero in electronically and provide a fix and the compass heading to base.
The D/F method didn't always work as advertised, probably because of
inexperienced operators. This was the case when a 49th FBG flight,
returning from a mission in North Korea, received fixes that placed
them thirty miles from K-2, at which point they began their let-down
through the overcast on a course aimed at K-2. When they broke out of
the overcast, K-2 was nowhere to be seen. At that point, the leader estimated that they were more than fifty miles from base and low on fuel.
As a result, three aircraft landed wheels up in the Naktong River and
one made a safe but risky landing on a 1,600-foot strip north of
Chongju. It wasn't long after that that we got a much safer let-down
arrangement at K-2.

The new system to assist pilots in locating and landing at K-2 in
low visibility consisted of two non-directional radio beacons installed
near the base. Each F-80 was equipped with an automatic direction
finder (ADF)—a radio-navigation instrument that displays the relative
bearing from the aircraft to the radio beacon selected by the pilot. Each
beacon transmitted three letters in Morse code identifying that beacon.
For an approach to K-2, a pilot tuned into and positively identified Beacon A, located about ten miles northwest of the airstrip, and then
maneuvered to be over the beacon at 20,000 feet on a course parallel to
the landing runway but on a reciprocal heading. At this point, the pilot
would start a steep descent to 5,000 feet while he maintained the reciprocal of the landing runway heading. He would be on the downwind
leg for landing.

Then he quickly tuned in Beacon B, which was located on the
approach path to the landing runway. As soon as the ADF needle

showed Beacon B to be off his left wingtip, the pilot continued for one minute and then turned ninety degrees to the left in order to be on the base leg of the approach. At this point, he lowered the airplane's landing gear and flaps while descending to 1,000 feet. As the ADF needle neared the left wingtip position, he turned ninety degrees to the left and maneuvered to approach the beacon on the landing runway heading. Upon crossing Beacon B, he descended to 500 feet on the runway heading and hopefully would break out of the clouds with the runway directly ahead. He would then be able to land safely. This procedure required a high degree of concentration and skillful piloting. But things didn't always go as planned, and when that occurred, disaster could follow.

One of the first to use the new instrument approach was a fellow Spitfire and Mustang pilot from World War II, Lt. Col. Leland P. "Tommy" Mollard. He had been assigned to the 49th FBG headquarters a few weeks earlier to get some seasoning in preparation for assignment as a fighter group commander. At least, that is what I assumed. I was really pleased to see him. He was the only pilot from my World War II outfit, the 31st Fighter Group, that I had come across in Korea, and I looked forward to spending time with him.

Above an overcast, returning from an early-morning weather-check mission along the front and to the north in the Pyongyang area, he rammed into a mountain twelve miles south-southeast of K-2. We don't know what happened but surmised that Tommy may have flown too far beyond the point when he got a wingtip fix on Beacon B, or maybe he wasn't tuned to Beacon B, or maybe he received a false transmission. In any event, the result was deadly. The lesson for all of us was one we already knew: use special care when executing an instrument approach.

Shortly after we began to use the new approach system, pilots discovered that ore deposits in the mountains eighty miles to the north of K-2 caused the radio compass of passing aircraft to swing, giving the false impression that the aircraft was over Beacon A. At that point, the pilot would begin a descent but quickly discover the he was nowhere near Beacon B. This was a highly dangerous situation that was remedied by raising the initial altitude over Beacon A to 20,000 from the original 10,000 feet.

One case of blundered navigation involved me. As I was taxiing out with a flight of four on a mission to far North Korea, all three of the other members of my flight aborted. This was a big surprise as our abort rate was quite low, and I had never known more than one in a flight to abort. I was reluctantly ready to call it a day when I observed three 7th Squadron F-80s taxiing out and heard a fourth inform the leader that he was aborting. Noting that they were carrying no bombs but were armed with rockets, the same as my aircraft, I unwisely decided to join the flight. I say "unwisely" because I hadn't attended their mission briefing and had no idea where they were headed or what mission they had been assigned. But I was all suited up and ready to go and wasn't ready to throw in the towel. I asked the leader for his call sign and informed him I would join his flight as number four.

I had always taken pride in my navigational abilities and made it a point to keep track of my location at all times regardless of what position I was flying in a flight. As it turned out, on this mission, I would be fortunate that this was my practice.

We flew deep into North Korea above an overcast. Given our armament load, I assumed that we would be making a reconnaissance along a route assigned to the 7th Squadron. About 200 miles from base, according to my mental estimate, the leader began a descent that took us another fifty miles right down to the deck, where we began a run along a segment of road. We were still heading north away from base. I wonder what in the world he was thinking. We were 250 miles from base and streaking ever farther away at six miles a minute, deeper and deeper into MiG territory. In the far north, I always conducted an armed reconnaissance *toward* home base so that we would be shortening the distance home as we sped along. But here we were, far from base, burning fuel at a ferocious rate while rapidly increasing the distance from home.

We shot up a couple of trucks along the way, but my mind was much more focused on our fuel situation. I didn't know precisely where we were because I hadn't sighted any recognizable landmarks after descending below the clouds, but I had a pretty good idea based on the time we had flown and our air speed. So I was mentally calculating just how much fuel we would need to return safely to K-2, and that number kept increasing as we continued. As fuel was approaching the critical point, I radioed the code word Josephine to signal that my fuel supply had reached the must-start-for-home-now level. I didn't know what fuel level the flight leader had specified at his flight briefing, but I knew from my calculations and the absence of a Josephine message by others in the flight that he must have miscalculated.

Our flight home was uneventful until we passed over Beacon A and started our instrument approach. The weather had gone downhill since we departed on our mission, and we were now confronted with solid cloud cover from 25,000 feet down to a reported ragged 500-foot ceiling with light rain over K-2.

On an instrument let-down, the flight leader flies on instruments, and the other three tuck in close to maintain visual contact and rely entirely on the leader to get them down safely. We began our descent in normal fashion, smoothly lowering the nose, with throttle retarded and speed brakes opened. But as we continued down, the leader's movement suddenly seemed to become quite erratic. Was he losing it? Was he getting vertigo? Was *I* getting vertigo? What was happening? I didn't know, but I wasn't going to stick around to find out.

At this point, my fuel supply was extremely low and shrinking fast. I couldn't afford to remain in what seemed like an iffy situation. I pulled out to the right, increased my dive angle and speed to provide separation from the others, and continued the instrument approach on my own. I broke out of the clouds at about 450 feet with the runway directly ahead and landed in drizzling rain.

As I began to taxi toward my squadron area with a fuel gauge hovering around empty, I spotted another F-80 on the landing approach. It was the element leader on whose wing I had flown. He landed without difficulty and taxied to his squadron area. At almost the same moment, I saw two more F-80s coming down the final approach. It was the flight leader and his wingman. Both made it down okay, but the wingman's engine flamed out on the runway, and the flight leader came to a stop, out of fuel, before reaching his squadron area. Just a minute or two more on the deck in North Korea, and it is likely that all four of us would have had to take to the parachute or ditch in the Naktong River. This episode confirmed a lesson I already knew: never trust anyone else's navigation.

On February 2, when I learned that I would be leading two flights of F-80s on a mission to escort B-29s on a raid against the rail yard and bridge at Sonchon, my thoughts went back to the first time I encountered B-29s. It was on a Saturday morning during the fall of 1948. I was on strip alert at Itazuke Air Base in Japan, strapped in a F-51 Mustang, ready to launch when ordered. We had been sitting patiently for more than an hour when the field telephone's shrill ring interrupted my conversation with the crew chief. The message was succinct: "Scramble, unidentified aircraft, vector 045 degrees." We were airborne within minutes, two Mustangs climbing to intercept the potential intruders. The controller directed that we climb to 25,000 feet. Just as we reached 20,000 feet, the controller advised, "Bogies five miles, 050 degrees." Moments later, three B-29s came into sight, thousands of feet above us, well beyond our reach, and soon disappeared to the west. I was impressed by their speed, almost 100 miles per hour faster than the heavy bombers of World War II, the B-17s and B-24s.

Known as the Superfortress, the B-29 was a huge airplane with a wingspan of 141 feet and a crew of eleven. It had a combat range of 3,250 miles and cruised at 220 miles per hour, enabling it to easily reach targets in North Korea from bases in Japan. It could carry forty 500-pound general-purpose bombs.

In my briefing of the pilots of the two flights, I noted that should MiG-15s, with a 100-mile-per-hour speed advantage over the F-80 appear on scene, we would face a real challenge in defending the B-29s. Our best tactic was to take up positions high above and to the rear of the B-29s. From there, hopefully, we would be able to intercept the MiGs at some point along their attack path and cause them to break off the attack. I said that I would position my flight, Bully Able, at 5,000 feet above and to the rear of the B-29s, and I ordered Bully Baker to fly

2,000 feet above my flight. Since the MiGs would probably attack in pairs, we should attempt our intercepts in pairs, I advised. As they began an intercept attempt, they should call out their intentions so that we avoided a traffic jam. I noted that we would be well within reach of the MiG base at Antung, so I was assuming—and hoping—that F-86s would be in the vicinity to keep the MiGs busy.

We rendezvoused with four B-29s over the east coast, fifty miles south of Wonson. They were at 20,000 feet, and we quickly took up our briefed positions. Because the bombers were much slower, we began to lazily weave to avoid overrunning them.

As we neared Sonchon, antiaircraft fire began, scattered black explosions, mostly above the B-29s, none of which seemed particularly threatening. The B-29s were sailing along at almost four miles a minute, so their time over target would be limited. When they released their bombs, it was an impressive sight: 160 500-pound bombs spread across the huge rail yard and the nearby bridge. Undoubtedly, the rail yard, all equipment, and rolling stock were torn apart, along with any adjacent buildings. I couldn't tell about the bridge. When the bombs began exploding, I thought, "This should stir things up a bit, and leave the place a bit untidy for a while." Fortunately, the MiGs didn't make an appearance, and we stayed with the B-29s back to the east coast.

On February 4, I led another B-29 escort mission, this time to Suchon. Then, three days later, on February 7, I led an escort mission to Wonson. Both were uneventful. As it turned out, we were lucky. Some two weeks later, on February 25, four B-29s on another raid against Sonchon were attacked by eight MiG-15s. I don't believe any B-29s were lost, nor were any of the escorting fighters, but the MiG attack would change the way B-29s were employed. Future B-29 missions would be against targets farther to the south.

★ ★ ★

On February 19, I was scheduled for a dive-bombing mission to Kanggye, up near the Manchurian border, about 375 miles from K-2. This was the second time I had been sent to Kanggye. The first time, a

couple of weeks earlier, low clouds had blocked access to the target, and
we had gone to an alternate site.

Four months earlier, in October, following the breakout from the
Pusan Perimeter and the Eighth Army's rapid move northward, Kim Il
Sung, North Korea's premier and commander in chief of the country's
armed forces, fled Pyongyang with members of his government, including military leaders, and established a new capital at Sinuiju. A short
time later, as UN forces extended their drive to the north, Kim took his
government to Kanggye, deep in the mountains of north-central Korea.
This area, extremely mountainous and heavily wooded, had been a
stronghold of Korean guerrilla operations during Japanese rule. Now
the former guerrillas, Kim Il Sung and his closest allies, were back where
they started in the 1930s, holed up in deep bunkers. According to an
intelligence report I had read, a "Combined Headquarters" had been
established in Kanggye under Kim Il Sung and staffed by North Korean
and Chinese officers who coordinated North Korean operations with
those of the Chinese.

Located less than twenty-five miles from the Manchurian border
and about 165 miles northeast of Pyongyang, Kanggye was a transportation hub, connected to other cities, including Pyongyang, by road and
rail; it was thus a conduit for supplies from China to the CCF and
NKPA. Not long after Kim Il Sung arrived at Kanggye, 19th Bombard-
ment Group B-29s attacked it on November 4, 1950, dropping 170 tons
of incendiaries and destroying 75 percent of the target, a large ammunition storage and communication center.

Two months later, on January 13, 1951, a single 19th Bomb Group
B-29, flying from Okinawa, carried out the first effective Tarzon mission
against a bridge at Kanggye. A radio-guided bomb, the Tarzon measured
twenty-one feet long and weighed six tons. When the bomb was
dropped, a bright flare in its tail was ignited. It was visually tracked by
the bombardier, and when it deviated from the planned course, he used
a control stick to send corrective commands to the weapon, which had
movable flying surfaces on its tail shroud. The bombardier did his job
well and Tarzon destroyed two spans of the structure. Designated the
ASM-A-1, the Tarzon was used for attacks on selected strategic bridges

that were especially hard to hit, let alone destroy, with conventional unguided bombs. There were problems with the Tarzon, but the weapon was credited with destroying six important bridge targets in Korea

My mission to Kanggye, the seventh mission of the day, was scheduled for an afternoon takeoff. We were armed with 500-pound bombs and rockets and tasked to dive-bomb a large supply storage area adjacent to the railroad on the outskirts of the city and then conduct an armed reconnaissance southward along a sixty-mile segment of Route Purple 5 to Huichon. This was an opportunity to get the rapt attention of Kim Il Sung and send him and his cohorts scurrying like rats to their bunker. In my mind, that alone would make the mission worthwhile.

The weather forecast didn't look promising, with possible snow showers producing restricted visibility in the target area. I could do nothing about that. I would just have to go and take a look. Fierce headwinds were reported at higher altitudes going out to the target. I would have to remain alert to this as it might complicate my navigation. To eliminate the risk of overshooting Kanggye and entering Chinese airspace, I planned my navigation to intercept the railroad about fifty miles south-southwest of Kanggye and then follow it northward to the target.

We flew 22,000 feet, four F-80s bucking the headwind. As we passed near Wonsan on the east coast, 250 miles out from K-2, I got a good fix and adjusted my estimated time of arrival over the turning point, the railroad to Kanggye. Shortly thereafter, as we slid by Hamhung, thirty-five miles off to our right, we entered snow country. Glittering white snow covered the landscape from the tips of the mountains down into the valleys below. About thirty miles short of the turning point, I began a gradual descent. Five minutes later, at 10,000 feet, the railroad came into view, a narrow dark sliver carved out of the snow. This was adjacent to the Purple 5 route we would cover on our way out.

Ahead at our altitude was a cloud bank that pushed us down to 8,000 feet. This is about as low as I wanted to go. The standard altitude for starting a dive-bomb run was 8,000 feet, and that was against a sea-level target. Our assigned target was at 1,000 feet elevation, which meant that we would be starting our run 1,000 feet closer to the ground than usual. If we released our bombs at the usual altitude, the separation distance from our bomb blasts would be narrowed, but we could compensate for that by releasing the bombs earlier in our dive. Accuracy might suffer since there would be less time to align on the target. Given the size of the target, that likely wouldn't be a problem.

The intelligence briefer had said that an array of antiaircraft batteries stood around the town. This was Kim Il Sung's bailiwick, so I was pretty sure that we would get a warm welcome. Given this expectation, I didn't intend to spend any time gawking around the place—just get in and out as quickly as possible. I didn't know if Kanggye was equipped with air-raid sirens, but if so, they were probably wailing some minutes before we came into sight, sending Kim Il Sung and his gang racing toward their shelter. I say this because flak bursts began to fill the air over the city while we were still five miles away. The air defense commander must have been a little jumpy—not surprisingly since his commander in chief was nearby.

The flak continued as we approached the target, persistent and threatening. It raised the adrenaline level, but not so much as to jangle the nerves. Then the target came into view, a large group of symmetrical buildings, now covered in snow but recognizable from the briefing photograph. I armed the bombs just before the target slid under my left wing, and I entered a steep diving turn, opened the speed brakes, and maneuvered the airplane to center the gunsight pipper on the target. I pressed the bomb-release button at 6,000 feet and immediately began to pull out of the dive, feeling the G-suit bladders squeeze the calves of my legs and tighten against my abdomen. I leveled briefly at 4,000, about 3,000 feet above the target, safely separated from the bomb blasts. I then continued down to 500 feet to get clear of the flak. Both of my bombs exploded right in the center of the target area. My wingman was close behind me, and his bombs also hit in the target area, as did those of three and four. A parting message passed through my mind: "You and the other rats had better get used to that bunker, Mr. Kim Il Sung, because we'll be back again soon."

We began our reconnaissance about ten miles down the road toward to Huichon. I hadn't been on this section of Purple 5 and found it

starkly different from the roads to the south. The mountains and everything else were blanketed with deep snow, and the road itself was barely
discernible. We saw not a living soul along the entire route, not a single
vehicle. Clearly, this was not the place for things to go sour. A downed
pilot wouldn't last long in this environment.

The flight back to K-2 took about fifty minutes. We were all glad to
be back to the somewhat warmer and much more placid south.

☆ ☆ ☆

During this period, from the day I started combat flying on January
17 until mid-February, we operated at high tempo. I flew on a combat
mission every day except one, and on twelve of those days, I flew two
missions. In addition to the missions I have described in detail, I flew
nine others in direct support of the Eighth Army and eleven attacking
air interdiction targets.

January 25	Close air support west of Suwon. Excellent results.
January 26	Armed reconnaissance near Kaesong; attacked suspected supply dump, communications.
January 28	Close air support near Suwon; strafed. "Good coverage."
January 31	Armed reconnaissance in Pyongyang area; hit suspected supply dump. Many fires.
February 1	Dive-bombed bridge near Yongyu. Bridge destroyed.
February 1	Dive-bombed at Kaesong. Twenty buildings destroyed, twenty damaged, twenty troops killed.
February 2	Close air support near Suwon. Enemy troop concentration. Results unknown.
February 3	Dive-bombed near Seoul. Near misses against railroad bridge.
February 4	Dive-bombed supply dump at Kunu-ri. Excellent results.
February 5	Close air support near Wonju; attacked machine-gun positions and dug-in troops.

February 6   Armed reconnaissance near Seoul; attacked vehicles
              and troops. Good results.
February 7   Attacked food storage and other targets in Inchon-
              Munsan area. Fires and explosions.
February 8   Close air support near Wonju. Excellent results.
February 10   Dive-bombed railroad near Suriwan. Extensive
              damage.
February 11   Dive-bombed bridge Yangdol, fifty miles north of
              Pyongyang. Direct hit.
February 12   Close air support near Seoul. Results unknown.
February 12   Close air support near Seoul; attacked troops on ridge.
              More than thirty killed.
February 13   Close air support near Seoul; attacked mortar position,
              dug-in troops. Results unknown.
February 16   Dive-bombed at Sinanju, supply dump. Ten building
              destroyed, more than twenty troops killed.
February 16   Close air support near Suwon; attacked troops on
              ridge. Results unknown.

Chapter 12

All fighter pilot lieutenants and captains were eligible for forward air controller duty after flying about thirty combat missions. I was getting close to that number, so I knew it would soon be my turn to go. A couple of weeks before my mission to Kanggye, our ops officer, Jim Anderson, told me that I was next up for FAC duty and was to report to Fifth Air Force headquarters on February 20 for assignment and indoctrination. I knew this was coming, and had it not been winter, I would have been looking forward to three weeks in the field with an Army unit, directing and observing the results of close air support missions for the fellows carrying the rifles. But cold, rain, and snow made this the very worst time of the year to be in the field, so I was not enthusiastic about the assignment. But it was my turn, and I would try and make the best of it.

I packed heavy clothes and toilet items and headed off on what I expected to be a three-week adventure with the infantry, but would it be with the U.S. Army or the ROK Army? The latter wasn't an assignment anyone would choose, given the language problems, but the boys who had drawn that duty said it wasn't too bad.

A squadron mate drove me over to Fifth Air Force headquarters, where I located the officer responsible for overseeing forward air controllers,

Lt. Col. Carl T. Goldenberg. I immediately recognized the name as one that my mother had mentioned as being from my hometown of Lynchburg. Whenever she spotted a newspaper story or even a brief mention of a hometown man in Korea, she sent the clipping to me, and I filed the name in my memory. To meet up with someone from home, even if you had never him met before, was a big event, a chance to trade information about what was happening at home and talk about mutual friends.

Carl Goldenberg was an affable fellow. He gave me a big smile when I asked if he was from Lynchburg. "Yes," he said, "and I recognize your name." We had a lively conversation about Lynchburg and folks we each knew. Carl was a graduate of the U.S. Military Academy, class of 1936. I didn't try to influence my FAC assignment, and I don't know if he was partial toward me when making the assignment or if he simply assigned me to the next open slot. But considering where he sent me, I was pretty sure that he saw to it that I got the best deal he could offer. Relatively speaking, my assignment was a cushy one—not to a regiment on the line, but to a usually safe division headquarters as air liaison officer, specifically to Headquarters, 2nd Infantry Division, whose command post was at Chungju.

In response to my question about how I was to get to Chungju, Goldenberg told me that he didn't have access to any spare transportation, but he said all sorts of vehicles were coming and going from that area, and I wouldn't have any trouble getting a ride. In short, he was suggesting that I hitchhike. That didn't seem like a good idea to me since a light rain was falling and I would be heading into the unknown. I caught a ride on a 1st Marine Division truck. The young driver wasn't talkative, but I did manage to find out the he had been in Korea only a few months and liked his truck-driving assignment.

Chungju is located eighty-five miles due north of Taegu, and the road leading there was typical of Korean roads—soil surfaced with gravel, narrow and eroded in places. As we proceeded north, the amount of accumulated snow along the sides increased, and there were long stretches of rutted, muddy roadway. The rain hadn't let up, and in the muddy sections, our forward progress was slowed to a crawl as we eased past trucks mired in deep mud with wheels spinning and others with chains attached to the rear attempting to pull other trucks from the muck. It looked like a disaster scene. Was this a preview of what I would find in the ground combat zone? If so, it was going to be a long three weeks. The driver dropped me off at a crossroads in Chungju, and it wasn't long before a soldier in a 2nd Division jeep stopped, picked me up, and delivered me to the division command post, which was located nearby in what appeared to have been a schoolhouse.

It didn't take long to find the fellow I was replacing. He introduced me to the G-3, Lt. Col. Claire E. Huchin, and showed me around the command post. This was where I would do my work, screening requests from the three regimental combat teams for air support, conferring with the G-3 (Air) about whether the requests could be met by division artillery, deciding on the priority to be assigned to each request, and forwarding approved requests via a dedicated communications net to the JOC. I was also responsible for overseeing the FACs assigned to the division's three regimental combat teams.

The command post was equipped much as I expected: status boards and maps covered with acetate overlays. One displayed the entire corps area, showing the location of enemy and friendly forces, with division boundaries marked out. Another focused on the 2nd Division's area and others on each of the RCTs' areas of responsibility showing the disposition of friendly and enemy units, observation posts, tank locations, and the RCT command post. Telephones and radios filled the command post, installed to provide communications with higher headquarters, lateral units, subordinate units, and the JOC. It would take a day or two before I mastered the communications system.

The division G-2 (intelligence chief) and G-3 (operations chief) or their representatives were on duty in the command post around the clock, and the division commander was present when plans were being formulated or decisions needed to be made. Also present were GIs who kept the map overlays and status boards up to date, as well as a radio operator who logged all messages. Other people were constantly coming and going.

As soon as I was informed that I was going to the 2nd Division, my thoughts turned back to the missions I had flown in support of the isolated outpost at Chip'yong-ni, under siege and cut off from the rest of the Eighth Army. I learned from the G-3 that the 23rd Regimental Combat Team had been the 2nd Division unit at Chip'yong-ni. Knowing that I would be visiting the 23rd at some point, I looked forward to getting the commanding officer's assessment of the impact of our air strikes on the battle. But no such luck: Col. Paul L. Freeman, the commanding officer during the siege, had been wounded during the battle and was now assigned elsewhere.

During the first week at Chungju, the weather was extremely cold, and I was glad to be inside where it was generally warm. I spent all of the daylight hours in the command post and, at night, slept in a sleeping bag on a canvas cot in a room with four other officers. A small potbellied stove kept the room warm until lights out. After that, I relied on the sleeping bag.

Initially, much of my time was devoted to familiarizing myself with the various situation maps and data displays in the command post, learning the procedures being employed, and gaining an understanding of how to use the extensive array of telephone and radio communications. Not surprisingly, I found that the Army chow was no better or worse than what I was accustomed to with the Air Force.

With an abundance of trucks available, free to move without fear of air attack, I was surprised to learn that all was not roses with respect to the Eighth Army's logistics. Bad roads—some almost impassable in foul weather—and hundreds of bridges destroyed by American fighter-bombers could severely restrict the movement of supply trains. In other cases, a suitable road network simply did not exist. The 2nd Division ran into this situation in late February and had to resort to the use of South Korean bearers to tote vital supplies to advancing troops, much like the Chinese and North Koreans were forced to do every day.

On the heels of the victories at Chip'yong-ni and Wonju, the 2nd Division, along with the rest of the Eighth Army, had begun what would be a slow advance northward with the objective of killing the greatest number of enemy troops at the smallest possible cost in men and equipment. In pursuit of this objective, Operation Killer was launched on February 22.

By the end of the fifth day, the 2nd Division's 23rd RCT had reached the outskirts of Ungyo-ri on the Hoengsong–Pangnimni Road. In support of this operation, we had been requesting and receiving up to a dozen close air support flights each day. As flights arrived overhead, I was gratified to hear on the radio 49th call signs, including that of my own squadron.

I went forward on the February 28 to locate the tactical air control party (TACP) with the 23rd RCT. I chose that TACP because its sector at Ungyo-ri had lots of action. I found the TACP on a hill within sight of the town, then under assault by the 1st Battalion, 23rd Infantry. The FAC was a young second lieutenant, a Mustang pilot from the 18th Fighter-Bomber Group, the outfit I had flown with seven months earlier. From our conversation and subsequent actions, I judged him to be confident and capable. He had been in contact with a Mosquito controller and briefed him in detail on the situation and the desired targets. An inbound flight of Mustangs would be directed against troops of what the FAC believed was the 197th CCF Division that had a company of the 23rd RCT pinned down under intense fire on the outskirts of Ungyo-ri. Once the Mustangs arrived overhead, the Mosquito controller provided a detailed briefing. The CCF troops were located on a hill, he said, and he pinpointed the location by firing a rocket that exploded white smoke. "Place your napalm in this area," he instructed.

As the Mustang leader maneuvered to get into position for his attack, the other F-51s went into trail formation following the leader and took spacing that would permit each of them to begin their attack just as the Mustang ahead was pulling off the target. Their maneuvering showed no slackness as they initiated their attack. I heard a dampened roar as the first napalm ignited, and I saw flames spreading across the hillside, but I was too far away to feel any warmth. Then it was number two's turn. The leader's napalm was still burning furiously as number two laid his napalm down adjacent to the leader's but farther up the hill. Three and four followed, carrying out their attacks with precision. Then they set about strafing the designated area, their machine guns chattering away. They did a terrific job, and it was a thrill to watch from such a close vantage point.

The napalm attacks, which resulted in billows of roiling flame that generated intense heat as the fuel spread across long swaths of the terrain, were impressive. Even before the Mustangs completed their attacks, another flight of fighter-bombers, F-80s, was waiting with rockets and machine guns to continue to pound the Chinese. A little later, a third flight of fighter-bombers and the 2nd Division's artillery put an end to the pressure from the Chinese, and the 23rd moved into Ungyo-ri.

I next paid a visit to another one of the 2nd Division's regimental combat teams, the 9th, near Haanhung-ni, west of Ungyo-ri. There I witnessed a flight of F-80s attacking Chinese troops with rockets and machine guns. The FAC, another young lieutenant, had been on the job for two weeks and was glad to see someone from the Air Force he could talk to, which he did at length. He had had some interesting experiences, none of which were headline material, but nevertheless important enough to him that he felt called upon to recite them to me. He was disappointed when I declined to spend the night.

By March 5, the forward movement of the division's regiments had stretched beyond normal limits the distance between the division command post and the units on the line. The 2nd Division's staff had been searching for a suitable location for a new command post. They selected Tudok, outside of the division's assigned area, but the closest suitable locale in terms of access to communications, roads, and a decent building. The move was an easy one, something the staff was well accustomed to doing. We accomplished it in only about three hours. This didn't really change anything for me or the command post staff—another building and a different sleeping room, but the same people, equipment, and routines.

I had no inkling that two weeks earlier, orders had been published in Washington announcing my promotion to major. When I learned of this, I was surprised and immensely pleased. I had been serving as a captain for six and half years, having been caught up in the post–World War II slowdown. I had often wondered how long I would have to wait. Back in 1944, after only three and a half months as a first lieutenant, I had received a combat promotion to captain, and this probably distorted my expectations. I had been with the 2nd Division for two weeks when Squire Williams sent word to Carl Goldenberg that I had been promoted and appointed squadron operations officer. Two days later, I returned to K-2.

Chapter 13

When I arrived back at the squadron, I learned that other interesting developments had taken place in my absence. A number of the old hands, including squadron operations officer Jim Anderson, had departed for the States, and a flock of replacement pilots had arrived. As squadron operations officer, I was responsible for overseeing the squadron's flying activities. This involved a long list of duties, the most pressing of which was to put together the daily flight schedule. Late in the evening, I would receive from the group operations officer an operation order from the JOC listing missions to be undertaken the next day. The list would specify the type of mission (for example, close air support, armed reconnaissance, or bomber escort), number of aircraft required, the target location, launch time, and other related information. In assigning flight leaders, I endeavored to match the requirements of the mission with the leader most capable of carrying it out. Some flight leaders had a preference about the members of their flights, and I tried to honor their desires. Others were comfortable with my selections. The mission schedule I prepared listed the flight leader, element leader, and wingmen for each mission. I tried to give everyone equal treatment when it came to roll-out-of-bed-hours-before-dawn missions. Once I had completed the schedule, I got word to the leaders of the early missions, and they alerted the other members of their flight.

During the next day, group ops would receive additions and changes to the operations order from the JOC, and I had to be prepared to act on these. I never encountered any display of reluctance on the part of a pilot to accept his assignment. In fact, pilots were always eager to be assigned a mission.

A few days before my return to the squadron, 1st Lt. Richard L. O'Leary, on his twenty-ninth combat mission, crashed his airplane on takeoff, apparently mushing in after lifting off before the airplane was ready to fly. He was on an early-morning mission to provide close air support to an Army unit near Seoul. The F-80 was a total loss, and O'Leary sustained serious injuries that included two broken legs. He would subsequently spend three months in a hospital in Japan before returning to finish his combat tour. Although offered the chance to return to the States following recovery, he was determined to finish what he had started—and he did so.

On March 7, the day following my return from FAC duty, Operation Ripper was set in motion by the Eighth Army. Rather than deliver a frontal assault across the Han River at Seoul, General Ridgway directed the U.S. IX and X Corps in central Korea to attack northward in order to create a bulge east of Seoul that would permit envelopment of the city. The operation was kicked off by the IX Corps' 25th Division, which moved to establish a beachhead across the Han River about fifteen miles east of Seoul. Following heavy artillery barrages and air strikes in advance of the river crossing, the division reached the northern shore almost unopposed. Fifth Air Force fighter-bomber pilots flew 200 close air support sorties in support of the 25th Division's crossing.

As the Eighth Army continued to move forward, the need for air support all along the line increased. I flew a mission in direct support of the ROK 1st Division, which was approaching Seoul from the south. The controller, Cottonseed 3, directed us against a roadblock that was holding up the division's forward elements. Our carefully placed napalm, followed by intensive strafing, took care of the obstacle.

The next day, my flight was dispatched to the rear of the NKPA division defending Seoul to search for tanks reported to be parked under trees along the road heading north out of the city. After a lengthy search, we found six well-camouflaged Soviet-produced T-34 tanks. At this point, I wished that we had brought along napalm, but we were carrying bombs, and given the small size of the T-34, the effectiveness of our dive-bombing attacks was likely to be iffy. We did manage to get a couple of bombs on target and then finished up with strafing attacks.

A few days later, the Communists suddenly abandoned Seoul without a fight, and the Eighth Army entered Hongchon, fifty miles east of Seoul. Now the Reds were on the run, many out in the open and vulnerable to air attack. For the next three days, many other fighter-bomber pilots and I were dispatched to attack the withdrawing enemy. I flew two missions against retreating troops under the control of Mosquito Granite 4 along the roads east of Hongchon. In addition to my flight, five other flights of F-80s were directed against the fleeing troops along these roads. When our 7th Infantry Division troops moved forward, they found 600 dead and 300 wounded enemy soldiers, as well as a dozen or so dead pack animals. The next day, during a mission north of Seoul, we came across dozens of enemy troops along the main road and strafed them with unknown results.

How did I feel about attacking enemy troops retreating along the roads? I had no qualms at all about attacking soldiers. It was the hordes of Chinese and North Korean soldiers, formed into armies, that threatened our very existence. They were the aggressors, and to achieve victory, we had to inflict the maximum number of casualties on them.

The entry of ROK Army elements into Seoul marked the fourth time the city had changed hands since the war began. The capital city was in shambles. Bombing, shelling, and fires since the Eighth Army had withdrawn in January had taken a large toll in buildings, and the transportation system was largely destroyed. Less obvious was the heavy damage that had been inflicted on communications and utilities. Many months of work would be required to provide even minimum services. Only about 200,000 of the city's original population of 1.5 million remained. Unlike the ceremony attended by General MacArthur and

President Syngman Rhee in September to mark the first liberation of Seoul, there was no ceremony this time around. MacArthur visited Korea on March 17, but he did not enter Seoul, limiting his visit to the 1st Marine Division as the IX Corps prepared to move forward toward Ch'unch'on.

By mid-March, I had flown more than fifty missions, and a feeling of sameness seemed to set in. Almost every mission felt like a repeat of one I had flown before—in some cases multiple times, as in the case of close air support missions. However, this didn't lead to boredom or complacence since the many potential hazards precluded a relaxed approach.

On my fifty-eighth mission, I again faced elements of the NKPA's 10th Division, the isolated outfit that had been conducting guerrilla operations in the rear of the ROK I Corps since January. Back then, on my second F-80 mission, my flight had attacked elements of the 10th on the east coast in the 1st Marine Division's area, and shortly after our attack, Marine leaders decided that the NKPA division was too scattered and too decimated to be effective. But now, two months later, the remaining elements of the division were engaged in an attempt to return to its own lines. Captured NKPA soldiers reported that the division had maintained a formal organization of a headquarters and three regiments, but that air and ground attacks had taken a sharp toll, leaving a surviving strength of only about 2,000. Under the direction of a controller, we attacked a group of 10th Division troops engaged in a skirmish with elements of an ROK division. I learned later that what was left of this NKPA division had fought its way through the ROK 3rd Division and disappeared to the north.

Shortly after dawn on March 21, I was making a walk-around pre-flight check in preparation for an early mission when I noted a string of

C-119s in the traffic pattern and three others on the ground taxiing toward the parking area across the field. That was just the beginning. By noon, eighty C-119s were parked wingtip to wingtip in long rows. A few minutes after the last C-119 landed, C-46s began to arrive, fifty-five of them in all. They too parked wingtip to wingtip, filling the entire west side of the field to the point of overflowing. No one was talking, but it was plain to see that an airborne operation involving paratroopers was about to take place, and it was likely that the pilots of the 49th FBG would be involved. In fact, the mission I was preparing to fly was in support of the operation, softening up the landing area and beyond, but it wasn't until the next day, when I learned of the destination of the airborne operation, that I made the connection.

Known as the Flying Boxcar, the C-119 was designed to transport cargo, personnel, and litter patients and to drop cargo and paratroopers. It had a crew of five and was 86 feet long and 26 feet, 6 inches high, with a wingspan of 109 feet, 3 inches. Its maximum speed was 296 miles per hour. The C-119 could carry sixty-two troops or thirty-five litter patients. The C-46's name was Commando. This twin-engine transport was designed to carry troops and cargo. It had a wingspan of 108 feet, 1 inch, a length of 76 feet, 4 inches, and a height of 21 feet, 9 inches. The Commando could carry fifty fully equipped troops or thirty litter patients. Its maximum speed was 269 miles per hour.

Following the recapture of Seoul, with Communist troops retreating to the north, the Eighth Army launched Operation Courageous, which was designed to trap as many Chinese and North Korean units as possible in the area between the Han and Imjin Rivers north of Seoul, opposite the I Corps. An essential feature of the operation was a parachute drop by the 187th Airborne Regimental Combat Team (ARCT) onto the south bank of the Imjin River near Munsan-ni, twenty miles north of the current front line, followed by a rapid advance by an armored task force, called Growler, to join up with the ARCT.

Before dawn on March 22, a stream of trucks entered the base, loaded with, 3,437 of the 187th ARCT paratroopers, 12 officers and men of the 60th Indian Parachute Field Ambulance Platoon, and 4 Air Force tactical air control parties, each including an FAC and a radio operator. No one milled around. Every man was assigned to a stick—the small group with which he was to jump—and the stick was assigned to a designated truck together with a second stick, both of which were assigned to a specific airplane. The forty-six men—two sticks of twenty-three men each, plus fifteen monorail bundles and four door bundles, which were deposited at the rear of each C-119—lined up in the order in which they would jump. Each man weighed over 250 pounds with all the gear he carried: a basic load of ammunition, three days' assault rations, a canteen of water, rifle and extra ammo, grenades, pistol and ammo, and apparently anything else he could carry that might be needed. Even from a distance, I could see that they had a hard time walking with that load and had to be helped up the three steps into the airplanes. Inside the C-119s, the paratroopers were positioned along both sides of the aircraft facing the middle and sitting on the canvas seats. The C-46s were similarly loaded.

Shortly after 0700, the C-46s and C-119s began to lift the airborne troops from K-2, all heading initially for a rendezvous point over the

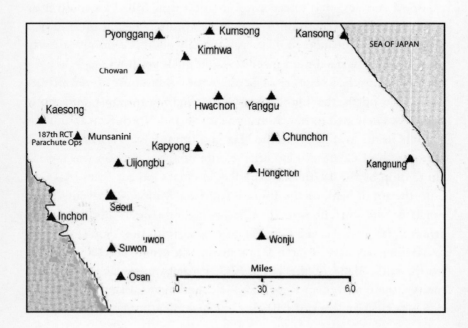

Yellow Sea west of the objective area near Munsan-ni. From the reports we received, the drop was successful, but jump casualties numbered eighty-four, almost half of whom returned to duty immediately after treatment. Battle casualties among the airborne troops were light, totaling nineteen. A minor stir was created when Korean civilians appeared in the drop zone and began gathering up parachutes. The attempted theft was ended by shots being fired over their heads. By the end of the day, all elements of the armored task force had linked up with the paratroopers, and the combined forces advanced to their goal, meeting weak resistance because the CCF had retreated before they got there. Enemy casualties included 136 dead on the field and 149 taken captive.

I led two missions in support of the 187th ARCT and Task Force Growler. I attacked two troop concentrations, one dug-in and the other in the open, with napalm and strafing, inflicting more than 100 casualties according to our controller, Mosquito Rakeoff. On a third mission, we attacked a supply dump with good effect, leaving behind a dozen fires and black smoke, apparently from oil stores.

In addition to these missions, I led five dive-bombing missions during March. Two were against bridges in North Korea. On the first, we scored six direct hits, which dropped two spans. On the second, we managed only to damage the approach and rails. Another dive-bombing mission, against a suspected supply dump near Chunchon, resulted in many fires, leading to the conclusion that the photo interpreter got it right when he labeled this place a *major* dump.

★ ★ ★

Maj. Irving W. "Pete" Boswell joined the 9th FBS the same time that I did. We had some things in common. Both of us had fought as fighter pilots in World War II, we each had volunteered to fight in Korea, we were both majors, and we each held a regular commission. His World War II service was in New Guinea and Malaysia, flying P-39s and P-40s. He had a sturdy build and was affable, unpretentious, and generally optimistic in his outlook. I enjoyed his company, and we often traded stories about World War II and the current war. His most stressful recent experience occurred in February, when he, along with two other members of his flight, with their fuel exhausted, were forced belly-land in the Naktong River, a few miles short of K-2. A direction-finding station had provided erroneous position information, which led to what could have been a disastrous ending for him and his fellow pilots. When the 8th FBS's commanding officer position became vacant in March, Boswell was designated to fill the slot. That appointment took him out of the squadron, but he remained nearby, and I saw him frequently.

The railroad marshalling yard at Sinanju, right in the heart of a heavy concentration of antiaircraft weapons, was a dive-bombing assignment that would never attract many volunteers, but that is the job I assigned my flight. Our plan was to arrive right at dawn, when railcars and a locomotive or two might not have taken refuge in a tunnel. And at that hour, the antiaircraft gunners might not be fully alert. Expecting heavy flak, we planned to get in and out as rapidly as possible.

As I entered my bomb run, I spotted a live locomotive spouting steam. It was connected to thirty to forty railcars. Our aiming point was the center of the marshalling yard right where the locomotive was positioned. My two bombs hit in the yard, just off center, and my wingman put his bombs nearby. Those four bombs did what was intended, creating craters, tearing up rails and switches, and smashing the locomotive and a number of the railcars. The element leader's bombs and those of his wingman veered off the intended target, hitting in the center of town, which may or may not have produced desirable results. Even though a hail of antiaircraft fire was directed at us, we escaped without a scratch.

Another dive-bombing mission took me back to the Sinuiju airfield, which was on the Fifth Air Force's list for periodic attention. This time, the targets were facilities that, according to the intelligence briefer, were undergoing renovation and repair. Our attack was intended to keep the airfield in unusable condition and to discourage work on restoring it to operational status. We were greeted by a whole lot of flak bursts as we approached and even more on our dive-bombing runs, but we weathered the barrage, put our bombs on target, and made it safely back to home base.

On the last day of March, the squadron recorded the loss of another experienced combat pilot, Capt. Kenneth J. Granberg, who went down on his twenty-fifth combat mission. He was on an armed reconnaissance of the main supply route from Pyongyang to Sinuiju in an area commonly known as Flak Alley, a route that saw many aircraft damaged and lost. The railroad lines and roads along this route comprised the main channel of transportation for the west coast of North Korea. Granberg hit a hill while evading heavy antiaircraft artillery ground fire five miles northeast of Sunchon. His flight leader reported seeing no signs of life at the wreckage. He was listed as missing in action, and years later, that listing was changed to presumed dead.

Twenty-six years old, Granberg was from Winton, Maine—the first person I had met from that state. When I learned he was from Maine, I was curious to know if he exhibited traits that I associated with New Englanders: strong regional accent, dry humor, steadfastness in the face of adversity, and so on. Over a beer in the officers' club, I found him to be somewhat reserved, but friendly, with a good sense of humor, and an accent that was distinctive, but moderated from what I had heard in films.

The loss of a pilot on a combat mission never came as a surprise to squadron members. Losses were expected and stoically accepted. No overt mourning of a loss took place, and little discussion took place beyond superficial comments about how good a guy he was. This resigned, unemotional acceptance of the loss of a comrade may seem puzzling to some, but those who daily faced the hazards of combating a determined enemy did not wish to dwell on the risks involved. It was better to push those thoughts out of the mind, keep the head down, and continue charging. The unspoken belief—maybe it was a hope—was that these things happen to others, not to me. While we were all well aware of the shock and anguish that such a loss inflicts on family members, we did not allow ourselves to become emotionally involved.

In addition to the airplanes destroyed in O'Leary's accident and the loss of Granberg, several other squadron aircraft were damaged due to enemy action. One pilot, unable to lower the landing gear because of battle damage to the main and emergency hydraulic systems, was forced to land wheels up. Another F-80 had major damage to the right intake duct, the result of a 30-millimeter shell. By the end of March, the 49th Group's aircraft strength had been reduced to sixty F-80s from its authorized strength of seventy-five. During that month, the group mounted 615 missions, comprised of 2,167 sorties. On these missions, more than 1,971,800 rounds of .50-caliber ammunition and 3,007 rockets were fired, and 80,100 gallons of napalm were delivered, along with 491,120 pounds of bombs; 1,589,700 gallons of fuel were consumed. During the first eight months of the war, the 49th FBG lost twenty-four F-80s on combat missions. The rate of loss would accelerate as the enemy added antiaircraft weapons and became more proficient in their use.

Chapter 14

A couple of weeks after I returned from my short tour with the 2nd Infantry Division, I received word that the group commander, Colonel Murphy, wanted to see me. Unexpectedly, the colonel had some good news for me. "Squire Williams," he said, "has completed his hundred missions and will soon be departing for a new assignment in the States. I have decided to appoint you commander of the 9th Squadron, effective upon his departure. I'm confident that you will do a good job." I couldn't have been more pleased.

I officially assumed command of the squadron a week later, on April 7. One of my first actions was to appoint a new squadron operations officer to replace me. Capt. Ray O. Roberts was my choice. Roberts was a highly likable fellow, smart, serious in his work, yet with a humorous side that made him a welcome social companion. He also had a high energy level and was always seeking a better way to get his job done.

The second action I took was to ask 1st Sgt. Merrill B. Simmonsen to call an evening meeting of the squadron's 165 enlisted men. The meeting was held in the mess hall, the only building large enough for that number of people. I told them that during World War II, I fought in the European theater, flying Spitfires and F-51 Mustangs, and that since joining the 49th in January, I had flown about seventy-five missions and had gotten to know many of them personally from the time I had spent on the flight line. I wanted to motivate every one of them to give his very best effort to the job he was assigned and also to provide each individual with a clear understanding of why we were in Korea and an appreciation the role of the 9th FBS in the war. Most important, I wanted them to know that we were a team and that every member of the squadron, whatever his job, was important to the success of the team. "From my months in the squadron," I said, "I know I can count on you. We have a great team of hard working airmen and pilots. Working together, we will get the job done."

I concluded by pointing out that we were members of one of the most illustrious fighter squadrons in the U.S. Air Force. Maj. I. Richard Bong, the highest scoring ace of World War II, had been a member of the 9th. He had forty confirmed victories and received the Medal of Honor. "We must uphold this great tradition of being the best, and I know that we will," I told the men.

As commanding officer, I avoided close friendships with others in the squadron. While I was friendly with everyone, close friendships could get in the way when a transgression called for discipline. I also wanted to avoid complaints of cronyism that I had observed earlier in my career when a commanding officer seemed to favor friends. This could undermine morale. The single exception was my friendship with Ray Roberts. The nature of our jobs meant that we worked closely together every day. We often had meals together, and we enjoyed each other's company. I also maintained my friendship with Irving Boswell, commander of the 8th FBS. We often shared stories about particularly interesting experiences that we or our pilots had had, and we discussed the various problems we encountered in our squadrons.

The 9th FBS had been in combat for over six months when I joined it in January. All of the pilots who were there from the start had racked up a substantial number of combat missions. This was a highly experienced group of flyers, but that would change as those who had been in combat the longest completed their combat tours and departed for new assignments. Then the replacements flowed in. By early May, all of the pilots who had been with 9th FBS at the start of the war had

PILOTS, 9TH FIGHTER-BOMBER SQUADRON
TAEGU AIR BASE, KOREA, MAY 1951

SQUADRON COMMANDER MAJOR GEORGE LOVING
OPERATIONS OFFICER CAPT. RAY O. ROBERTS

FRONT ROW (LEFT TO RIGHT): *Osborne, Costa, Gallager, Overstreet, Metzer, Coons, Lavoie, Murphy, Dennis.*

STANDING: *Evatt, McEachern, VanDerKarr, Moxley, Forrester, Roberts, Loving.*

SITTING: *Litchfield, Lovas, Steinharter, Dixon, Todd, Galbraith.*

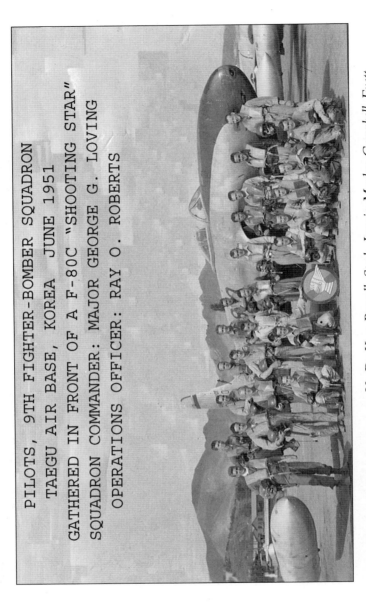

PILOTS, 9TH FIGHTER-BOMBER SQUADRON
TAEGU AIR BASE, KOREA JUNE 1951
GATHERED IN FRONT OF A F-80C "SHOOTING STAR"
SQUADRON COMMANDER: MAJOR GEORGE G. LOVING
OPERATIONS OFFICER: RAY O. ROBERTS

FRONT ROW KNEELING (LEFT TO RIGHT): *VanDerKarr, Russell, Stark, Innnig, Moxley, Campbell, Evatt.*

STANDING: *Doc Hood, Plum, Overstreet, Oleary, Lovas, Roberts, Loving, With, Dennis, Burns, Brantley.*

SITTING ON WING: *Bradley, Ward, Fowler, Willis, Litchfield.*

49th Fighter-Group pilots, left to right: George Loving, Bob Eckman, Walter "Lefty" Selenger, Ben Mayo, Charles Williams, Jim Anderson, and William "Red" Byers.

K-2 air base, summer 1951.

Makeshift shower at K-2 air base, 1950.

Runway at K-2 air base being repaired.

Control tower at K-2 air base.

9th Fighter-Bomber Squadron being readied for a mission.

9th Fighter-Bomber Squadron aircraft and pilots.

Airmen installing high-velocity aerial rockets.

An F-80 fighter-bomber lifting off on an armed reconnaissance mission.

Cockpit of an F-80C.

An F-80 on a strafing run.

An F-80 (at top) has just completed a strafing attack.

An F-80 releasing napalm tank during an attack run.

Napalm attack on railcars.

Tank destroyed by fighter-bomber napalm attack.

A MiG-15.

Battle damage on an F-80.

Loving examines a "whistle"—a modified shell casing—installed on his F-80 and intended to have a psychological impact on enemy soldiers. It didn't work.

Korean laborers rolling 1,000-pound bombs off truck prior to loading on F-80s. Fins will be installed later.

Battle damage on an F-80.

Maj. George Loving talks with Lt. Gen. Earle E. Partridge, commander of the Fifth Air Force.

Maj. George G. Loving, April 1951, age twenty-eight.

Forward air controller jeep and T-6 airborne controller aircraft.

Capt. Ray O. Roberts, 1951.

A C-47 takes off from K-2, fall 1950.

departed. In their place were one major (me), four captains, a dozen first lieutenants, and fifteen second lieutenants. A hard core of combat-experienced pilots remained with the squadron because about half of the pilots had joined the squadron in the early spring and had flown a good number of combat missions.

The four captains were all highly experienced fighter pilots. I would rely on them to provide combat leadership on tough missions.

Capt. James Gallagher's premature balding made him look older than he was. He had been a flying school instructor in the Air Force's training command, a job that required him to adhere strictly to a checklist and pay close attention to detail. During our initial meeting, he came across as a serious-minded individual, mature in outlook, but not without humor. He would be a valuable team player, I decided, and I appointed him squadron adjutant as an additional duty. In this capacity, he would be responsible for the squadron's administrative matters. After a couple of missions, Roberts, with my concurrence, placed him on the list of flight leaders. It wasn't long until I heard comments that during his briefings, he treated the other members of his flight as if they were student pilots. I didn't see anything wrong with that. Maybe he bruised the egos of some of the younger pilots, but he intended no malice. While Gallagher's motherly approach was not the style used by me or the other flight leaders, it was effective. He proved to be an excellent leader.

Capt. Henry L. Litchfield was from Beaumont, Texas. He had flown P-38s with the 82nd Fighter Group in Italy during World War II, stationed not far from my Mustang base. He was credited with damaging a Macchi C.202 during aerial combat. A laid-back fellow, he was seemingly comfortable with every assignment. I was concerned that he would resent that I had selected Ray Roberts to be operations officer even though Litchfield had an earlier date of rank, but he never gave any indication that he was unhappy with my decision. The fact that he had flown from a base near mine during World War II and that we both were involved in escorting heavy bombers gave us a common bond. From time to time, we enjoyed exchanging stories about our experiences. Litchfield proved to be a solid, reliable leader.

The third captain was William E. "Red" Byers, who sometimes organized beer busts and songfests. He was a retread—a reserve officer who had served during World War II, been discharged sometime after it ended, and then was recalled to active duty to serve in Korea. He had the sun-burned complexion of an outdoor blue-collar worker and carried a few too many pounds. Outgoing and flamboyant, he was aggressive, but somewhat slack in adhering to the rules of military life. Byers and his brother owned and operated a trucking business in Washington state. I heard him mention a number of times that he had driven big rigs all over the western United States. At the time I assumed command of the squadron, Red had already racked up more than fifty missions, most of which he had led. From the time he joined the squadron in January, he demonstrated an eagerness to take on any combat mission that came his way, but before he finished his combat tour, his record would be marred.

The fourth captain was Ray Roberts, a rock-solid pilot with excellent judgment, even temperament, and a great deal of common sense. I knew I could depend on him to do the right thing.

Unlike the captains, many of the second lieutenants lacked experience in jet-fighter operations and were not well trained in gunnery, rocketry, and dive-bombing. It just wasn't right to send them into combat with inadequate training and experience, which could translate into missed targets and unsafe flying practices in the F-80. That is why the 49th FBG established a training detachment at Tsuiki Air Base in Japan. Virtually every newly joined pilot was sent to Tsuiki for training. For those who were not proficient in jet operations, the training lasted four weeks. The more experienced jet pilots might need only a few practice bombing, strafing, and rocketing flights to get up to speed.

Among the second lieutenants, some stood out from the time they joined the squadron. One was Donald VanDerKarr. A bright, energetic, and very capable officer who volunteered for any and all tasks, he was an excellent pilot who accepted and carried out his flying duties in a professional manner. Roberts selected him to work in operations as a scheduler, and he eventually became assistant operations officer. After about twenty-five missions, Roberts put him on the flight leader list.

Second Lt. Carl Overstreet was another newly assigned pilot who caught my attention. He was from Bedford, Virginia, just twenty-five miles from my hometown. He projected a sober persona but was smart and quick-witted. Even though we didn't have mutual Virginia friends, I enjoyed exchanging stories with him about happenings back in our region of Virginia.

The briefing booth, an innovation Roberts originated, was one of the first subjects I discussed with him. When he first mentioned the subject, I immediately recalled the briefing for my first combat mission as a Spitfire pilot in World War II. Of the ten pilots scheduled on that mission, I was the only new boy, and I was surprised by the brevity of the stand-up briefing, which included only a brief description of the mission, a short mention of the possibility of enemy air opposition, our call signs, the assigned altitudes for each flight in the patrol area, start-engine time, and a time hack—with no mention of recommended airfields to use in an emergency, no alternate radio frequencies, or a host of potentially useful information. I concluded later that the details I had expected hadn't been addressed because they were well known to everyone except me, the only inexperienced pilot on the mission. This was not the kind of operation I wanted to run.

The briefing booths that Roberts somehow arranged to have constructed were very much like those found in a diner, with room for four people, two to a side, with a table in between. Affixed to the table, under Plexiglas, was an aeronautical chart covering our area of operations and a detailed briefing checklist. The flight leader was required to sit down with the other members of his flight and conduct an unhurried, detailed briefing following the checklist. A pilot might have heard three dozen times the list of airfields to which he could divert in an emergency, along with their location and associated radio beacon frequency. That information would be briefed on every mission, as well as everything else of possible value. The least inexperienced lieutenant on the flying roster deserved all of the assistance he could get, and this was one important way in which we could help.

Given that almost all of our missions were flown in flights of four aircraft, at least a quarter of the pilots would have to be capable of functioning as flight leaders if we were to have a balanced flight schedule. This leadership position involved a great deal of responsibility and required excellent judgment and cool behavior under fire and other difficult conditions. Over time, Roberts and I flew on combat missions with every pilot in the squadron, closely observing each of them, evaluating their potential to assume flight-leader responsibility. We never ran short of competent leaders and even found some among the young second lieutenants.

Mission aborts were another area of special interest. On the wall in operations, we maintained an abort board on which was listed, by aircraft number, every aircraft that had aborted from a mission. The listing included the date, pilot's name, and mechanical reason for the abort (generator failure, for example). The board had two purposes. First, multiple listings of the same airplane would alert us and a pilot scheduled to fly the craft that this could be a problem plane. Second, a pilot's appearance on the board several times could raise a questions about whether he was just having hard luck with the airplanes he flew or was squeamish about combat flying. The listing of pilot names, we believed, would identify potential problem cases and deter unjustified aborts. The board worked well in identifying the occasional problem airplane, but it didn't turn up any weak sisters during my term as squadron commander.

Although I had seen the Fifth Air Force's commander, Lt. Gen. Earle E. Partridge, many times, I had not had the opportunity to speak to him until he made an unannounced visit to the 49th FBG. I had a high regard for him and was pleased when he showed up in the personal equipment room of my squadron just as I was returning from a mission. I introduced myself as the squadron commander and responded to his questions about the mission I had just flown. He also inquired about the folder of aeronautical charts that I had in my hand, which I then showed him as I explained the folder's usefulness. He had further questions about pilot morale and recent sightings of enemy vehicles along the main supply routes. It was a boost to the morale of all, especially the pilots, to have the commanding general stop by for a visit.

Not all of battle damage to our aircraft was inflicted by the enemy. During April, the actions of two 9th FBS pilots resulted in unintentional damage to their airplanes that could have been fatal, but resulted in no injury to them.

Second Lt. Donald I. VanDerKarr went too low on a dive-bomb run before releasing his bombs and encountered some bomb blast that put a couple of gashes in his canopy. If he had continued in his dive for just a second longer, which would have put him much closer to center of the bomb blast, he would have been in serious trouble.

First Lt. Walter "Jack" Doerty, while making a strafing attack at dusk, flew through multiple high-tension wires that stripped off his canopy, ripped off some of his external ordnance, sliced into the right wing to the main spar, and damaged the empennage. The aircraft got him home okay, but the wing had a broken main spar and was "Class 26"—useful only for spare parts.

We were always looking for ways to be more effective in combating the enemy. I remembered reading that during World War II, the Luftwaffe's Ju-87s emitted a demoralizing whistling sound during dive-bomb runs. To augment the whistling, some crews attached sirens to the landing gear to generate what they hoped would a "demons from hell" sound. Maybe we could install whistles on our F-80s to enhance the psychological impact of our attacks. I asked our line chief to see what he could develop. He obtained a large-caliber brass shell casing, cut a notch in the side, and partially blocked the open end, a design somewhat like that of a hand-held whistle. He then had it fastened on the underside of the fuselage of my F-80, and I launched off on a test flight. Good try, but it didn't work. We asked around the base, but were unable to locate anyone with a suggestion on how to modify the design, so we abandoned the project.

Chapter 15

From the Chinese perspective, the Korean War became a battle of logistics. Employing fighter-bombers and light bombers of the Air Force, Navy, and Marine Corps, the Fifth Air Force conducted an extensive campaign aimed at curtailing the movement of personnel, supplies, and equipment from secure bases in Manchuria to the CCF and NKPA in Korea and destroying all that were found. During daylight hours, fighter-bombers conducted regular armed reconnaissance missions along all of the supply routes from Manchuria to the front lines, searching for vehicles, trains, tanks, soldiers, and supply dumps. The B-26s did the same at night. In addition to bombs, the B-26s dropped specially designed tetrahedral nails on highways to puncture the tires of enemy vehicles.

Rail and road bridges were attacked systematically, as were rail lines and marshalling yards. In addition, segments of road networks were assigned to each fighter-bomber squadron so that pilots could become intimately familiar with those segments and more readily detect changes. My squadron was assigned two road and railroad segments labeled Purple 9 and Purple 11. Located in the northwest corner of Korea, Purple 11 was the principal supply route that ran from Sinuiju to Sinanju, one of top three areas of greatest loss of American fighter-bombers. Purple 9, a less important supply route, ran northeast out of Sinanju.

On an armed reconnaissance mission along Purple 9 in early May, we carried rockets in addition to machine guns. We were a flight of four, call sign Bully Dog, taxiing down an inactive runway, parallel to and a few yards from the active 5,700-foot pierced-steel-planking runway. Bully Charlie, another flight of four F-80s, had preceded us by a few minutes. Just as Bully Charlie Leader's aircraft reached takeoff speed, his two 500-pound bombs detached, giving us something to think about as they hurtled past us at 120 miles per hour, striking sparks and repeatedly bouncing several feet into the air as they continued their eerie and potentially deadly journey to end of the runway, where they came to a halt in a cloud of dust. This was not an encouraging way to start a day. But at this point, I had other things to do and had no time to reflect on what could have been a catastrophic outcome. I would try to determine later the cause of those runaway bombs.

The weather was clear, and our flight to the target area was uneventful. I navigated to the end of Purple 9, about seventy-miles from Sinanju, and dropped down low to begin our run toward the southwest. We were searching for targets along the road as well as in adjacent areas—troops, vehicles of any kind (including horse-drawn wagons), supply caches, and all types of military facilities. We were down below 1,000 feet in an area of open countryside, away from towns, with only scattered villages.

We were moving at 360 miles per hour when Dog 3 radioed: "Bully Dog, suspicious activity near buildings on right, now at five o'clock. Suggest we swing around for a closer look."

I responded, "Roger, Dog 3," and turned back to scrutinize the area.

I had just rolled out of the 180-degree turn, headed back for a look, when suddenly we were surrounded by exploding 37-millimeter projectiles. More than a hundred explosions surrounded us, above and below, and my adrenaline jumped. There was only one way out of this—if we were lucky—and that was to dive for the ground and get as low as possible while turning and increasing our airspeed. But as I shoved the stick and throttle forward and headed down, I wasn't all that confident that we could escape this fire. There was so much of it that I didn't see how we could possibly break clear. The intense barrage continued, even as I passed below fifty feet on my way down to treetop level, chasing behind us like a pack of vicious dogs. But we did escape, all four of us, without being hit.

Once clear of the guns, I began a search of the area to try to determine what warranted such strong antiaircraft defenses. Was it the headquarters of a reserve CCF division? A training area? A supply depot? I couldn't tell from a distance; I would have to get closer to figure it out. After backing off ten miles to the west to get out of sight of the gunners, I instructed Bully Dog 3 and 4 to orbit while I made a run across the defended area with Dog 2. I dropped down to fifty feet, pushed the throttle forward and went screaming across at 450 miles per hour, apparently unnoticed by the defenders until it was too late for them to fire effectively. Despite our closer look, we were unable to figure out the situation. It would require careful study before we could mount an attack. I annotated the location on my aeronautical chart. At the mission debriefing, I would give the information to the intelligence officer so the location could be posted on flak charts and the JOC could dispatch a photo-reconnaissance aircraft to get a shot of the area. Photo interpreters could then determine what was going on at this remote place, and the ops guys could plan an attack to put it out of business.

Shortly after we continued our run down the road toward Sinuiju, we spotted six trucks heading in our direction, stirring up a long trail of dust as they sped along. I knew the moment the driver of the lead truck spotted us—the truck suddenly swerved sharply and careened into a roadside embankment, a futile and rather pathetic effort to escape what was coming. We had caught this small convoy in the open with no place to hide, and within minutes, our .50-caliber machine guns had ripped the trucks apart, leaving three of them burning and the others largely destroyed.

A few miles down the road, we happened upon three box cars parked on siding out in the middle of this rural area. What was this all about? Suspicious, I circled to look for a clue to explain their presence. Suddenly, it became clear: this was the only field in the vicinity with rows of straw stacks. The rounds I fired into one of the stacks exploded straw in all directions. We had stumbled on an ammunition dump. We set to work, setting off one haystack after another, until the area looked like a tornado had touched down. It wasn't until my wingman radioed Josephine that we set course for Taegu.

Confederate calvary general Jeb Stuart, who had boldly led 115 troopers in circling George McClellan's army, creating havoc in the rear areas, would have given us a thumbs-up for the commotion we stirred up along that seventy-five-mile stretch of enemy territory. But there was a difference. Our incursion was a routine event, repeated day after day by flights of fighter-bombers. For the enemy's soldiers, the rear areas were as dangerous as the front lines.

Back at base, I talked with the flight leader whose bombs got everybody's attention. He said the bomb release was accidental, but I wondered how this could have happened. No fewer than three errors would have had to have been made for the bombs to release during takeoff: someone would have had to have moved the bomb selection switch from "off" to "both"; the pilot would have had to overlook or fail to check the position of that switch during his preflight check; and during his takeoff run, the pilot would have had to press the bomb-release button on top of the control stick. The pilot in question was mature and experienced, but he had flown far fewer missions than other pilots during the three months he had been in the squadron because of medical problems. This raised a caution flag. Moreover, there was something about him that didn't quite fit the fighter-pilot mold. All of this made me think that he didn't belong in a fighter squadron. By the end of the week, while I was contemplating what action to take, he was transferred out of the squadron after the flight surgeon determined that he had incurable ear problems and was medically unfit to fly at high altitude.

To counter the Fifth Air Force's intense campaign to curtail their logistics flow, the Reds restricted most of their movement to the hours of darkness. In response to this, the Fifth employed light bombers at night. The crews searched for any sign of enemy activity, which, when detected, was illuminated with flares and attacked. Such attacks were effective, but sightings were limited because trains operated without lights, as did most road vehicles. Moreover, operating at night in mountainous terrain was a challenging kind of flying. While the crews gave this mission their very best effort, an Air Force evaluation board found that night-intruder operations were successful only in harassing the enemy's movement.

Understanding that its night-attack capability was limited, the Fifth Air Force devoted a great deal of effort to developing more effective methods to conduct daylight operations. In addition to the assignment of road segments to each fighter-bomber squadron, another innovation was the predawn mission, with which I became very familiar.

Trains, a principal means used by the CCF to transport food, ammunition, and equipment to their deployed forces, moved at night, and when dawn approached, they headed for the nearest tunnel to hide out in daylight hours. Ordered to travel as far as possible before hiding in a tunnel, the train engineers felt safe to be in the open during a short period just after dawn. That would prove to be a mistake. Beginning in April, we received operation orders tasking us to launch flights at 0430 hours in order to be over an area with one or more tunnel entrances before dawn, search for trains, and, at dawn, attack any that had delayed entry into a tunnel. We enjoyed some success doing this, but none of the pilots liked rolling out of bed as early as 0300 hours for a briefing.

At 0350 hours on April 17, I sat down with the three other members of my flight to brief them on the mission the ops officer had assigned us. We were to fly to Kiching, just north of Songchon, and follow the railroad running to the east through a number of tunnels. The plan was to be over the area thirty minutes before dawn and watch for lights—hopefully from a locomotive when the fire door was opened—or smoke when dawn broke. Afterward, if no trains were pinpointed, we were to check the rail line west of Kiching.

I began my takeoff roll at 0440 hours with my wingman hanging in close. As soon as we reached the midpoint of our takeoff roll, the element leader and his wingman began their takeoff and soon joined on my left wing, at which point I turned onto a heading of 335 degrees, which would put me over Kiching in about forty-eight minutes—thirty minutes before dawn.

The weather couldn't have been better. The sky was clear with a nearly full moon. Lights on the ground marked our route until we reached the front lines. That is where everything went dark on the CCF side. With no lights on the ground to mark cities and towns, I would have to rely on dead reckoning to get us into position over the target area. We didn't see even a dot of light over Kiching or to the west, but I caught the reflection of the moon off the rails, so I knew we must be where we should be. When dawn began to creep in, we were at 5,000 feet, searching diligently. We saw not a locomotive or train car. I followed the railroad through Kiching and on to the east. That's where we hit pay dirt.

It was only a few minutes after dawn and twenty-five miles from Kiching, where the rails turn to the north, and we spotted not one but three locomotives, all trailing smoke as they raced toward a tunnel about two miles ahead. If we were to destroy all three, we would have to stop the lead locomotive. That required that we act rapidly because the lead engineer had poured on the coal in what for him was the race of—and for—his life. Once we stopped the lead locomotive, we could take our time finishing off the other two.

I radioed my flight, "Bully Able, let's speed this up. Attack the lead engine until it is stopped. Able 2, use rockets on your first pass."

We were in a valley hemmed in by mountains and hills, with little room to maneuver, and the locomotives were heading directly toward the base of a towering peak. This was going to involve some careful maneuvering because it would be easy to misjudge distances and elevations in this situation and end up spread across a mountainside. We had to attack at steeper dive angles than normal, then pull up sharply to avoid tall hills on either side of the tracks. I would make the initial attack, and the others would follow my lead, spaced so that number two would begin his attack run just as I was pulling off the target.

My gunsight was on and my machine guns were armed as I began my attack run perpendicular to the tracks. This was the preferred attack path since the engines presented the largest target when approached directly from the side. An approach along the length of tracks, toward the mountain, would have been risky because of the mountain's proximity.

I maneuvered to place the gunsight piper on the boiler of the lead engine. I was in a somewhat steeper dive than normal—forty degrees—because I had to approach over the adjoining hills. At about 1,200 yards, as the target came into range, I pulled the trigger. Instantly, the six guns spewed out streams of armor-piercing projectiles. With earphones in place and the guns isolated in separate compartments, the muted sound came through as a powerful growl, accompanied by some vibration of the airframe.

I scored multiple hits on the boiler and on the cab. Steam instantly engulfed the boiler, spewing from the many holes I had punched into its side. Bully Able 2 was close behind, and his rockets slammed into the engine, creating a spectacular blast. The first engine was now stopped dead, blocking forward movement by the other locomotives. As I pulled off the target, I saw the engineers and firemen jumping from the cabs of the other locomotives and scurrying for cover. But we weren't after them.

I radioed, "Alpha 3, use your machine guns on the second engine. Alpha 4, attack the third engine. Then go after the box cars with rockets."

In very short order, the boilers of the two other locomotives were blown to pieces, and then we set to work rocketing the strings of box cars. From start to finish, the destruction of all three locomotives took less than ten minutes.

The success of my flight on an early-morning locomotive hunt was not a fluke. Pilots of the 49th FBG scored a number of such kills before the North Koreans changed tactics and began heading for their tunnel refuges well before dawn.

Intelligence reports received in April stated that the North Koreans had 23,000 men, organized into units of fifty rail-repair troops stationed at all major rail stations, ready to be dispatched immediately to repair damage inflicted by air attack. This was a clear indication of just how vital movement of supplies by rail was to the Reds and the impact we were having.

In addition to bombing, napalming, and strafing trains, the Fifth Air Force employed psychological warfare, as demosntrated by this leaflet dropped to dissuade North Korean workers from making repairs to bombed rail lines.

Not long after our dawn attacks began, locomotive sightings at first light decreased sharply. We knew they were hiding in tunnels, and given the high probability that practically every tunnel in North Korea contained a locomotive and freight cars during daylight hours, the Fifth Air

Force needed to find an effective way to get at them. Strafing tunnel entrances didn't cause much damage, and dive-bombing against such small targets required a number of missions to produce lasting results. Another method that we tried was skip-bombing or low-angle bombing. The bombs we used for skip-bombing had fuses with a ten-second delay, allowing the pilot to get well clear of the target before the bomb detonated. The ideal attack was a long straight-in run starting at 3,500 feet and continuing down to 25 feet at high speed, with release of bombs as close as possible to the tunnel entrance. The terrain surrounding many tunnels didn't permit such attacks. In some cases, the terrain blocked a straight-in approach or rose too sharply behind the entrance to permit a safe exit for the pilot. But for those tunnels located in suitable terrain, a skilled pilot, we were informed, could put bombs into the entrance and cause massive damage.

My first skip-bombing mission was against a tunnel entrance located on the rail line running south out of Pyongyang to Sariwon, where it branched off toward Sinmak. There were three tunnels along this stretch, and I was going after the one nearest Sinmak, about thirty miles east of Sariwon. I always had faith that bomb fuses would operate as advertised and didn't give the subject more than a passing thought on dive-bombing missions. But when it came to skip-bombing—in which the ten-second delay was absolutely vital—I always personally contacted the armorer who had installed the fuses and got his assurance that he had indeed installed ten-second fuses.

As we taxied out, a light rain was falling, and a cloud layer extended from 700 feet up to a reported 25,000 feet. The forecaster had said that the cloud ceiling in the target areas should be about 5,000 feet but that we might encounter some lower clouds. After takeoff, I stayed under the cloud ceiling until the element leader and his wingman joined the formation. Then I set course for the target area and began a climb to 20,000 feet. I planned to descend in order to be within sight of Sariwon at 5,000 feet. From there, I would pick up the railroad line and follow it to our assigned tunnel entrance. The tallest peak within fifty miles or so of Sariwon rises to almost 3,000 feet, so descent in the clouds to 5,000 feet should be safe.

When we emerged from the clouds at 5,000 feet, Sariwon was just ahead. As I turned over the edge of the city to follow the railroad to the east, we were greeted by a few bursts of antiaircraft fire—not really threatening, but a reminder that we were being tracked.

The Fifth Air Force's planners had determined from aerial photographs that it would be feasible to skip-bomb the tunnel entrance assigned to us, but once I had located it, I would have to determine the best approach and departure routes. We made one circle over the entrance to get the lay of the land. It didn't look too bad. The railroad ran almost directly west to east, and we would have a fair amount of maneuvering room to the north of the tunnel entrance. I decided that we would begin our attacks from a position north of the rails and make a descending turn to get into position directly over the tracks at 3,500 feet about five miles from the entrance.

At the initial point, I armed the bombs, selected "Both," and set the throttle at 98 percent. I then initiated the descending turn that placed me over the tracks about five miles from the tunnel entrance at the correct height. From that point, I descended smoothly to twenty-five feet with the K–14 gunsight aligned on the left edge of the tunnel entrance. I wanted to get as close as I safely could, but I was moving at more than seven miles a minute, and judging the distance at that speed was difficult. It was like a game of chicken.

When my brain screamed, "Now!" I punched the bomb-release button and initiated a sharp pull-up to the left. Exactly ten seconds later, two explosions occurred, one from within the tunnel—spitting out a dense cloud of dust and debris—and the other to the right of the entrance. Very lucky for a first timer, I thought. But driving toward a mountainside, even a small mountain, at very high speeds can be hard on the nerves. I decided that I wouldn't want to make a career of tunnel busting.

With this entrance blocked, I called off the other members of my flight and led them to the other entrance of the tunnel. The three of them each made a run and scored near misses that cascaded rocks and other debris onto the tracks blocking the entrance, but there were no direct hits.

After this initial effort, squadron pilots skip-bombed three other tunnel entrances, completely closing two and damaging the other. The damaged entrance was at a tunnel near Wonsan, on the east coast. The direct hits were on tunnel entrances located on the railroad line that ran southeast out of Sohung to Kumch-on. I led one of these attacks that completely closed an entrance. A week later, another flight closed a nearby tunnel entrance.

In addition to railroad tunnels, squadron pilots conducted skip-bombing against raised railroad beds. I didn't fly any of these missions but knew that the bombing could be highly effective. First Lt. Richard G. Immig, one of the 9th FBS flight leader stalwarts, reported: "We carried 1,000-pound bombs with delayed fuses, and I took take one wingman (widespread) and skipped one bomb into the embankment while the wingman did the same. We then made a 180-degree turn and moved down the line a little bit and did the same thing from the other side. I'm sure we were making life miserable for the gooks."

An intelligence report I read at about this time gave an idea of just how much manpower the Chinese had available and were willing to commit to counter our air assaults on their transportation system. The report stated that they had mobilized 400,000 laborers in Manchuria to be employed in building caves, revetments, and trenches along the highway from Sinuiju to the front lines in order to hide and shelter their trucks from our air attacks. This massive effort had a noticeable effect on our operation. Over time, we spotted and attacked fewer vehicles along Purple 9 and 11. As a further indication of the impact we had, the Reds used not only trucks to move supplies, but also wagons, oxcarts, and pack animals. On recent missions, the boys reported seeing camels along the road.

We didn't know it then, but our attacks and ever-present threat of attacks had a pronounced effect on Chinese and North Korean soldiers dispatched as combat replacements According to our intelligence officer, prisoner-of-war reports indicated that CCF and NKPA combat replacements were assigned to regiment-size units in Manchuria and marched southward. They moved only at night, always on foot because there was no transportation to spare for personnel. Most prisoners had experienced at least one daylight attack against their camp sites while marching southward. Seventy percent of the Chinese prisoners and 81 percent of the North Koreans interrogated by the Fifth Air Force's analysts said that they had not been attacked while marching at night. Although they had not experienced repeated air attacks, they nevertheless felt like hunted animals and had suffered deterioration of morale and physical well-being by the time they reached the front. They had made long and hurried marches at night over difficult terrain and in bitterly cold weather. They avoided villages and usually slept in trenches in daytime camps, thus falling victim to sickness caused by exposure.

A captured report prepared by the political department of the Chinese 15th Division described the hectic march of this unit southward from the Yalu, beginning on March 21. It spoke of "frequent air raids" and the "consternation" they caused and of troops being unable to obtain food for two or three days at time. Exhausted by forced marches and from digging air-raid shelters at each day's camp, troops straggled and took sick. By the time this division reached the front lines on April 9, it was already suffering from combat fatigue.

Chapter 16

I got a taste of unfriendly skies on a sunny April day over Anju. My assigned mission that day was to lead a flight of four on an armed reconnaissance mission along Purple 11. This would take us into what could be a hornet's nest, an area bristling with antiaircraft defenses, and into the heart of MiG Alley.

The only break we got was that this was not one those get-up-in-middle-of-the-night missions in order to be over the target at dawn. In fact, we had a rather civilized late-morning takeoff time. Armed with rockets and machine guns, we took off in pairs and climbed up through an overcast. We broke out into the clear at 21,000 feet and then cruised northward at 22,000 feet.

I planned to start our reconnaissance at Sinuiju, close to the border with China, 370 miles from K-2, and work our way south toward home. The cloud cover disappeared near Pyongyang, and visibility was just about unlimited as I began our descent about sixty miles short of the target area.

I dropped down to treetop level, and the other three trailed me at about 3,000 feet. In short order, I spotted a large group of trucks partially hidden beneath some trees alongside the road. I called them out as I passed overhead, and Bully Able 3 and his wingman swooped in for a strafing attack. Normally, we made a single pass at targets in heavily defended areas, but this was the largest group of vehicles I had seen. I wanted to finish them off, so I turned back with my wingman, and we each made a strafing run, raking the line of trucks with hundreds of rounds of .50-caliber machine-gun fire. We observed only spasmodic defensive fire, probably from rifles and machine guns. We left behind at least a dozen burning vehicles, all fully loaded with supplies for the CCF.

Farther down the road, on the adjacent rail line, I spotted three railcars parked on a siding. I didn't know if they were loaded or empty, but I had to assume the latter. These were tougher targets than trucks; they would require rockets to blast into them. As I was getting set for a rocket attack, I instructed Bully Able 3 to climb to 8,000 feet with his wingman to provide top cover. I assumed that F-86s would be in the area to keep the MiGs occupied, but maybe they weren't. At this point, we had moved down the road to Anju, only seventy miles from the MiG base at Antung, and I couldn't assume that MiGs in the air would be tied up with F-86s.

I had just let loose a fusillade of rockets and was dodging the fireball from an exploding freight car when Bully Able 3 radioed: "Four bogeys approaching fast at 10,000 feet from the northeast." The immediate question was whether they were F-86s or MiGs. The answer came a few moments later: "Bully Able, they are MiG-15s." At this point, Able 3 and 4 dove for the deck and departed the area.

Flown by Chinese and Soviet pilots, the MiG-15 was a more advanced airplane than the one I was flying. With swept wings and 5,005 pounds of engine thrust, the MiG-15 had a top speed of 664 miles per hour. The engine in our straight-wing F-80 produced 4,600 pounds of thrust and provided a maximum speed of 580 miles per hour. Moreover, there were four of them against two of us, and the MiGs were armed with a 37-millimeter cannon and two 23-millimeter cannon, while we had .50-caliber machine guns. On top of that, in this instance, the MiGs had lots of altitude that could be readily converted into airspeed and maneuverability. All of this meant that if a fight took place, we would be the underdogs. Better to avoid a fight if possible, given that the odds were stacked against us. But it didn't appear that we would have a choice.

At this point, we had at least one thing going for us: although this was the first time I had been faced with the possibility of jousting with MiGs, I was no stranger to dogfights. A few years earlier, in World War II, I had been in many air battles and had been successful in combat with German pilots. Now I would have the chance to see what the Chinese or Soviet pilots had to offer. The big question in my mind was the turning capability of the F-80 versus that of the MiG. If we got into a turning match, how would we make out? I didn't know, but the moment of truth was approaching. As the leader of Bully Able flight, I had my work cut out for me.

I switched to the emergency radio channel and broadcast a warning: "This is Bully Able. MiG-15s sighted over Anju at 10,000 feet." This was intended to be an invitation to any F-86s in the area and a warning to all fighter-bombers. I then radioed my wingman: "Bully Able jettisoning tip tanks." I punched the tank-release button, pushed the throttle to the firewall, backed off a fraction so I wouldn't lose my wingman, turned to the southeast, and began a high-speed climb. Altitude could be converted into airspeed, and that is what we would need in any maneuvering situation. My strategy was to keep working toward the southeast—toward our home base and away from Antung.

Far above, I saw two of the four MiGs roll into a dive. In a few moments, we could expect to have some lead spewing toward us. I would wait until just before they reached firing range and then turn sharply into them to spoil their aim. Turn too soon and the MiG pilots could readjust their aim and hammer us. Turn too late and we could get blasted. Discipline and experience were what counted.

Down they came at a very steep angle and a very high speed. As I waited for them to get closer, I thought they'd never nail us with those tactics—which were too steep and too fast to hit the side of a barn.

Seconds before I saw the muzzle flashes of the lead MiG's cannons, I called out, "Able 2, break right," and racked my airplane around almost 180 degrees to confront the attackers. The MiGs broke off their attack and pulled up sharply. I followed suit, pulling the nose of my airplane up to fling a long burst of machine-gun fire as the retreating MiGs zoomed back up in a steep climb. No blood. I knew that my burst of fire was likely to be a futile gesture at this distance, and pulling up sharply to get the MiGs in my gunsight bled off vital airspeed—but I couldn't accept the idea of engaging in a dogfight, even a one-sided tussle, without throwing some lead.

I turned back toward the southeast and reestablished a high-speed climb. At this point, I perceived that our greatest vulnerability was a diminishing fuel supply. On the deck, a jet engine running at near full-tilt burns fuel at a ferocious rate. We couldn't afford to hang around much longer. My hope was that by moving the fight farther and farther to the southeast, away from Antung, they would want to break off before our fuel supply got critically low.

The MiG leader and his wingman zoomed back up and rejoined the other two, at which point MiGs three and four came off their perch and headed downhill for an attack. It was a repeat of the first—very steep and very fast. Once again, an instant before I observed their muzzle fire, I called a right break and made a violent turn to face the attackers, almost head-on. I fired my machine guns as they pulled up and headed back to their perch high above. No blood again.

By this time, we had worked our way about twenty-five miles to the southeast of Anju. This was progress. I had now drawn the MiGs about 100 miles from their base, which was near the boundary of their normal operating area. But if the harassing attacks continued much longer, it could be touch-and-go for us, given our shrinking supply of fuel.

We didn't have to wait long for the third attack. The MiG leader and his wingman came sliding down, as if on the steepest slope of a roller coaster. They must have been having a grand old time, conducting target practice at high noon south of Anju. My actions didn't vary: wait patiently for the right moment and then turn sharply to spoil their attack; throw a long burst of machine-gun fire at them as they climbed away; and turn quickly back to the southeast. We suffered no hits, and I didn't observe any on the MiGs.

Did this end it, or would there be another attack? A couple of minutes later, I got the answer: the MiGs turned toward the north.

En route back to Taegu, I wondered what the MiG leader's mission report would say. Maybe something like, "Controller vectored us to vicinity of Anju; sighted four enemy dive-bombers engaged in attack on rail cars; broke up attack and sent the cowardly running dogs retreating to the southeast."

My mission report was a bit different: "During armed reconnaissance along Purple 11, attacked truck convey 20 miles north of Anju, and left a dozen trucks in flames. Was completing successful rocket attack on freight cars at Anju when we came under attack by four MIGs who made repeated ineffective firing passes in pairs, yo-yoing from 10,000 feet to the deck and back up. Returned fire, but observed no hits. Despite their altitude advantage and superior aircraft performance, MiG pilots apparently didn't have the stomach to engage in close combat at low altitude."

Maybe it was our lucky day that the MiG pilots didn't close in and dogfight with us, or maybe it was *their* lucky day that they took a pass. We'll never know, but given the timidity of the MiG pilots, I believe we would have scored.

So what is one to conclude from this MiG encounter? Although the MiG-15's performance was vastly superior to the F-80's, the MiGs outnumbered the F-80s four-to-two, had the altitude advantage, had superior firepower, and were fighting in their own backyard, they turned out to be paper tigers. Why? The probable reason was that the MiG pilots were lacking in experience and maybe courage. Flying a superior airplane in an aerial encounter doesn't guarantee success, nor does having an inferior airplane mean failure. A well-trained, experienced pilot with a cool head can carry the day.

✭ ✭ ✭

The news hit like a bombshell. On April 11, President Truman relieved General MacArthur from his command. We didn't understand why at the time, but it was big news. MacArthur was replaced as head of the Far East Command by Lieutenant General Ridgway, who had done a magnificent job in shaping up the Eighth Army. Now there would be a new commander of the Eighth Army, Lt. Gen. James A. Van Fleet. He had participated in the D-Day landings on Utah Beach and served as a division and corps commander during World War II. We would have to wait and see how he would lead the Eighth. Under Ridgway's leadership, it had performed extremely well and had advanced steadily to positions along and above the 38th parallel, making South Korea whole again. But that wouldn't last. The Chinese had been increasing their strength, preparing for a new offensive.

We knew from intelligence reports that Chinese ground troops had been led to believe that they would have tactical air support when they began their 1951 spring offensive. This would require many forward airfields within North Korea because their MiGs did not have the range to provide cover to ground forces from bases in Manchuria. In March, aerial reconnaissance had revealed that workers were engaged in repairing eleven airfields in North Korea. The U.S. strategy was to wait until an airfield was nearing operational status, then launch a bombing raid.

B-29s played a major role in the bombing of North Korean airfields. Because of its large payload—20,000 pounds—the B-29 was the preferred airplane for airfield attack. Typically, a B-29 load consisted of forty 500-pound general-purpose bombs, about half of which were equipped with delayed-action fuses, set to detonate from 1 to 144 hours after arming. The other half, set to explode on impact, were aimed at runways, buildings, and other airfield facilities. Each of the delayed-action bombs was filled with 250 pounds of RDX Composition D explosive, which is more powerful than TNT. The external casing of these bombs was scored so that when detonated, shrapnel would shower the area around the explosion. The delayed-action fuses were intended to discourage North Korean attempts to defuse unexploded bombs and delay repair of bomb damage. To prevent easy defusing of a bomb, several features were incorporated that would trigger the bomb's detonation if attempts were made to disarm it.

By mid-April, the time had come to neutralize the North Korean airfields. An average of twelve B-29s a day were launched to crater runways and spread delayed-action explosives over North Korean airfields. On each of these raids, the 49th FBG provided eight F-80s to protect the B-29s from attack by MiGs. I participated in a number of these raids. At rendezvous over a specified point in South Korea, the B-29s would be at 20,000 feet. We flew overhead at 28,000 or 30,000 feet, weaving out to one side and then across to other side, all the while watching for MiGs. The bombings were impressive and effective. Each B-29 dropped forty bombs, blasting craters in the runways, blowing up fuel and munitions storage facilities, and destroying buildings.

In my view, because of the MiG's superior performance, we were largely a token force that would be of limited value in protecting the B-29s. If a MiG attack came, we would do our best to defend them, but it was unlikely that we would be effective. Certainly, the Fifth Air Force's commander knew this, but given the limited number of F-86s available, he had little choice but to use us and hope for the best.

After the first Soviet-built MiG-15s entered the war, Air Force technical intelligence people started to think about ways to get their hands on a MiG—or at least get a close look at what made the airplane tick. As a consequence of this interest, the Fifth Air Force organized and trained teams to go quickly to the site of any downed MiG-15 within reach and salvage key parts for study and analysis by technicians at Wright-Patterson Air Force Base, the Air Force's technical center in Ohio. Capt. Donald Nichols was put in charge of the effort. He had been transferred from the Office of Special Investigations to the intelligence section of the Fifth Air Force to work on special and clandestine operations. The teams, a part of "Special Activities Unit Number One," consisted of Americans and Koreans trained in parachute jumping, concealment in enemy territory, and salvage of key aircraft parts, which was taught and practiced at K-2 using a wrecked F-80 and two engines contributed by the 49th FBG. That is when I became aware that something odd was going on. I noted the presence of strangers, including Koreans, who were taking a wrecked airplane and engines apart. What was this all about? I met and talked with Captain Nichols. He said this was a training exercise for the ROK Air Force, but that didn't sound reasonable to me since they didn't have jets and were unlikely to get them anytime soon. However, I didn't connect this activity with what would occurred later.

When the teams had been trained, they waited for the sighting of a downed MiG-15. This occurred in a short time when an F-80 pilot caught sight of a wrecked MiG not far from Sinanju. Photoreconnaissance confirmed it was a MiG-15, and a recovery effort termed "Operation MiG" was set in motion. A team of five Korean specialists led by Captain Nichols set off via helicopter to Paengyong Island, where the bird was refueled. Located off the west coast of Korea, the island allowed a largely overwater approach to the downed MiG, which was located about twenty-five miles inland from the coast. An overland approach would have been much too risky for a slow-flying helicopter. Once refueled, the helicopter set off for the target area, which was near a major Communist installation. It landed in a barley field 250 feet from the MiG. Prior to the helicopter's arrival, F-51 fighter-bombers staging from Cho-Do Island had strafed the area and then remained overhead to cover the operation. A well-trodden path indicated that the MiG had been under guard, but no one was at the site when the helicopter arrived.

The team had a list of desired MiG parts—fourteen in all—as well as documents pertaining to the aircraft. The list included the engine, major components, turbine blades, instruments, skin samples, tailpipe samples, radio, armament, fuel igniter, name plates, ID tags, and so forth. After Captain Nichols confirmed that the airplane was indeed a MiG-15, the team began work to obtain the desired parts. While Nichols took photographs of everything not removable, the others obtained airplane skin samples and ammunition samples. When they needed to get inside the fuselage, they used a hand grenade to blast it open. The airplane had been partially burned and the instruments had been destroyed by the fire, but there were still plenty of parts to salvage. The team loaded onto the helicopter turbine blades, the engine exhaust pipe, exhaust pipe heat seals, a combustion chamber, and other key parts including the horizontal stabilizer. After only thirty-five minutes on the ground, the team completed the job, reboarded the helicopter, and lifted off with the MiG's horizontal stabilizer protruding out the open doorway.

Shortly after liftoff, near Sinanju, the helicopter became the target of antiaircraft gunners and took a hit on a rotor blade, but it continued on without difficulty to Cho-Do Island. There it was refueled before flying on to Paengyong Island. Here it was met by an SA-16A, which transported the men and their loot onward to a base in South Korea. Afterwards, the MiG parts were flown to the States for analysis.

Unfortunately, although this was a textbook example of an audacious, well-planned, and perfectly executed operation, with which Air Force technical intelligence was well pleased, there was no payoff for the U.S. pilots who were fighting the war.

★ ★ ★

Beginning during the second week of April, smoke from deliberately set brush fires obscured the CCF's frontline positions to a depth of ten miles across the IX Corps' sector. Eight new Chinese armies, each with 10,000 men, were moving into place. The attack, labeled the Chinese Spring Offensive, was launched on the night April 21 when 337,000 Red soldiers swept ahead all across the IX Corps' front. The main effort was in the west and center against the U.S. 24th Infantry's and ROK 6th Division's sectors. The CCF's objective was to overwhelm and destroy the UN forces. Seoul was the immediate objective.

I got involved on opening day, when I led a mission to Hwachon to provide support to the ROK 1st Marines Regiment, which was withdrawing under the strong pressure of the 10,000-man 39th People's Liberation Army (PLA). Our controller reported that our napalm and strafing attacks had stopped the PLA advance and relieved the pressure on ROK marines. "Good results," he said.

By the end of the first day, Fifth Air Force fighter-bombers had flown 340 sorties providing close air support to Eighth Army units.

Like all of the other fighter-bomber groups, our tempo of operations increased significantly. This put a heavy strain on the ground crew. Just as soon as an aircraft landed, it had to be quickly refueled and rearmed and made ready for another mission. Crews were working long hours to keep up with the demand placed on them. Almost all of them were young fellows who took their job seriously and were emotionally attached to their airplane and, in most cases, to the pilot assigned to the aircraft. I made it a point to spend some time recounting for the crew chief some details of the mission I had just flown so he would know what his airplane had been involved in and to express my appreciation for his hard work.

Every so often, I would draw a mission that would turn out to be a "milk run," one on which we encountered no antiaircraft fire. The mission on April 21 to dive-bomb the runway on the airfield at Pyonggang was one such milk run. Located a few miles northeast of Chorwon, it was North Korea's southernmost airfield, well positioned to serve as a staging base for North Korean attack aircraft. I had flown over it a number of times and had never noticed any signs of activity, but the airfield's location was such that it had to be closely monitored on a continuing basis. Periodically, the Fifth Air Force dispatched fighter-bombers to rough it up a bit so that it would remain unusable.

The airfield was located a mile north-northwest of Pyonggang. It had a single runway, 5,000 feet long, running almost due east and west, and a parallel taxiway with several revetments. My wingman, flying as Bully Able 2, was 2nd Lt. Carl Overstreet. I had asked Ray Roberts to put him on the mission so that I could get to get better acquainted with him, a fellow Virginian who was new to the squadron.

I approached on a northerly heading in order to be in a position to attack to the west along the length of the runway. As we neared the airfield, I spotted smoke just to the north. This gave us information on wind direction and speed to use in selecting an aiming point during our dive-bombing attack. At this point, I armed the two 500-pound bombs. We were at 10,000 feet, and just as the east end of the runway passed under the forward edge of my left wing, I turned and entered a forty-five-degree dive, opened the speed brakes, and selected an aiming point on the right edge of the runway to compensate for what I estimated to be a ten-mile-per-hour northerly wind.

At 4,000 feet, I punched the bomb-release button and began to pull-out of the dive, feeling the G-suit inflate. Thankfully, I didn't observe any antiaircraft fire. As I was pulling off the target, Bully Able 2 was entering his bomb run. He would be followed closely by the two other members of the flight. The first six bombs scored direct hits on the runway, creating craters along its length. The two bombs of Bully Able 4 struck the taxiway. A successful mission.

The next day, April 22, I was dispatched on another airfield attack mission, this one against Pyongyang Airfield, located on the northeast edge of North Korea's capital city. Again, Carl Overstreet was flying as Bully Able 2. He had performed well on his first airfield attack mission, and I was certain he would do so again. The Pyongyang Airfield had been attacked many times, and after each raid, the North Koreans set about repairing the damage. So a pattern emerged: we continued our periodic attacks, and they kept repairing the damage. Our targets this time were the buildings and revetments on the airfield; the runway was still cratered from an earlier attack. The intelligence briefer noted that the airfield and the Pyongyang area were defended by numerous antiaircraft weapons. This wasn't new information for us, but it served to remind us that we should plan an attack that would minimize our exposure to the defenses.

At our briefing, we studied an aerial photograph of the airfield, focusing our attention on the location of the buildings and revetments. I decided that we would approach from the north, attack on an easterly heading, and withdraw toward the east until out of range of the defenses. An island in the Taedong River, just north of the airfield, was our initial point, aligning us for our approach to the target. The mission went well. A great deal of antiaircraft fire was directed at us, but we escaped unharmed. We put all eight bombs on target but had to report "results unknown." Damage assessment would require detailed study a photo interpreter. We never learned what damage we inflicted.

On April 23, my flight provided close air support for the 24th Infantry Division near Chorwon, where we killed 100 enemy troops of the Chinese 60th PLA when it had attacked along the west flank of the 24th and rammed through the Turkish Brigade. That same day, my flight was also sent to Munsan-ni to provide much-needed support for the ROK 2nd Division, which was under strong pressure from the NKPA 8th Division. Our controller reported unknown results, but we got good coverage of the designated target areas.

On April 24, three days after the CCF launched the offensive, I received a radioed message from the JOC some twenty minutes after takeoff, informing me that there was a report that a B-26 had been hit by ground fire and was going down twenty miles west of Chorwon. Another B-26 was on the scene, and a chopper had been launched. I was directed to proceed to that area—about fifty miles north of Seoul—and assist in the rescue attempt.

I suspected this would be messy. The Chinese had launched their major offensive a few days earlier and had sent two armies sweeping

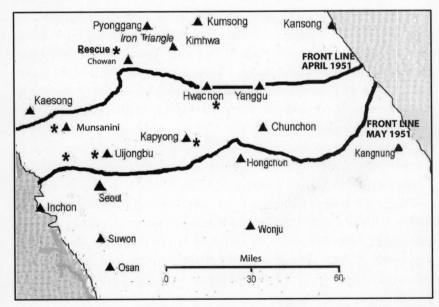

Rescue and close-air-support missions (asterisks) carried out during this period.

through Chorwon. The lead CCF elements were now twenty miles south of the city and still on the move. But the area in which the downed airmen were located would likely be a hot bed of Chinese soldiers—the rear area of the 12th PLA, which had an estimated strength of 10,000 soldiers. I thought that in addition to rear-area troops, reserve elements and replacement troops were likely to be in the area.

We had been launched on an armed reconnaissance mission, but I immediately abandoned that mission and turned toward the Chorwon area. We quickly located the B-26 crash site, marked by rising smoke, and spotted two parachutes nearby. Flying low, I saw two individuals waving their arms. These were two of the B-26 crew, but there should have been one or two others. Where were they? We searched the area but saw no sign of them. They either went down with the plane, were hiding, or had been captured by the Chinese. Our job now was to protect the two downed airmen until a rescue helicopter arrived and then provide cover for the chopper during the pick-up.

Well before the helicopter arrived, another flight of F-80s arrived and joined us in circling overhead. I had switched my radio to the emergency channel in hopes of making contact with the downed airmen, who should have been carrying small portable radios. After several tries, I heard the voice of one of them say that they were hunkered down in a small depression and were receiving heavy fire from two sides. It turned out I was talking to the pilot, who was with the co-pilot, neither of whom was injured. Another crewman had parachuted with them but had landed some distance away and might have been captured.

I wasn't surprised about the heavy ground fire they were receiving. When we had gone in for a check on the downed crewmen, we had gotten heavy fire from nearby hills, one of which had a series of zig-zag trenches. If the chopper was to effect a successful rescue—and keep the airmen safe—we had to eliminate the source of the fire, so I decided to place some napalm on the trenches. The trenches were located about 100 yards from the downed airmen and ran parallel to their position. This would allow us to spread our napalm along the length of the trenches without endangering the airmen.

I radioed my flight, "Bully Charlie, place your napalm along the length of the trenches—west to east. I want complete coverage. I'll start at the west end."

As I maneuvered to get positioned for my attack, I wondered what was in the minds of the Chinese soldiers who were watching us. Undoubtedly most of them were peasants, recently drafted, then quickly trained and shoved into combat. Ours were probably the first fighter-bombers that they had seen in such close proximity. They would have known from word of mouth that we could cause fearsome destruction. I suspected that all of them were apprehensive, and fear would soon grip many of them as we began out attacks.

For my part, I had no apprehension and certainly no fear. My thoughts were focused on getting set up for the attack. I was at 3,000 feet, with my wingman and the other two trailing me, spaced so that each would begin his run toward the target as pilot ahead dropped his napalm and began to pull up.

I initiated the attack pattern a mile from and perpendicular to the trenches and made a ninety-degree turn at a point where I was aligned with the length of the trenches. Easing down to 500 feet, I selected the segment of trenches closest to the downed airmen as my target. My wingman would go after adjoining segments. At the release point, 300 feet from the target, I was at 50 feet, moving at 450 miles per hour. When I punched the bomb-release button, the airplane lifted slightly as the napalm tanks dropped away.

The four of us laid swaths of burning napalm right on top of the trenches and watched in surprise as scores of Chinese troops tumbled out of nearby trenches and ran down the hill. That was a big mistake on their part. They were probably unseasoned soldiers, fresh out of recruit training in China, and they had been frightened into panic. Both flights of fighter-bombers set about delivering all we had on strafing run after strafing run. I kept up a conversation with the downed airmen, getting information on the location of ground fire being directed at us and about a squad of Chinese soldiers that was edging toward them. We were able to deal with each of these threats, and by the time the helicopter approached, it was a quiet scene.

As soon as I sighted the rescue helicopter, I made radio contact with the pilot and informed him that I believed we had pretty much suppressed the defenses, but if he encountered any fire, he should let us know at once.

We kept up the strafing attacks during the chopper's approach, pickup, and departure out of small-arms range.

At the mission debriefing, we all agreed that we had left at least 200 dead Chinese soldiers, but we reported only a hundred, leaving it to members of the other flight of F-80s to claim the rest. The two rescued airmen, the pilot and copilot, were from the 452nd Bomb Wing; the third crewman, a staff sergeant, was captured by Chinese soldiers and became a prisoner of war. He was released two year later.

★ ★ ★

The morale of the pilots who flew combat missions was affected by many factors. One of the most important factors related to rescue capabilities: did a capability exist to rescue downed aircrews, and if so, how effective was it? The Fifth Air Force's search-and-rescue capability was rudimentary at the beginning of the war but became increasingly effective over time. The 3rd Air Rescue Squadron, which was responsible for the rescue of downed airmen, was equipped with a search-and-rescue version of the Flying Fortress—the SB-17—which was employed for long-range operations. The squadron also had Sikorsky H-5A helicopters—small, two-seat, rotary-wing choppers used for short-range rescues. A pilot and technician flew inside the aircraft, and two passengers could be carried in external litter capsules. In addition, the squadron operated two much more capable ten-passenger Sikorsky H-19 helicopters, as well as SA-16 Albatross amphibian aircraft for water rescues. From what I had heard and observed, I sensed that the fighter and bomber pilots who flew over enemy territory had confidence that if they were downed, the Fifth Air Force would mount a prompt effort to rescue them if at all possible. This was demonstrated by the rescue mission on April 24 in which I participated.

But sadly, despite the best, sometimes heroic rescue efforts of all involved, only 10 percent of the 1,690 USAF airmen who went down in enemy territory during the Korean War were rescued. It is likely that many who went down did not survive their landings.

On April 30, a few days after the rescue mission, I was sent to dive-bomb the railroad yard at Sunchon. My wingman was 2nd Lt. Lindsey G. Russell. First Lt. Donald W. McEachern was the element leader, and 2nd Lt. Donald I. VanDerKarr was his wingman. VanDerKarr was on his second mission. Upon arrival over the target, we found about sixty box cars, separated into two groups, just sitting there waiting for us to have a go at them. I directed McEachon and VanDerKarr to put their 500-pound bombs on one group of thirty cars, while Russell and I went after the other group. We scored well and blew apart many of the cars. Shortly afterward, we discovered what perhaps was a more important prize: stacks of supplies, extending for several hundred yards along both sides of the tracks, apparently unloaded a short time before. Would our mix of .50-caliber incendiary and armor-piercing ammunition do significant damage to these stacks of supplies? We quickly found out. As soon as I fired my first volley, explosions marked the row I strafed, and many fires began to blaze. At the conclusion of the three strafing passes that each of us made, the rows along each side of the tracks were in flames—a most satisfying sight.

By the time the Red offensive had stalled on April 30, I had flown six missions in direct support of Eighth Army units. My controllers reported in each instance that we had achieved good results. So it was fair to conclude that we had had a part in bringing the CCF's offensive to a halt.

To meet a pressing need for a capability to provide close air support during bad weather and hours of darkness, the Fifth Air Force began employing the MPQ-2, a precision radar that had been used for practice bomb-scoring in the Strategic Air Command. Three MPQ-2 radar sets became the heart of tactical air direction posts called Tadpoles and were positioned behind the front lines near the command posts of the U.S. Amy's I, IX, and X Corps to direct night and bad-weather bombing strikes.

The MPQ-2 was used extensively by B-29s and light bombers. Fighter-bombers also employed the system when cloud cover obscured the front lines. When the ground commander needed an air strike, he called the coordinates of the target to the JOC. The JOC then assigned the mission to a bomber or fighter-bomber group. I led several MPQ-2 missions when the front lines were socked in. In each case, the JOC directed me to one of the three MPQ-2 sites—code-named Beverage, Chestnut, and Hillbilly—and when I had made radio contact and my flight was picked up on the MPQ-2 radar, the Tadpole controller directed that we fly at a specific altitude, airspeed, and compass heading. With the coordinates of the target marked on a map of the area, the controller "talked" us to the target area using the location of the aircraft as seen on the radar. At a certain distance, the radar controller began a countdown from ten to zero, at which time we all dropped our bombs or napalm.

From our viewpoint, the MPQ-2 missions were bland and without a shred of excitement. I never knew the results of our MPQ-2 missions but heard from our intelligence officer that enemy prisoners stated that the night and bad-weather bombings often caught them in the open and interfered with their planned movements. I was also told that many of the MPQ-2 air raids were done within a few hundred yards of friendly troops who were impressed at the accuracy and effectiveness of the missions.

It seems as if we got a report every two weeks or so that the Commies had bolstered their antiaircraft defenses. At a mission briefing around April 30, the intelligence officer advised us that the CCF had been steadily increasing their air defenses and now had an estimated 275 antiaircraft artillery guns and 600 automatic weapons deployed to protect against our aircraft. This wasn't surprising news to anyone who had been flying combat missions during the past two months. The increase in antiaircraft fire and the battle damage inflicted on the group's aircraft provided solid evidence that the Reds were indeed employing more guns. The 49th FBG battle damage report for April listed twenty-four aircraft that had incurred battle damage. Of those, seven were from my squadron: April 4, Captain Litchfield—two-foot hole in left aileron, probably from a 37-millimeter shell; April 17, 2nd Lieutenant Lavois—explosive bullet damage in the landing gear area; April 23, 1st Lieutenant Evatt—collided with trees while strafing locomotive with major damage to airplane (right intake crumpled, nose section dented, and skin peeled away) but none to the pilot; April 23, Captain Morris—forty-three holes over the entire aircraft, probably from a 37-millimeter shell; April 25, 1st Lieutenant Coons—jagged hole two inches in diameter in the left wing, caused by a 20-millimeter shell; April 30, 1st Lieutenant Lovas—small hole in fuselage from small-arms fire; April 30, Captain Gallagher—damage to the right aileron and left stabilizer vertical stabilizer from a 20-millimeter shell.

In addition to the twenty-four aircraft that sustained battle damage, four 49th FBG pilots and aircraft were lost during April 1951. During almost every attack we made, we took fire. While many enemy soldiers might leap into the nearest foxhole and keep their heads down while we strafed or dive-bombed, a good number gunned for us.

The same day the battle damage report was issued, we learned that three out of four F-51s making an air-to-ground attack against a target at Sinmak had been downed by ground fire. This was the first indication of enemy radar-controlled antiaircraft guns. From this report, we concluded that things were likely to get worse.

I met quite a few of the many newspaper correspondents who passed through K-2 en route to various Eighth Army or Fifth Air Force units. At some point, reporters from every major U.S. newspaper and the wire services touched down at K-2. Marguerite Higgins of the *New York Herald Tribune*, the first female war correspondent to arrive in Korea, was one. She had a reputation as a glamorous and daring war correspondent, so I was pleased to have the opportunity to chat with her when she came by the squadron for a brief visit. We were disappointed that she never filed a story on the 49th FBG.

William C. Barnard, an Associated Press correspondent, also stayed for a while. Somehow he got authorization from the Fifth Air Force to go on a bombing mission with the 49th, and my squadron got tagged to take him along in a T-33, a two-seat version of the F-80. I thought this was a bum idea. Ground fire would pose a risk, and for a non-pilot, ejecting from a T-33 and parachuting to earth involved complicated procedures that were difficult to remember in an emergency. But my negative reaction didn't count, and I was assigned to pilot the T-33.

My T-33 was the fifth airplane in a flight led by Capt. Edward R. "Rabbit" Johnson, and our target was a bridge across the Imjin River. We had no photograph of the target, just some map coordinates denoting its location, so we had no idea what sort of bridge we would find. Having a correspondent along to observe a bridge bombing, especially if it was a narrow bridge, really put the pressure on us. The last thing any of us wanted to see was an AP story sent out to the world about how five 49th Fighter-Bomber Group pilots all missed the target and failed to bring the bridge down. But we were successful, and Barnard wrote a story detailing the mission.

Because of his engineering and piloting skills, Rabbit Johnson was selected by the Fifth Air Force to conduct various tests aimed at improving combat capabilities. One such test involved tip tanks. Carrying 265-gallon droppable fuel tanks attached to each wing-tip posed a potential hazard to pilots and airplanes. If one tank didn't feed, then landing with one empty and one full tank was possible only if high speed was maintained until touchdown. At normal landing speed, the aircraft could not be controlled. But landing at high speed wasn't desirable because we used relatively short runways in Korea. This led to a test to devise a safe, easy solution. To find out if tip tanks that were not feeding properly could be drained in flight, Rabbit took an F-80 up to 5,000 feet, slowed down, opened the canopy, drew his .45-caliber pistol, and fired shots into the tanks. Success. Within about six minutes, both tanks were drained.

Another test he conducted involved me, other pilots of my squadron, and parachute flares. For some time, B-26s, which operated at night, had dropped parachute flares over suspected targets—vehicles and trains—to provide the illumination needed to effectively conduct attacks. Could F-80s, operating at night under the illumination of parachute flares they had dropped, safely and effectively carry out attacks against such targets? Using a cross section of pilots from my squadron, we gave it a try. I don't think any of us was enthusiastic about the whole idea, but we gave it our best shot.

The procedure was to release a parachute flare over a target area—a road with vehicles moving along it—then descend below the flare and carry out an attack on an illuminated target. The first parts of the procedure—releasing the flare and getting into position below the illumination—worked well, but the attack phase didn't always go as hoped. It was a bit nerve-wracking to dive at high speed toward a target at night, even if it was well illuminated, while trying to maintain accurate aim and simultaneously stay fully aware of your proximity to the terrain below and to nearby unseen hills or even mountain peaks. The problem could be compounded on a dark night without a horizon when a pilot had to rely on his instruments to avoid disorientation. In a B-26, while the pilot was concentrating on the target, the copilot kept close watch on the airplane's proximity to the terrain and monitored the airplane's instruments and the orientation. This was too much for the lone pilot in an F-80 to carry out successfully under any except ideal circumstances. So nothing more came of the project during my stay in Korea.

In addition to close air support missions during April, the rescue mission, the successful attack on the rail yard at Sunchon, and the two airfield attack missions, I led four dive-bombing missions against bridges in Red territory. The spans were taken down in every case. I also flew on two other dive-bombing missions against railroad yards with good results. I further conducted armed reconnaissance along Purple 11, visited Kanggye to attack rail facilities, and bombed a radar station near Sariwon. It was a busy month.

Chapter 17

By May 1951, after eight months of hard use, the pierced-steel-planking runway at K-2 was falling apart. Laid on unstable ground and pounded by as many as 10,000 takeoffs and landings a month for eight months, it had deteriorated so badly that it had become dangerous to the pilots and aircraft. Jet blasts on takeoff had blown soil from beneath the planking so that the ends were becoming curled, which led to shredded and blown tires and runway sagging in many places, causing a few low-hanging fuel tanks to strike the runway and rupture. The remedy was to move the group to Tsuiki Air Base while the runway was being repaired, a job that involved rolling up the planking, replacing the soil with a firmer mix to stabilize the runway, and installing new sections of planking.

I was quite familiar with Tsuiki Air Base, which was located about fifty miles east of Itazuke Air Base at Fukuoka on Kyushu, the westernmost of Japan's main islands. While based at Itazuke in the late 1940s, my Mustang squadron was dispatched to operate for two weeks from Tsuiki, a former Japanese naval air base, which then lacked any facilities except an old operations building and a bare hangar. We were on a field exercise and had erected pyramidal tents for operations, maintenance, and supply, pitched pup tents for sleeping, and trucked in fuel and supplies from

Itazuke to sustain us during two weeks of intensive operations. Now I was back at Tsuiki for a spell. This time, it was no longer a bare base. It had dozens of pyramidal tents, all with wooden frames and floors to house the various squadron functions, as well as an operating mess hall and an officers' club of sorts with plenty of beer and booze. Life wouldn't be too bad during the couple of week we would stay. Constructed during World War II, the base had a concrete runway that pointed out toward Japan's Inland Sea and a concrete ramp connected to the runway with a stretch of pierced-steel planking. Next to the runway was a small monument honoring a Japanese kamikaze squadron that flew from Tsuiki.

Tsuiki is more than 525 miles from the Manchurian border. This meant that on combat missions, we couldn't make a round trip to targets near the Yalu River. Instead, we were assigned missions that wouldn't take us far north of Seoul.

I flew only eight missions in May. A bug laid me low for a week, after which we were on a reduced flying schedule because of the Tsuiki operations.

On May 1, I led a dive-bombing mission aimed at a camouflaged supply dump at Singgye, which yielded unknown results—no fires to give clues about damage. The next day, I went on another dive-bombing mission, this one to Sunan against the rail yard. It produced results we could see—fourteen railcars destroyed and sixteen damaged. We then strafed supplies stacked along the side of the tracks and left numerous fires.

On May 4, with a wingman tagging along, I launched off on an early-morning weather reconnaissance north of Soeul and strafed some rail cars on the way home. Then on May 6, I flew a close-support mission near Inje in support of ROKA forces and another the next day in support of ROKA forces near Munson. The controllers in both instances reported good results.

The most interesting mission I flew in May was one aimed at maintaining air superiority, a principal task of the Fifth Air Force. Such operations were labeled as "counter-air" missions. The objective of counter-air missions was to keep UN forces in Korea unhampered by enemy air attacks. Except for the first week of the war and a few scattered incidents later, the Fifth Air Force succeeded in doing this. But on the afternoon of November 1, 1950, when MiG-15s flashed by a Mustang pilot near the Yalu River, it was clear that the Chinese Air Force was embarking on a plan to challenge the Fifth's air superiority and thereby threaten UN forces.

The MiGs were operating from a newly constructed 6,000-foot all-weather runway at Antung, just across the Yalu River in China. To confront the threat posed by the MiG-15s, the U.S. Air Force moved quickly to deploy F-86 fighters to the theater. The swept-wing F-86 fighters had performance characteristics believed to be comparable to those of the MiGs. This was the beginning of an intense campaign to contain the Chinese Air Force. But matters were complicated by an American political decision that forbid the entry into Chinese airspace by U.S. aircraft, which meant that the MiG-15s at Antung would be operating from a sanctuary.

The plan developed by the Fifth Air Force to contain the air threat was twofold: first, conduct frequent patrols along the Yalu River to confront the MiG-15s and keep them contained within about 100 miles of their Antung base; and second, conduct systematic reconnaissance of all airfields in North Korea and mount attacks on any airfield that was near the point of reaching operational status. These were referred to as counter-air missions. Over time, I actively participated in airfield attacks in three different roles.

On a number of missions, I led dive-bombing attacks on North Korean runways and airfield facilities. On others, I was part of an escort force sent to protect from MiG attacks other fighter-bombers or B-29s engaged in bombing North Korean airfields. The third type of counter-air mission on which I flew involved suppressing airfield defenses. Suppression was achieved by attacking antiaircraft weapon emplacements and thereby enhancing the probability that other fighter-bombers conducting dive-bombing attacks on the airfield would not be hit by enemy fire.

The MiGs generally confined their operations to the area lying within 100 miles of their Antung base. This area became known as MiG

Alley, a hotly contested zone of action with almost daily air battles between MiGs and F-86s. A number of North Korean airfields and portions of Communist main supply routes were located in MiG Alley, so it was necessary that our fighter-bombers enter the region on a frequent basis. The hope always in the mind of a fighter-bomber pilot entering MiG Alley was that F-86s would be in the area to keep the MiGs at bay. If not, the pilot could find himself challenged by a much superior fighter airplane with the outcome very much in doubt.

In the counter-air campaign, the North Korean airfield that got the closest attention was located at Sinuiju, right jam-up against the North Korean border with China. It was defended by an extensive array of antiaircraft artillery, more than any other airfield in North Korea, and by the MiGs based just across the Yalu River at Antung. Apparently the Communists felt that Sinuiju airfield was fairly secure, given its defenses, so they set about building a host of new facilities for ammunition, fuel, and supplies, and they brought in thirty-eight Yak-9s, Il-10s, and LA-5s and dispensed them in revetments scattered around the airfield. All of these single-engine fighter aircraft were capable of conducting ground-attack missions and thus posed a potential threat to UN air bases and ground forces. As soon as these airplanes were detected by Air Force reconnaissance aircraft, the Fifth Air Force put together a sizable strike force to destroy the threat. The force included a total of 312 fighter aircraft.

The raid was scheduled for May 9, 1951. It would be the largest counter-air strike up to that point in the war. The 49th Fighter-Bomber Group's commander, Lt. Col. John R. Murphy, was designated to lead the strike. At the prescribed start-taxi time, Murphy's F-80 began to move out of the parking area, soon followed by forty-seven F-80s, each loaded with two 1,000-pound bombs. The temperature was unseasonably hot, so we had to use JATO (jet-assisted takeoff) bottles to get our heavily loaded airplane airborne. With the temperature in the 90s and the air thinned, the required takeoff distances stretched out so that the 15 percent additional thrust provided by water alcohol wasn't sufficient to safely get off the ground with heavy loads. Two JATO bottles were strapped onto each airplane, one on either side of the fuselage back near the midpoint. Fired during the takeoff run, these small rocket motors, which emitted white smoke, provided the additional thrust needed to get the heavily loaded F-80s into the air. We jettisoned the used JATO bottles over the dry river bed just beyond the end of the runway.

I was in the lead of my squadron, the last off the ground. Once airborne, I turned to join to the left of the 7th Squadron, which Murphy was leading. After several lazy circuits of the field, all three squadrons had been gathered into formation, and Murphy set course for Sinuiju, 360 miles to the north. Moments later, he radioed me that his airplane had mechanical problems, and he was aborting. "You now have the lead," he said.

I hadn't even thought about the possibility of Murphy aborting, but I didn't consider it a big deal that I was now the group leader. At this point, I advanced the throttle to move my squadron into the lead position. I would now be first over the target.

Our mission was flak suppression. We were to attack the antiaircraft emplacements and thereby suppress the antiaircraft fire. Timing was critical. We had to have the shortest possible interval between the time when our bombs exploded over the antiaircraft emplacements and when the dive-bombers began their attacks on the airfield. All of our bombs had proximity fuses installed so that they would explode just above the ground, sending out thousands of steel fragments.

Five more aborts—a much higher number than usual—occurred within the next fifteen minutes, reducing our number to forty-two.

Each flight leader in our group had an aerial photograph of the gun emplacement his flight was assigned to attack. The photographs were not of particularly good quality, but with careful study, they would serve their purpose.

Navigation to the target would not be a challenge. There wasn't a cloud in the sky, but getting over the target at precisely 1400 hours would require careful attention. At my first checkpoint, just east of Seoul, I was ninety seconds ahead of schedule, so I eased back on the throttle. By the time we reached the 250-mile checkpoint, just east of Pyongyang, we were only twenty seconds ahead of the time prescribed to begin our attack. I slowed a bit more.

We were going in at 10,000 feet to attack emplacements containing Soviet-built 85-millimeter and 37-millimeter guns. The former had an effective ceiling of 25,000 feet while the latter could fire 160 rounds a minute up to an effective ceiling of about 4,500 feet. The Chinese Air Force MiG-15 base at Antung would be in sight at we approached Sinuiju. We were counting on the F-86s to keep the MiGs off our backs while we were delivering our surprise packages.

As we neared the Sinuiju airfield, flak from the big guns appeared out ahead of us, greasy-looking black explosions flinging shrapnel in all directions, most of it somewhat above our altitude. I had encountered this kind of flak on many occasions during World War II. Back then, to lessen the chance of being hit, we constantly changed direction and altitude, weaving above the bombers we were escorting. Now, with a large formation in tow and a schedule to keep, I didn't have that option. My extensive combat experience had immunized me against what could be anxiety-arousing events, and I ignored the explosions and concentrated on locating my target just north of the airfield on a sandbar in the Yalu River.

Across the river, on the Chinese airfield at Antung, I could see what I estimated to be eighty MiG-15s. That was puzzling. Why weren't they airborne, trying to fight us off?

The antiaircraft guns on the Chinese side of the river opened fire as we neared the target. I maneuvered in order to be in a position to start my attack toward the west along the river's southern bank leading out to the Korea Bay, which flowed into the Yellow Sea. That was our exit route.

When the target passed under the left wing, I turned and executed a forty-five-degree dive as I opened the speed brakes. I was looking right down into the muzzles of an array of guns from which I saw bright flashes as round after round was fired. That is when I muttered, "Those will be your last rounds, you Commie bastards. We are coming at you." Second later, I punched the bomb-release button on the control stick and began to pull out of the dive, feeling the pressure of the G-suit inflating around my calves and abdomen.

During the exit, I maintained 6,000 feet, which was safely above the effective range of the 37-millimeter guns, and hugged the south bank of the Yalu River out to the Korea Bay, where I turned to the south.

Antiaircraft fire was directed at us all along our eighteen-mile exit route, persistent bursts and tracers that created some concern, but we were moving fast, about 420 miles per hour. None of us was hit.

All forty-two of the 49th Group's Shooting Stars released their bombs within seconds of each other, on target and on time. Just as we were pulling off the target, radio silence, maintained up to this point, was broken by a stern voice that said, "Goddammit, Bertram, where are you?" Col. William E. Bertram was the commander of the 27th Fighter Escort Group, equipped with F-84s that had been scheduled to start their dive-bomb attacks within a second after we had hit the flak batteries, but they were two minutes late, which wasted some of the protection we had provided. The stern voice was that of General Partridge, the Fifth Air Force's commander, who was observing from a T-33 in the target area.

In addition to the 27th, we were followed by a hoard of fighter-bombers that attacked airfield targets and by other flak suppressors. Relays of F-84 and F-86 aircraft maintained patrols overhead to guard against MiG-15 attacks, and although fifty MiG-15s took to the air from Antung, only eighteen crossed the river. They took no aggressive action.

The raid lasted about two hours. During those two hours, F-80s of three fighter groups suppressed flak with proximity-fuzed bombs and rockets, while Marine Corsairs and Air Force Mustangs and F-84s launched bombs, rockets, and napalm against pre-briefed targets in the ten-square-mile airfield area. These knocked out all of the Red aircraft on the field, destroyed 106 buildings, fired a large aviation dump, exploded twenty-six other ammunition and supply dumps, and almost certainly inflicted heavy casualties on enemy personnel who evacuated the buildings and moved into the open. Only one F-84 Thunderjet was damaged, and it returned to safely to base, as did all American planes.

Following the raid, the pilots of the 49th were highly pleased when a report was received from the Fifth Air Force that the operation was a success and not a single American plane was lost. This was confirmation that we had done our job well. A few weeks later, in a package from home, I received the May 21, 1951, issue of *Newsweek*, which contained a story—titled "Biggest Bombing"—about the big raid. It was the first publicity I received during the war, and the reporter got the details wrong:

American airpower staged it biggest show of the war last week in full view of a Chinese Communist audience across the half-mile Yalu River. It thus showed what it could do should the Chinese, by their own air actions, ask for a repeat performance inside their privileged sanctuary of Manchuria. The stage was the mile-long concrete airfield at Sinuiju along the Korean bank of the Yalu where Russian-made LA-5 fighters were massed to made a sneak blow without giving any excuse for retaliation against Manchuria. Curtain time was 2 p.m. May 9. The plot: Act 1: Enter Major George G. Loving, Jr., of Lynchburg, Va., flying in low from the Yellow Sea to avoid detection by Red radar. He is followed by 44 F-80 Shooting Stars of the 49th Wing. Together they silence Sinuiju antiaircraft gun by strafing and rocketing. Across the Yalu, Chinese ack-ack opens up. Of course, I was not allowed to shoot back at them, Loving says. Across the river he spots 80 MIG-15 jets on the Antung airfield. I couldn't cross the border to get them, Loving says.

This raid must have been unsettling for the Red Chinese air commander, Gen. Liu Ya-lou, who was undoubtedly under enormous pressure to provide support to Chinese armies in the field and who now had good reason to fear that he might lose his job, if not his head. Furthermore, the attacks surely dealt a sharp blow to the morale of the MiG pilots who were unable to defend an airfield located only a few miles from their base at Antung.

After this attack, the Communists essentially gave up the repair effort. A captured report by a Red Chinese aviation inspection group deplored the lack of success in rehabilitating North Korean airfields and asserted, "If we had had strong air support, we could have driven the enemy into the sea."

Why were counter-air operations so important? Probably the most succinct, right-to-the-point answer was provided by Gen. Curtis E. LeMay in a statement he made to the House Un-American Activities Committee on September 23, 1956: "As long as there are airplanes and air weapons, the successful conduct of any military operation hinges upon the possession of air superiority. Strength on the ground or at sea can only prevail, or for that matter survive, if the air above is friendly."

✯ ✯ ✯

For a week, intelligence briefings had included information on activities by North Korean and CCF forces preparing for an anticipated second CCF Spring Offensive. That offensive was launched on May 10 and was not halted until ten days later, after it had penetrated thirty miles in the east-central area.

The night before the offensive was launched, photography of the area facing the 2nd Infantry Division revealed heavy traffic where little or none had been before, partially concealed supply dumps, and concentrations of Chinese soldiers. One of these concentrations, which posed a threat to the 2nd Division's forward bases, was in the hilly terrain east of Chunchon. The next morning, I led a close air support mission called in to deal with that threat. Our controller was Mosquito Cottonseed. He directed us to a ridgeline laced with deep trenches—ample space for 150 or more Chinese soldiers. Nothing new or exciting characterized what we would do next. This would be a repeat of the pattern I had followed on many earlier close air support missions. The four of us laid napalm along the length of the trenches and then made repeated strafing runs throughout the adjoining area. What was the impact of our fiery attack on the enemy? The controller was unwilling to make a judgment. "Unknown results," he radioed. Nevertheless, if the trenches were occupied, as had been reported, we were confident that we had had struck a significant blow on the enemy.

After being out for a while with that flu-like ailment, I returned to flying on May 29 and led a flight to Kaesong. Dick Immig was my wingman, and Don VanDerKarr was leading the element, with Gene Brantley on his wing. The weather briefer had adivsed us of solid cloud cover over the Kaesong area but thought that the base would be high enough for us to carry out the mission. Since we almost always proceeded to a target area at an altitude above 20,000 feet in order to minimize fuel consumption, we often had to descend through clouds in the target area. In this instance, our attempt to descend below the clouds was unsuccessful since we were still in the soup when we reached our minimum safe altitude. Aborting our assigned primary mission, I turned eastward and proceeded to the Chowon area, where the weather was clearing, and we conducted reconnaissance along the road and rail line coming southward out of Pyongyang. We came across a band of soldiers who scattered in all directions when they sighted us, but we managed to kill at least ten of the group. Farther down the road, we spotted an extensive array of supplies beneath the tree line. Fortunately, we were carrying napalm, which we spread over all of the supplies that we had spotted. Then, to finish the job, we strafed the surrounding area. The good news was that we did not observe any ground fire being directed at us. The not-so-good news was that we had no idea about the impact our attacks on the supplies would have on the enemy.

The squadron lost two pilots on combat missions in May, both listed as missing in action.

Second Lt. Jack C. Steinharter went down on May 8. This was his third mission. I questioned members of his flight about the incident and learned that the flight was on a close air support mission near Chikkol, one mile northeast of Mudang. They had set up a circular strafing pattern, and each had completed a couple of strafing runs when the controller radioed that one of the F-80s had crashed into a hillside. A head count revealed that it was Steinharter's plane. No radio message from him had been heard. It was quite possible that his plane was brought down by antiaircraft fire. On that same mission, the airplane of 2nd Lt. Carl E. Overstreet, a flying-school classmate of Steinharter, was hit on the left side by a 12-millimeter projectile, which was embedded in the right wing of the aircraft, having gone through the fuselage just below the pilot cockpit.

Twenty-eight years old and from St. Petersburg, Florida, Steinharter had been a member of a musical group in the Philadelphia area called High, Low, Jack & the Dame. Entertaining was in his blood. From time to time, he put on wire-rimmed glasses, pasted on a bushy mustache, stuck a cigar in his mouth, and set about entertaining his squadron mates in wonderful imitations of Groucho Marx. He was listed as killed in action. His remains were recovered some years after the fighting ended.

First Lt. Charles E. Coons went down on May 19. A 1948 graduate of the U.S. Military Academy, Coons was twenty-five and came from East Orange, New Jersey. He had joined the squadron the month before

Charlie Coons's drawing.

and was on this twenty-fourth mission. His flight was on an armed reconnaissance mission along Purple 11. In questioning members of his flight, I learned that he was downed by ground fire near Kumhwa, located approximately fifty miles northeast of Seoul along the main highway as it branches off to the east. His remains were recovered some years later.

In addition to being remembered for his engaging personality, Charlie Coons left behind a number of drawings that reflected a great deal of artistic talent. The drawing with the most appeal to his squadron mates was a depiction of vertigo in the bizarre surrealist style of Salvador Dali. The drawing showed an inverted F-80 plunging toward a menacing, bullet-shaped mountain with grasping hands; various limp aircraft instruments display conflicting flight information. A sweating hand grasps the control stick, and at the bottom, an F-80 is stuck in the ground with a sad-sack pilot peering out the hole. After Charlie went in, Ray Roberts had the drawing framed and hung it in the pilots' lounge, The Vertigo Room—a name every pilot could relate to.

Earlier, we had taken some extra space in the operations building and converted it into a lounge. It was a comfortable setup, with some pretty fancy furniture that Ray Roberts had scrounged from a friendly supply officer at Itazuke Air Base. A group of pilots was always hanging around squadron operations. Some would be waiting for a mission briefing or a mission assignment, and when the weather turned sour and flying was put on hold, the place was jammed with pilots waiting for the weather to clear. The lounge was where waiting pilots would sit around talking, writing letters home, sometimes reading letters from home, playing cards, bitching, and drinking coffee. With pilots from every region of the country and various backgrounds, it could be entertaining sometimes to just sit and listen. Eventually, as the base population expanded and the officers' club became over-crowded, this was where 9th FBS pilots often gathered after hours.

We lost a third pilot in May. First Lt. Walter "Jack" Doerty, who had completed sixty combat missions, was sent to be a forward air controller with the ROK's 9th Division, 3rd Corps. It was located close to Imje, on the Imjin River, roughly along the 38th parallel. This was not a desirable assignment since ROK army units had a history of collapsing when the going got tough. In mid-May, the Chinese launched a massive offensive that engulfed the 9th Division, which promptly collapsed. We received word from the Fifth Air Force that in mid-May, Jack was missing in action. A couple of weeks later, 1st Lt. Horace G. Linscomb, a 49th FBG pilot who was an FAC with Jack, returned to K-2 after evading capture for seventeen days. He and Jack had been together for a portion of that time but had gotten separated after a few days. He suggested that Jack had probably been captured by the CCF.

Based on his observations while in enemy territory, Linscomb shed some light on why we had difficulty locating the enemy. He told us that when aircraft entered the area, lookouts would fire three quick shots, blow a whistle (one long and one short blast), or sound a bugle call. These signals were relayed from position to position and mountain to mountain. Immediately, everyone would move to cover, and anyone with a gun began to fire at the aircraft when it entered the area. The machine guns went wild—firing long steady bursts, he said.

Meanwhile, things were changing in the group. Lt. Col. Wilbur J. Grumbles assumed command of the 49th Fighter-Bomber Group, replacing Colonel Murphy, who was transferred to Fifth Air Force headquarters. Grumbles was well qualified to command the 49th. He had fought as a fighter pilot in the Pacific theater during World War II, flying P-38s, and more recently had commanded the 18th Fighter-Bomber Group. We also received notice that the 49th would be changing over to F-84s in June.

★ ★ ★

In addition to the two aircraft and pilots lost on combat missions, the squadron lost two other aircraft in May because of bad weather and faulty navigation on the part of a flight leader.

I learned of this when I received a phone call from Red Byers. "I'm calling from Pohang," he said.

"What are you doing at Pohang, Red?"

"It's a long story. We had been up at Wonson, and on the way back, the weather turned sour. I couldn't tune in the beacon at Kimpo or K-2, but finally got a steer from the D/F station at K-3 [Pohang]. The weather at Pohang was down on the hilltops, and our fuel was just about gone. [1st Lt. Clarence R.] Osborne was element lead; he ejected. He's okay. [2nd Lt. Carle E.] Overstreet, my wingman, got down okay, but ran off the end of the runway and wrapped up his bird. I landed without incident. Could you send a jeep? The two of them will need transportation back to K-2. I should be back within an hour—just as soon as I get refueled." "All right, Red. Check with me as soon as you arrive."

I informed group ops of the situation and awaited Red's return. He didn't have much to add to the story except that when he received the D/F steer, he was fifty-miles offshore, out over the Sea of Japan, almost due east of Pohang.

Shortly after Byers arrived, I received a telephone message instructing me to report to Colonel Grumbles. He asked me about the fiasco at K-3. I told him what I had learned from Byers, explaining that Byers's navigation had been faulty and that I had grounded Byers, but anyone with his combat record—124 combat missions—was entitled to a mistake. I wanted him to see him return to the States with a clean record. Grumbles agreed.

★ ★ ★

The number of 49th FBG aircraft incurring battle damage remained high. During May, eighteen airplanes had battle damage. Four of those were 9th FBS airplanes: 2nd Lieutenant Dixon's, with a half-inch hole in the right wing fuel tank; 1st Lieutenant Costa's, with extensive damage to the underside caused by flying through a cloud of debris created by rocket blast; 1st Lieutenant Osborne's, with a .50-caliber hole in the underside of the leading-edge fuel tank; and Captain Roberts, with a six-inch-diameter hole in the right wing.

★ ★ ★

Until mid-May, the Fifth Air Force flew a daily average of 171 armed reconnaissance and interdiction sorties and 57 close air support sorties. Later in the month, its aircraft averaged more than 140 close air support sorties. In April and May, the Fifth Air Force had lost fifty-nine aircraft to enemy ground fire. This was an increase over previous months, so some tests were conducted against friendly flak batteries to see what could be learned. The testers found that a trailing wingman was a sitting duck for enemy gunners. The message was plain: number four in a formation had better not lag as this could be hazardous to his health.

Chapter 18

The war was about to enter a new phase. Although none of us knew about a Joint Chiefs of Staff directive to General Ridgway on June 1, we would soon sense that a change was underway. The directive stated:

> You will, consistent with the security of your forces, inflict maximum personnel and materiel losses on the forces of North Korea and Communist China operating within the geographic boundaries of Korea and adjacent waters, in order to create conditions favorable to a settlement of the Korean conflict which would as a minimum: a. Terminate hostilities under appropriate armistice arrangements. b. Establish authority of the ROK over all Korea south of a northern boundary so located as to facilitate, to the maximum extent possible, both administration and military defense, and in no case south of the 38th Parallel.

On that first day of June, the squadron lost another pilot. Second Lt. Jack Forrester went down on his eighteenth mission while flying as a wingman in a flight conducting an armed reconnaissance mission fifty miles north of Seoul. The flight had delivered a napalm attack against a group of buildings thought to contain enemy troops and supplies and was strafing when Forrester was knocked down by gunfire and crashed near Nunsu-ri in Chonnyangam area. Three weeks earlier, he had had a close call when his plane was hit by gunfire that exploded a wing tip tank, creating a fire that enveloped the tank before it detached from the airplane. Now he had a second run of bad luck.

Although Forrester came across as a mild-mannered individual, he had a reputation for being very aggressive in his attacks. Some thought he was a little too daring in pressing home his attacks, cutting it a little too close. Others admired his dedication to getting the job done. In any event, he was taken down by enemy gunfire, not by slamming into the ground. He was listed as missing in action and later classified as presumed dead. Forrester was twenty-two years old.

On June 1, the Eighth Army again went on the offensive to retake lost ground and secure an advantageous position in advance of armistice talks. The code name given to the new offensive was Operation Piledriver. It would be the last Eighth Army offensive of the war, and when it ended, our forces would be positioned just north of the 38th parallel. Heavy fighting was involved in the vicinity of the Hwach'on Reservoir—later known as the Battle for the Punch Bowl—and around the Iron Triangle, the area between Pyonggang, Chorwon, and Kimhwa.

I led two missions to the Chorwon area in support of Operation Piledriver. The first, on June 2, was my 100th mission. Our task was to provide close air support for the ROK 2nd Infantry Division near Hwach'on. The division was attempting to move along the road toward Kinhwa, located at the southeast corner of the Iron Triangle. It was engaged in heavy fighting, held up by CCF troops on a ridge adjoining the road. We napalmed and strafed the dug-in troops but were unable to assess the results. This mission was launched from Tsuiki Air Base in Japan, and we landed afterward at K-2 to refuel.

On June 6, I went on another close air support mission, this one in support of the 3rd Infantry Division. The division's objective was Chorwon. They were stalled on the road to the south of Chorwon and needed some help to clear out CCF troops on ridges along the way. My

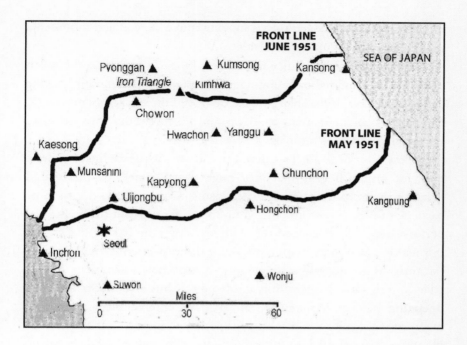

flight was one of many dispatched to help the 3rd Division advance to its Operation Piledriver objective. The controller reported "excellent results" from our napalm and strafing attacks.

On June 9, also in support of Operation Piledriver, I led an armed reconnaissance mission along the road and railroad going north out of Kaesong, on the left flank of the I Corps. We achieved moderate success—twenty troops killed and a large cache of camouflaged supplies napalmed.

My final mission in support of Operation Piledriver was flown on June 13. We provided close air support for the ROK 2nd Division near Kimhwa, very near the division's objective. The controller reported that our napalm and strafing attacks achieved "excellent results."

Four days later, I led an armed reconnaissance mission along the road and railroad running north out of Pyonggang to Wonsan. Our task was to search for CCF supplies or reinforcements destined for Communist units engaged in battle around the Iron Triangle. The road and railroad were deserted—no rolling stock or vehicles sighted—but we spotted a couple of dozen troops moving into a canyon and mounted a strafing attack with unknown results

An armed reconnaissance mission on June 22, farther to the north along the road and railroad running northeast out of Pyongyang, yielded better results. Near Pukohang-ni, we destroyed three wagons, one truck, two railcars, and a railroad hand car and killed twenty-four to thirty troops and three pack animals.

Every pilot took a keen interest in the out-of-the-ordinary experiences of others, hoping that they might learn something that would enhance their chance of survival. Incidents involving MiG-15s were of particular interest—because the MiG-15 was far superior to the F-80 in performance, which stacked the odds squarely against F-80 pilots. For this reason, encounters with MiGs were to be avoided if at all possible, but this was not always possible. We were especially susceptible to MiG attacks in the area lying within a 100-mile radius of Antung, the MiG operating base in Manchuria—an area we entered often on armed reconnaissance missions searching for targets along the CCF's main supply routes. We counted on the F-86 pilots, who conducted daily patrols of the area, to keep the MiGs occupied, but sometimes, the F-86s were not on station.

So it was no surprise when, on June 25, Jim Gallagher, Ray Roberts, and Dick Immig returned from trips to the north with tales of tangling with MiGs. This was big news because no encounters with MiGs by 49th FBG pilots had taken place since my tangle with them back in April. Did this mark the beginning of a systematic MiG offensive against fighter-bombers? What tactics did they use? Were they aggressive?

From my initial conversation with the three pilots, I learned that unlike the high-speed hit-and-run tactics the MiGs employed against me back in April, this time they engaged in close-in combat. This change in tactics was a development that needed to be brought to the attention of all of the squadron's pilots. I instructed Roberts to arrange for a pilot meeting that night after the evening meal. Gallagher, Roberts, and Dick Immig were eager to tell their stories, and I was certain that everyone would be interested in what they had to say.

At the meeting, I asked the three MiG fighters to recount their experiences and the lessons they had learned. They had the rapt attention of every pilot in the room, each of whom had at some point rehearsed in his mind just how he would deal with MiGs.

Capt. Jim Gallagher was leading Bully Easy flight—three F-80s—on an armed reconnaissance mission along Purple 11. First Lt. Harold B. Ward and 1st Lt. Arthur F. Dennis were the other members of his flight. They had just completed a third pass against a target some ten miles south of Sinuiju and were at 800 feet when four MIGs appeared above them at 2,000 feet. Gallagher ordered his flight to drop tip tanks and turned into the attacking MiGs, making a head-on firing pass. After circling in an effort to get on the enemy's tail, Gallagher began working in a southerly direction and radioed a heads-up to other flight leaders entering the area as well as a call for assistance. At some point, the other two pilots in Gallagher's flight became separated from him, leaving him alone to face the four MiGs. He steered his plane over Namsi-dong, a town known to contain flak batteries, hoping that the fire he was sure to draw would deter his pursuers, but two MiGs followed him right through the bursts of fire. About twenty-two miles south of Sinuiju, they made their final pass at him. That's when Gallagher saw a cone of red shells the size of golf balls pass over his left wing. Two seconds later, he saw a similar cone of red shells pass over the right wing. Gallagher got in the last shots as he fired at the departing MiGs.

Capt. Ray Roberts, leader of Bully Fox flight, heard Gallagher's warning of MiGs in the area and his call for assistance. He located Gallagher in short order, but he almost immediately came under attack by four MiGs. "I saw out of the corner of my eye a stream of MiG cannon tracers streaking past my right wing tip," he said. "My reaction was instantaneous—a hard break to the left. At the same time, glancing over my right shoulder, I saw the round intake of a MiG as he passed me at a high overtake speed. He missed! I immediately reversed my turn to get a shot at him as he pulled away." He did not score any hits, but in the skirmishing that followed, he skillfully outmaneuvered the MiG pilots, thereby avoiding taking any hits. He likened the MiG-versus-F-80 battle to a contest between a Porsche and a Volkswagen.

First Lt. Richard Immig said, "It was the first time I had seen a MiG. I then watched in amazement as the two pulled their noses just about straight up and leveled off about 5,000 feet above us." At this point, the two MiGs, one positioned on the right rear flank and the other on the left, alternated closely coordinated attacks against Immig. That is when he used a last-resort tactic he had learned from a flight commander in the States some months earlier: "I simultaneously yanked in full left rudder, full left stick, and pulled hard on the stick." He believed the resulting gyrations caused the MiGs to give up their attacks, but he acknowledged that it could have been because they were nearing the edge of their operating area. Immig got back to base unscathed.

In this encounter, pilots of the 49th claimed two MiGs damaged, with one 49th FBG pilot lost. All of the participating F-80 pilots agreed that the enemy fliers were extremely aggressive and employed good tactics.

While the Fifth Air Force could rightly claim that it exercised air superiority except in a relatively small arc of air space near the Manchurian border, a few folks around Seoul might have taken exception. Beginning in late June 1951, the Seoul-Inchon-Suwon area was "heckled" by slow-flying North Korean PO-2 light aircraft. Flying at night, below the hilltops at times, these fabric-covered planes largely evaded our radars and were a nuisance and a challenge. On most raids, they dropped small bombs from the rear cockpit and sometimes a burp gun was fired. On one occasion, four mortar shells were dropped in Seoul, and on another, six small bombs just missed the radar-direction center.

Early on, two of the PO-2s were shot down, one by a B-26 Night Intruder and the other by a Marine pilot flying an F7F night-fighter. But the raids kept coming, and though they caused little damage, they remained a thorn in the side of the Fifth Air Force. To deal with these slow-flying "Bedcheck Charlies," the Fifth kept an AT-6 aircraft on strip alert at Kimpo Airbase near Seoul at night, but that didn't stop the raids.

They continued off and on until well into 1953, when photo reconnaissance located their operating base at Pyongyang. Bombing, plus two
more shoot-downs, halted the attacks.

At the beginning of the last week of June, we learned that the war
might come to an end soon. We certainly hoped so. We heard a radio
broadcast and then read in *Stars and Stripes* that the Soviet delegate to
the United Nations, Jacob Malik, had proposed that a ceasefire take
place in Korea.

In mid-June, unbeknownst to us, the Eighth Army ceased any
attempt to gain further ground. Then, on June 30, General Ridgway, acting on orders from Washington, proposed a meeting of military officers
of both sides to discuss a ceasefire. The Communists agreed, and truce
talks began at Kaesong on July 10, 1951. The talks progressed at a slow
pace, and it wasn't until November 27, 1951, that the two sides agreed
that the 38th parallel would be the line of demarcation. That is when
military ground operations slowed down and became restricted to
small-unit actions and patrolling. Nevertheless, the Fifth Air Force's
operations would continue at a high tempo to keep the pressure on the
Communists until a ceasefire agreement was reached. That would be a
long time coming.

A combat tour for pilots of the 49th Fighter-Bomber Group normally consisted of 100 combat missions. However, squadron commanders
and group and squadron operation officers were excluded from this limi-
tation. Their utilization was governed by the group commander's decision.
So when I reached the 100-mission mark and received no directive from
the group commander to cease combat flying, I kept going.

A number of pilots racked up many missions beyond the hundred
mark. Red Byers flew 124 missions before I stopped him. Bud Evans,
who checked me out in the F-80, flew 160. The record was probably

set by Lt. Col. Walter G. "Lefty" Selenger, who racked up a total of
233 missions between May 1950 and May 1951, when he was killed in
a airplane crash. Why did some pilots continue to fly mission after
mission beyond their prescribed normal tour? Some wanted to remain
in a squadron until they had the seniority and experience to be
selected for a coveted leadership position. For others, the challenge of
combat flying was irresistible. Still others wanted to stand out from the
crowd, believing that a sizable number of missions beyond the norm
would label them as gung-ho warriors and enhance their record and
reputation.

My 106th F-80 mission, on June 26, didn't turn out the way I
would have liked. This was a squadron mission, with me in the lead of
six flights. My call sign was Bully Able. We had one abort, so the total in
the formation was twenty-three aircraft. Our job was to dive-bomb a
railroad bridge near Sukchon on Purple 11, about ten miles south of
Sinanju. Then we were to break out into flights and conduct an armed
reconnaissance along Purple 11.

All of us scored near misses—a big disappointment. How could this
be? I attributed it to inaccurate wind information. The weather forecaster had provided his best estimate of the wind direction and speed at
the target (critical information in dive-bombing), and that is what we
were forced to use. No smoke was visible on the surface at the target
which we could have used either to verify the forecaster's information
or to make our own more accurate, on-the-scene estimate. (The fact
that the bridge was still standing when we departed the scene is something that sticks in the memory long after the fact.) We then began
searching for targets along Purple 11. My flight came across a group of
soldiers and pack animals, and our strafing attack killed six of them and
sent perhaps four dozen enemy soldiers to the great beyond. The 49th
Group mission summary states that we killed forty-three enemy soldiers—a laughably precise number that no one would have reported. It
is probably just a typo, but incorrect in any event. The other flights
claimed to have destroyed seventeen carts, seventeen oxen, thirteen box
cars, one tanker, two trucks, and fourteen buildings. Not a bad day, but I
thought it could have been much better.

Back at base, a note was waiting for me: "Call Col. Grumbles ASAP." When he answered, his message was right to the point. "Pete Tyer [49th Fighter-Bomber Wing commander] has directed that you cease combat flying. He said that he has already lost too many of his boys." At this point, I had flown 112 missions in all—6 as a Mustang pilot and 106 in F-80s—and I was ready for it to end. Now, while I awaited the order taking me back to the States, I would have little to do except take care of various squadron administrative tasks and lend encouragement to my pilots and the hard-working support personnel who kept things going—the aircraft mechanics, armorers, communications specialists, and the intelligence, supply, administrative personnel.

As if to celebrate the completion of my combat flying, the very next day, Jack Benny brought a troupe of movie stars to K-2 to put on a big show. It was billed as "A Carnival of Stars," and the group included Errol Flynn, Marjorie Reynolds, Frank Remley, Benay Venuta, Harry Kahne, Delores Gray, and June Bruner—all of whom had appeared in popular films. The show was held in the evening of July 1 at an outdoor arena at K-2 with the Fifth Air Force Band participating. Hundreds of soldiers and airmen showed up, as well as a few Marines—an appreciative audience that gave every performer an enthusiastic round of applause. Jack Benny got the most laughs, but it was the girls, all beautiful and all with engaging personalities, who got the lusty cheers.

My grounding from combat flying didn't alter anything for others. While I was awaiting publication of orders sending me home, the tempo of squadron operations continued unabated, with both successes and losses for my squadron.

Bully Charlie flight, led by Dick Immig, hit it big on a mission some twenty miles northeast of Pyóngyang. It was just before dark when the flight came across a concentration of a couple of hundred vehicles. It was an unbelievable sight: the road was jam-packed with horse- and ox-drawn carts, all packed high with supplies and camouflaged with green branches. Apparently, this was a loading or unloading point—the flight couldn't tell which but quickly began strafing attacks. By the time the four pilots had completed their attacks, they had inflicted widespread damage and killed an estimated 200 enemy soldiers.

Then, on July 14, 1951, Maj. Marlyn C. Ford didn't return from an armed reconnaissance mission. He had begun flying with the squadron in June and went down on his eighteenth combat mission. Although Ford was the 49th FBG's executive officer and we had limited day-to-day interaction with him, we nevertheless treated him as a member of the squadron. He was thirty years old, a friendly fellow well liked by all who knew him. His flight leader told me that Ford's airplane was hit by antiaircraft fire and crashed south of Sunan. He was listed as killed in action.

On July 18, 1951, 1st Lt. John S. Starck went down on his seventy-second mission two miles west of Unhung-ni. His flight leader reported that Stark was hit by antiaircraft fire while on a dive-bombing run. He ejected from the airplane but was too low for his chute to open. The planes of two other pilots in Starck's flight—Burns and Moxley—suffered battle damage from ground fire, but they were able to return to base without difficulty. A month earlier, when Starck returned to the squadron after serving as a forward air controller for six weeks, he asked to be granted leave to visit his wife at Clark Air Base in the Philippines. I declined to approve his request, noting that we weren't granting leave to anyone except for short R&R visits to Japan by those who had completed their combat tours. Starck was quite upset by it, and subsequently, the operations officer, chaplain, and others pressed me to let him go. I relented and granted him leave to travel to the Philippines. Now, upon learning that Starck was down, I was glad that he had had some time with his wife. He was only twenty-three years old.

★ ★ ★

After a couple of weeks of waiting, I received word that a new policy had taken effect and I might not be going home after all. The new policy stated that upon completion of a combat tour, every pilot would have to then serve for six months in a staff job in Korea or elsewhere in the theater. I didn't like the sound of that, but I was hopeful that the five months I had served at K-2 before joining the 49th would satisfy the requirement.

At this point, I decided that I might as well have a little fun while I was waiting for someone to determine my fate. During the year I had been at K-2, except for forward air controller duty with the 2nd Infantry Division, I had been away from the base for only a handful of overnight stays in Japan, all on-base. Now I saw the chance to get away from the war for a more extended period. I knew the Fujiya Hotel, a renowned mountain resort near Tokyo, was being operated as a rest-and-recreation facility for American armed forces personnel. Upon inquiry, I learned that there were vacancies for five-day stays during the following week. So with R&R orders and in the good company of my friend Pete Boswell, the 8th FBS's commander, who had finished his missions and was also awaiting determination of his future, set off for Johnson Air Base near Tokyo.

In Japan, we boarded a train bound for Odawara, about a ninety-minute trip, followed by a taxi ride to another world. The Fujiya Hotel had been operating since 1878, and according to a pamphlet in the room, it had drawn dignitaries and celebrities from all over the world since its opening. It was easy to see why: in addition to the spacious guest rooms and wonderful food, the hotel boasted striking scenery, elaborate architecture, and beautiful Japanese gardens. A main feature was the Miyanoshita hot spring, which fed the swimming pool. The springs were said to be therapeutic. I can't vouch for all of the claimed healing qualities of the hot spring water, but we had a thoroughly relaxing stay that included some time soaking in the pool. As the days progressed, I could feel the tension—heretofore unfelt—slip away and the depressed appetite, rightly blamed in part on the poor chow at K-2, return to normal.

When we got back to K-2, my orders to the States were waiting. Another set of orders relieved me of command of the squadron on the day of my departure, July 29. As if to remind me that the war would continue without me, the squadron suffered yet another loss on the day before my departure when Capt. Cleland D. With didn't return from an armed-reconnaissance mission along a main Chinese supply route near Sunan. His airplane took a direct hit from antiaircraft fire, crashed, and exploded. He was listed as missing in action and was later classified as presumed dead. He was thirty-one years old, a highly experienced fighter pilot with a friendly, appealing personality. He had joined the squadron and started flying combat missions in June. He was on his thirty-fifth mission when he went down.

As I reflected on my Korean War experiences, what stood out most forcefully was the tumultuous nature of the first year of the Korean War. Initially, U.S. and allied forces were squeezed into the narrow confines of the Pusan Perimeter and came very close to being pushed into the sea. Then came the Marines' successful amphibious landing at Inchon and the swift advance of our forces into North Korea, reaching, in one place, all the way to the Manchurian border. This generated optimism that the war would soon be over and that we'd be home by Christmas. Then the Chinese entered the war, eventually fielding seventy divisions that forced U.S. and ROK forces to retreat—in many instances in disarray back well south of Seoul. Soon after that debacle, General Ridgway, newly appointed as the Eighth Army's commander, adopted a new strategy that led to the recapture of Seoul and the advance of U.S. and allied ground forces back to the 38th parallel.

From almost the first day of the war, the Fifth Air Force played a critical role in preventing the Communists from achieving victory. Our ability to secure and maintain air superiority enabled the Eighth Army to operate without fear of enemy air attack. This was perhaps the Air Force's greatest contribution. The close air support we provided to Army units, as well as the massive campaign to staunch the flow of enemy logistical support, ranked as close seconds.

My part in the war was to fly and fight in pursuit of each of these objectives, doing daily battle with enemy soldiers down at treetop level, rocketing and strafing them and their equipment and supplies on nearly every mission, dive-bombing and napalming their supporting elements on scores of missions. During World War II, I had achieved recognition as an ace after downing five enemy aircraft. In Korea, I had no idea how many trucks, tanks, artillery pieces, bridges, rail cars, locomotives, pack animals, supply dumps, tunnels, and buildings I had destroyed, or how many enemy airfields I had closed down, or how many soldiers I had put out of action. The achievements of individual fighter-bomber pilots weren't recorded—and in many instances weren't even measurable. Even in those instances where the results of an attack were clear, no record of individual achievement was kept. This wasn't because of slip-shod recordkeeping but because we didn't consider it important.

In speaking about war experiences, no rational person would boast of the destruction he wrought or the enemy deaths he caused. War is one horror after another. Destroying and killing—that is *all* it is about. And that is what my fellow fighter-bomber pilots and I set out to do day after day. But we didn't think of it in those stark terms. We were engaged in a noble cause set forth by the United Nations to free South Korea from the clutches of North Korean and Chinese Communist aggressors. This meant that we participated in and experienced the brutal realities of war on a daily basis. While this was an exciting undertaking, no pleasure was ever involved. Rather, the driving thought was that as a U.S. Air Force officer, I had a duty to fulfill, and I was going to execute that duty to the best of my ability.

I did nothing heroic on the 112 missions I flew, but I came away with the satisfaction of knowing that I had been an out-front combat leader who had done his duty and, I believe, done it well. The opportunity to command a fighter squadron in combat is the dream of every red-blooded fighter pilot, but only a very few are afforded that honor. I was one of the lucky ones, and that pleased me more than anything else about my Korean War experiences—aside from the fact that I survived.

Epilogue

The war continued for two more years after I completed my combat tour and departed Korea. It finally ended with the signing of an armistice agreement on July 27, 1953. By that time, a total of 490 USAF fighter-bombers had been lost.

My next assignment after Korea was to the Air Proving Ground at Eglin Air Force Base on Florida's upper Gulf Coast. As a test pilot, my job was to conduct operational-suitability tests of equipment and airplanes to be employed in tactical air operations. It was a plum assignment, one with which I was well pleased and well qualified, given my combat experiences. The most important test I conducted involved a new fighter-bomber, the F-84F, a swept-wing, nuclear-capable airplane that had many growing pains during the test period, including inflight engine failures, one of which resulted in my crash-landing, without injury, in the swamps of Louisiana. My four years as a test pilot ended when a small dog ran under the front wheel of my BMW motorcycle, resulting in a head injury and grounding me from flying duties for two years.

I spent the next four years at the Air Command and Staff College, located at Maxwell Air Force Base in Montgomery, Alabama, first as a student and then as a faculty member—a job for which I did not volunteer but in the end worked out well for me. It was during these four years that I regularly attended night classes at the University of Alabama, and through these classes, plus a couple of on-campus summer sessions, I earned a bachelor's degree. Since I had completed only the first year of college when I entered the Air Force at the age of nineteen during World War II, the opportunity to acquire a degree was highly important to me.

Next, I was sent back to the Far East, this time not to fight the Chinese, but to assist them. These weren't the Communists I had fought in Korea, but the Nationalists, who had been defeated on the mainland by the Chinese Communists and had withdrawn en masse—almost the entire national government and much of the armed forces—to Taiwan. I served for two years as advisor to the upper-level military colleges and got to know the Chinese quite well.

In subsequent years, I served in assignments at Tactical Air Command headquarters and on the Air Staff in Washington, revising and creating doctrinal statements and dealing with doctrinal and policy issues pertaining to the employment of a tactical air force in combat. In the Air Force, doctrinal statements not only provide guidance for the employment of forces, but also form the basis for the design and development of new weapon systems. In between these assignments, I attended the Air War College, a highly desirable step toward future advancement. I also earned a master's degree in international affairs from George Washington University.

After my Pentagon assignment, which lasted four long years, I received another plum assignment, a year-long fellowship with the Council on Foreign Relations in New York City. This provided the opportunity to deepen my understanding of international affairs while hobnobbing with an impressive array of academic, business, military, and government figures, both national and international. Toward the end of my fellowship, much to my surprise and delight, I was promoted to brigadier general. What was not a surprise was the assignment that followed, which made a great deal of sense given my general background and earlier assignments. I became Commandant of the Air Command and Staff College, where I had earlier served on the faculty. With 500 or so young majors in residence, including 50 students from foreign air forces, and a correspondence course serving another 5,000 students, I had a challenging and enjoyable time as the leader of this fine institution.

After two years at the Air Command and Staff College, I returned to the Pentagon—not a move any rational person would choose because of the hours and commuting hassles. I was now a major general and became the Air Force's Director of Plans, a high-pressure job with responsibility for numerous war plans, for all Air Force matters involving foreign governments, and for direct support to the Air Force Chief of Staff concerning all issues that came before the Joint Chiefs of Staff. After almost three years of this, I was ready for a break, and with only a few days' notice, I was off to Vienna, Austria, on a diplomatic mission.

Representing the Joint Chiefs of Staff, I joined the American delegation in Vienna as the Senior United States Military Representative at the NATO–Warsaw Pact arms-limitation negotiations. All sixteen of the NATO countries and six of the Warsaw Pact countries were represented by delegations headed by an ambassador, and each had military representation. The plenary sessions were held in the historic Schönbrunn Palace, and during the several months when I was involved, I had close contact with all of the military representatives, including those from East Germany, Poland, and the Soviet Union. It was a fascinating experience, but it was clear to me that it was highly unlikely that the talks would go anywhere since the Russians held almost all of the cards and had little incentive to reduce the their forces in eastern and central Europe. Consequently, I was glad that my involvement ended after two plenary sessions.

The Air Force Chief of Staff decided that I was the right man to fill a position that was becoming vacant in NATO. After interviews with the Chairman of the Joint Chiefs and the Secretary of Defense, I was directed to proceed to Izmir, Turkey, to take command of the Sixth Allied Tactical Air Force (NATO). That was just fine with me, especially since a promotion to lieutenant general went along with the job.

The Sixth Allied Tactical Air Force included, in wartime, the air forces of Greece and Turkey, as well as augmenting forces from Italy, the United Kingdom, and the United States. Turkey and Greece lie in a blocking position between what was then the Soviet Union and the Mediterranean Sea, which was likely a prime wartime objective of the Soviets. I had on my staff officers from all of the represented nations, but because of tumultuous relations between Turkey and Greece, Greek officers had been withdrawn a few months before I arrived. My time at Izmir was professionally interesting and enjoyable in every way. But the best was yet to come. After two years on the job, I got a call from the Air Force Vice Chief of Staff informing me that the Chief had decided to send me out to Japan. I was to return to Washington for interviews with the Chairman of the Joint Chiefs of Staff and the Secretary of Defense, and if I passed muster, I'd received some briefings before I went to Japan.

I was to wear two hats in my new assignment, one as commander of U.S. Forces Japan and the other as commander of the Fifth Air Force. For me, this was a dream assignment, one for which I felt exceptionally well qualified by reason of my prior experiences. As commander of U.S. Forces Japan, I worked closely with Japanese officials on matters pertaining to the defense of Japan, had close continuing contact with the American ambassador and his embassy staff, and was responsible for 50,000 troops of the U.S. Army, Navy, Marine Corps, and Air Force. I controlled fighter, bomber, reconnaissance, and tanker forces at bases in Japan and Korea. I felt that I had come full circle. Twice, I had served as a fighter pilot in the Fifth Air Force, first as a Mustang pilot during the occupation years in Japan and then a few years later as a fighter-bomber pilot combating North Koreans and Chinese in Korea. Now I was back in the Fifth, this time as the boss with a ton of responsibilities. I couldn't have been more pleased.

One of my first actions upon arriving back in Japan was to meet with the U.S. ambassador, Mike Mansfield, a former Marine and a fine man who was easy to work with. Then I traveled to Korea to call on various high-ranking American and Korean officials and inspect the Fifth's air bases and units. It was now 1977, and many changes had taken place there since the armistice was signed in 1953. There were now modern air bases, with no sign of short pierced-steel-planking runways like the one at K-2 from which I had flown in 1950–51; the bases had concrete runways and a highly trained, ready force of pilots and modern fighters and reconnaissance aircraft. The war still was not officially over. Even at this late date, the North Koreans had declined to sign anything more than an armistice agreement and had, all through the intervening years, maintained a threatening attitude and exhibited unpredictable, hostile behavior toward the Republic of Korea and the United States. This was confirmed for me in a personal way in a broadcast made on June 30, 1977—the day after I ended my visit to Korea—by "The Voice of the Revolutionary Party for reunification (clandestine) in Korea": "Bellicose Maniac Loving, Commander of the 5th U. S. Air force, left today after staying here for two days. . . . It goes without saying that the purpose of Loving's visit to South Korea was accelerating deliberate maneuvers for war provocation in our country and heightening tension. . . . This is an atrocious challenge to our people and the world peace loving people who unanimously desire peace on the Korean Peninsula and independent and peaceful unification."

So here I was, twenty-six years later, back in Korea, and the war still wasn't officially over, nor had the tension subsided. Vigilance and a high state of readiness would be required, as had been the case since the signing of the armistice in 1953. As I write these words in 2011, now more than half a century since the fighting ceased in Korea, North Korea remains as belligerent and unpredictable as ever—secretive, still armed to the teeth, and more dangerous than ever with missiles that can reach Japan and beyond, to say nothing of its newly developed nuclear capability.

After two years in the assignment, I retired from active duty on June 30, 1979, having reached the mandatory retirement age. I had served more than thirty-seven years on active duty. Afterward, I lived in Sarasota Florida and, at the urging of a group of the community's leading citizens, took on the job of rescuing the Marie Selby Botanical Gardens—an institution with magnificent waterfront gardens and programs of botanical education and research—from the verge of bankruptcy. I served as executive director for eight successful years, after which I retired again and served as a volunteer on various community boards. In 1997, my wife and I moved to a retirement community in Williamsburg, Virginia.

Afterword

Eight pilots of the 9th Fighter-Bomber Squadron were killed in combat during my five months with the squadron. Over the years, I have often thought of those brave young men, and to keep the memory of them alive, I dedicated this book to them.

There is a ninth individual who deserves special recognition for his courage and resilience. A fellow pilot, he was missing in action when I left the squadron to return to the United States, and it was not until much later that we learned he was a prisoner of war and remained so for twenty-eight months until the truce in 1953.

First Lt. Walter L. "Jack" Doerty was a personable fellow, smart, outgoing, and friendly. He was an Army brat born in Middletown, Connecticut, and had lived in many places. He joined the squadron in February 1950, a graduate of Flying School Class 49A at Williams Air Force Base, Arizona, and of the Fighter Gunnery Instructors Course, which set him apart from his classmates and most other pilots in the squadron as well.

By the end of April 1951, he had flown sixty combat missions and was sent to be a forward air controller with the ROK's 9th Division, which was located close to Imje, on the Imjin River, roughly along the 38th parallel—not a desirable assignment since ROK units had a history of collapsing when the going got tough. And that is just what happened shortly after Jack joined the division. In mid-May, the Chinese launched a massive offensive that surrounded the 9th Division, which quickly collapsed. Jack and some of his fellow Americans spent five days evading the Chinese before being captured on May 17. More than two years of subhuman treatment would leave him weighing ninety-five pounds.

He was first moved to Bean Camp, then to Pak's Palace near Pyongyang, where he underwent months of relentless interrogation while subsisting on minimum rations of sorghum or rice. Overall conditions were "wretched," he said. His final period in captivity was at Camp 2 at Pi-chong-ni, about ten miles east of Pyoktong and four miles south of the Yalu River. This camp was under Chinese control. It was here that the Chinese, once discussions began with the U.S. regarding a prisoner exchange, improved conditions and the prisoners at Camp 2 began to regain their health and physical stamina. That is when Jack and Charlie Brock, a U.S. Army intelligence sergeant, decided that they would escape together. Here is the story of their heroic escape attempt in the words of Jack Doerty.

We were planning to escape in early fall, hoping to harvest some crops along the way. Raiding gardens/fields and isolated farm houses was going to be our primary source of food. We were going to travel in the hills—off the roads. We were going to go southeast clear across the Korean Peninsula towards the vicinity of Hungnam, north of Wonsan Harbor. We had decided there was too much activity to the west and that the China Sea coastline was more open for escape. We thought: we can make it; we'll stay in the hills; and we're early enough before winter; it will stay warm enough; and we're ready. We'll eat grass; we'll eat bark and bugs; we'll do whatever it takes; we're going to do it. When we get to the coast we will liberate a boat and row into the gulf. The U.S. Navy will spot us. I had made an improvised signal mirror and magnetized a needle for a compass and I knew semaphore, signaling using flags, from Boy Scouts. We will just do it and the Navy will pick us up.

Charlie spoke fluent Korean, and we intended to capitalize on that. We worked hard on our sketchy plans. We "liberated things" at every opportunity: ponchos, caps, some sulfa powder, a flashlight with batteries, a signal mirror, and compass.

We went right out through the fence under the coverage of darkness and the overriding noise of the others. You could hear my heartbeat in Chicago. I'm going to tell you the dry weeds and grass sounded like we were threshing corn. I was thinking, "My God, we've got to get out of here; the guard is going to hear us because of my heart beat!" But it worked—audacity—and it worked. One of us stepped on a pheasant, and Oh, what a whirr!!! I don't know who jumped into whose arms. We were both in each other's arms—as I recall, it was only a pheasant! Well, that relieved the tension and we took off.

We stayed off the road for quite a while but eventually cut to the MSR that paralleled the Yalu and the same one that went through our camp. The terrain was such that we decided to stay on the road for just a little ways. The sky was overcast with a partial half moon, which was mostly hidden. We were wearing our ponchos, making good time and thinking how clever we were. All of a sudden—"Chu-la!"—the loudest shout you can imagine. It was a Korean guard post ordering us to halt. We had not seen the guard post, and it was such a surprise I think we were both transported from earth for just a moment. Charlie was so cool; he just answered: "Chosen sodemy," meaning Korean people. His answer was all that was needed. We kept right on walking like it was an everyday—I mean every *night*—occurrence.

Suddenly, we realized there were shapes which then became buildings on either side of us. We were in a village. The moonlight partially drifted through the clouds and we saw two people coming towards us— it was a Chinese and Korean patrol, and we couldn't do anything but keep walking. We just kind of moved over, and they moved a little bit, and we walked right by each other. Charlie spoke to me in Korean as we were going by. It was the perfect pre-briefed situation that we had rehearsed. He asked me "what time I thought it was" and then nudged me in the side and I grunted just enough to make it sound like a reply was starting. By then we were past the patrol and just kept walking. By this time, my heart was really pumping loud enough this time to be heard in New York. As we were leaving the village, we approached a bridge over a ravine. There was a guard standing at port arms, dead center, in the middle of the bridge. Charlie mumbled some phrase to me, and I dutifully grunted a response. The moon was hidden again, and we marched right up to him just like we had all the rights in the world. He stepped to the side and let us pass without a word. We kept right on going.

We got by this guy and went on, and we didn't say a word. I think we were both speechless. We went on and suddenly realized it was almost dawn. We've got to get off the road and we went up the embankment, worked our way as far off the MSR as we could get before dawn. We were looking for food and coverage. We found a real copse of woods, a genuine thicket this time. We got in the "excellent concealment," and the sun came up. Our thicket turned out to be just a patch of brush. Right down there below us was a farm house and a dog was already out. We were on a cultivated hillside, and our tiny patch of cover was the only uncleared spot in the middle of a peasant's farm. Whatever he had planted had either been harvested or was yet to be harvested, but not that day. We stayed there until dark and nobody or the dog ever spotted us. However, it was here that we were confronted with a major game-plan change.

Charlie had developed terrible blisters on both feet. After I was moved to the hill, we did not train as a team, and he forgot to train every day with his boots on. His feet had gone soft in tennis shoes, and a ten-mile hike in boots took its toll. The lymph nodes in his groin were already swollen, and he was in serious pain. We treated his feet with sulfur powder and made a fateful decision. We would scrub our plan of hiking in the mountains and stay on the roads until Charlie's blisters healed. That night, we took off again and went for five nights. We occasionally passed Koreans and eventually got to Manpo, about fifty miles.

We walked past convoys of trucks parked alongside the road, and we passed Koreans and Chinese soldiers and just kept chugging along. We began to think we were phantoms—that we were invisible. I think we developed a mindset that we just couldn't be seen.

We got through Manpo and on the fifth or sixth night came to a little village. We raided a corn field on the outskirts of town and passed a couple of people and just kept on going—our usual routine. They didn't say a word, and neither did we. We still thought we were invisible. We got to the edge of the town, and all of a sudden, all hell broke loose. A Korean police guard was right on top of us before we even knew anyone was there. We started to split, but he had a gun on us. Charlie couldn't run, and our phantom life was over.

The guard took us into the local police station. They didn't mistreat us and gave us something to eat. We were surprised at the lack of hostility. The next morning, he got on the telephone to call around and got through to the Chinese. Before the Chinese arrived we disposed of our ill-gotten Chinese booty. The next morning, the Chinese arrived in a six-by-six truck, with two interrogators and several soldiers. "Scarface" was among them. "Scarface" was the chief and nastiest Chinese interrogator. So they gave us a lot of heat, talked to us, and pushed us around for a while.

They took us into the courtyard and tied us, hands behind our backs, put a rope around our necks, and pulled our hands upward until the "hands to neck rope" was really tight and we very red faced and choking. Then they stood us toe to toe, nose to nose, and left us alone. Apparently, the objective was to humiliate us and also to show the Koreans how to subdue American escapees. We stood there for about five minutes, I guess. Pretty soon, I said (whispering), "Charlie . . . Charlie, don't laugh." We hadn't seen a toothbrush in over a year, and we were both pretty gross. I was thinking that it was pretty funny looking at each other cross-eyed and a smirk was appearing on his face. And pretty soon, what do two twenty-four-year-old American GIs do? It became funny to us, and we laughed. We started to smile and laugh! We knew this is going to get us into serious trouble, but we could not help ourselves. It was ridiculously comical to be looking at each other with our noses touching.

The Chinese came out with Scarface leading—they came rushing over to us, untied us, put us in the truck, and drove off. We had caused them to lose face in front of the Koreans. They were going to show

how tough they could be and humiliate and frighten these two escapees. (Remember, shooting us was no longer their option because of the impending prisoner exchange.) We didn't really know, but that's the only explanation that makes any sense to me. So they took us from the village, and we went into Manpo. They stopped and drew a large crowd of civilians. We stood with our hands tied behind us in the back of the truck, and Charlie said, "Oh, damn. Why the hell did I escape with you?" He said, "We're American fighter pilots, and we strafed this place, and we strafed the hospital, and we napalmed the schools, and all this crap," and he says, "Why the hell did I pick you to go with me?" He always made light of a tough situation—and this was shaping up to be a tough one. We always had a good banter. I was so certain of him. He was hearing what the Chinese were telling the crowd, they were out there—I saw them—paying money to the Koreans and telling them what Charlie was translating for me. I could see them talking and Charlie was translating. During the course of this, Charlie said something, and I made a remark derogatory of the Chinese. The guard got the gist of my words and hit me solidly on the base of the neck with a rifle butt, so hard it knocked me right to my knees—just pow!

It didn't do serious damage at the time. What I'm trying to say is, he didn't go further, but he really whacked me. I got back up, and they took us, with our hands still bound behind us—nothing around our necks this time—and put us beside the road. The crowd of several hundred Koreans gathered in front of us and more money and more propaganda was given by the Chinese. Then, the Chinese disappeared. Well, we had heard about this sequence of events. The idea was that the Koreans would just beat the daylights out of you—broken ribs, broken teeth, you know, they'd done this to other prisoners and we'd heard the stories. It was a roadside version of a People's Court with instant punishment. Charlie and I talked about this, and he was whispering to me all the time. The standard drill is that the Korean kids are right up front, and the little boys would pee on you. It was the routine. It happened to Jim Kiser when he was captured. They pee on you, and the crowd gets rowdy, and pretty soon, they beat you up—it's bad. The kids came up in front of us, and we smiled at them, and Charlie talked with them. He told them the Korean people were "number one" and the Chinese were "number ten." He reminded me, "Be nice to the kids, and do not look at any of the women. And be courteous to the men, and bow to anyone who has a stove pipe hat."

We did that, and nobody laid one hand on us. Nobody touched us. The kids were curious. Some of the old men returned our bows. And about thirty minutes later, the Chinese came back, and they were pretty furious. Grrr!—you could see it.

Now I have to remind you that this all happened in 1952 when the peace talks were progressing. The prisoner-exchange ratio was not favorable for the Communists. They didn't want to lose any more bodies, and they didn't want any broken-up ones either. So that's the context.

On the way back to Ping Chong-ni, where Camp 2 was located, we passed through the village where the bridge with the guard was. We saw that the village was a prison camp for South Korean POWs. When we got to our village, we went right past our compound so it was known that we had been recaptured. They took us into the Chinese area where there were Koreans watching. The chiefs came out; I suppose Ding (Colonel Ding, camp commander) was among them.

The Chinese officers told us what bad guys we were, gave us a political harangue, and told us we were headed for solitary confinement. During that process a guard slammed a rifle butt down on my foot. I thought later, a long time later, the guard that popped me on the neck with his rifle butt, and the guard that slammed my foot, were probably on guard duty the night we escaped. They were two guys that had good cause to have a grudge against us. They took us from there, and we spent thirty days in the hole. The "hole" was located under a small building and I assume it was originally a root cellar. We had to crawl through a narrow opening to get inside. There was a little slit left in the opening which we could sometimes peer through to the outside. You had to crawl through it on your belly and kind of roll into the cellar, which was maybe five feet long, four wide, and about five feet high. We were both about six feet tall, so we couldn't stand upright or stretch out to sleep.

We spent thirty days there, together in "double solitary." We both had dysentery; we just crapped all the time. It was just awful. The distinction between diarrhea and dysentery is frequency. More than ten times a day and you have dysentery.

We got fed twice a day, a little bowl of gruel or rice or something. Just enough calories to hold our weight since we were not getting any exercise. It turned out that the building we were in was occupied by the town seamstress. She had a treadle sewing machine. She would treadle away, and it was very loud and obnoxious for us—thump, thump, thump, right over-head. Charlie would interpret everything he would hear—it was our amusement. It was probably our sanity. He would say, "She just got another customer and she always apologizes as soon as they come in. She'll say, 'It's those Americans down there; they just stink. It just smells awful up here!'" And we thought: "Yeah lady, you ought to try it down here."

They let us out once or twice a day, and it was the fall season. Nearby there were some broad leaf plants. When we got out, we would gather as many leaves as we could, ten to twelve each, and we'd use one every time we had to crap. Often we had to use them twice. We kept them all piled up as they were used. Each time we were let out we took turns as to who went first. Then, the other one would hand up the pile of leaves. That was the nastiest part. We would get rid of them and har-vest some more. A nasty but very necessary chore. I had a little piece of soap that they hadn't found on me, and I put it in my boot when I slept on it at night—my pillow. The rats got it one night—right out from under my head. Oh, those were bad days

Doerty was released during the Operation Big Switch prisoner exchange on September 17, 1953. Afterward, he returned to duty with the Air Force and served a full and distinguished career, rising to the grade of colonel. Among other important assignments, he would com-mand a fighter wing.

Combat Missions in F–51D Mustang

All missions flown from Taegu (K-2) Air Base, Korea.

1950	MISSION	DURATION	POSITION	TARGET
Aug 2	1	2:15	Wingman	Close Air Support 1st Cavalry Division
Aug 3	2	1:45	Wingman	Close Air Support ROK 8th Division
Aug 4	3	2:30	Element Leader	Close Air Support ROK Capital Division
Aug 5	4	2:05	Element Leader	Close Air Support ROK 1st Division
Aug 6	5	2:45	Element Leader	Close Air Support 24th Division
Sept 23	6	2:05	Element Leader	Armed Reconnaissance Seoul

Combat Missions in F–80C Shooting Star

All missions were flown from Taegu Air Base (K–2), Korea, except for five from Tsuiki Air Base, Japan.

1951	MISSION	DURATION	POSITION	TARGET
Jan 17	1	1:45	Element Leader	Yongdok
Jan 18	2	1:55	Element Leader	Anyang-ni
Jan 19	3	1:30	Element Leader	Suwon
Jan 20	4	1:30	Element Leader	Paranjang
Jan 20	5	1:05	Flight Leader	Yonwol
Jan 21	6	1:35	Flight Leader	Wonju
Jan 22	7	1:20	Flight Leader	Kyongn-ni
Jan 22	8	1:30	Flight Leader	Kaesong
Jan 23	9	1:20	Flight Leader	Suwon
Jan 24	10	1:35	Flight Leader	Suwon
Jan 25	11	1:45	Flight Leader	Songchon
Jan 25	12	1:40	Flight Leader	Suwon
Jan 26	13	1:35	Flight Leader	Kaesong
Jan 27	14	1:50	Flight Leader	Pyongyang
Jan 28	15	1:25	Flight Leader	Suwon
Jan 29	16	2:10	Flight Leader	Anju
Jan 30	17	1:55	Flight Leader	Sunchon
Jan 30	18	1:45	Flight Leader	Pyongyang
Jan 31	19	2:15	Flight Leader	Pyongyang
Jan 31	20	1:30	Flight Leader	Pyongyang

1951	MISSION	DURATION	POSITION	TARGET
Feb 1	21	1:50	Flight Leader	Kaesong
Feb 1	22	2:00	Flight Leader	Yongyu
Feb 2	23	2:20	Flight Leader	Songchon
Feb 2	24	1:20	Flight Leader	Suwon
Feb 3	25	1:40	Flight Leader	Seoul
Feb 4	26	2:00	Flight Leader	Suchon
Feb 4	27	2:00	Flight Leader	Kunu-ri
Feb 5	28	1:40	Flight Leader	Wonju
Feb 6	29	1:20	Flight Leader	Seoul
Feb 6	30	2:05	Flight Leader	Kanggye
Feb 7	31	1:00	Flight Leader	Wonsan
Feb 7	32	1:20	Flight Leader	Ichon
Feb 8	33	2:25	Flight Leader	Yongwol
Feb 10	34	2:05	Flight Leader	Sariwon
Feb 11	35	1:35	Flight Leader	Yangdok
Feb 12	36	2:00	Flight Leader	Chongju
Feb 12	37	1:20	Flight Leader	Seoul
Feb 13	38	1:00	Flight Leader	Seoul
Feb 13	39	1:10	Flight Leader	Chip Yong-ni
Feb 15	40	2:05	Flight Leader	Chip Yong-ni
Feb 16	41	1:30	Flight Leader	Yoju
Feb 16	42	2:15	Flight Leader	Sinanju
Feb 19	43	2:15	Flight Leader	Kanggye
Mar 8	44	1:15	Flight Leader	Seoul
Mar 10	45	1:30	Flight Leader	Kumsong
Mar 10	46	1:15	Flight Leader	Hwachon
Mar 11	47	1:50	Flight Leader	Kapyong
Mar 12	48	1:30	Flight Leader	Kapyong
Mar 12	49	1:30	Flight Leader	Kapyong
Mar 13	50	2:00	Flight Leader	Wonsan
Mar 13	51	1:40	Flight Leader	Kumsong
Mar 14	52	1:15	Flight Leader	Hasinbull
Mar 14	53	1:30	Flight Leader	Kapsong
Mar 15	54	1:30	Flight Leader	Uijongbu
Mar 15	55	1:15	Flight Leader	Inje
Mar 16	56	1:15	Flight Leader	Hongchon
Mar 16	57	1:30	Flight Leader	Wasan
Mar 17	58	1:45	Flight Leader	Chunchon
Mar 18	59	1:35	Flight Leader	Kanam-ni
Mar 18	60	1:50	Flight Leader	Chinnampo
Mar 19	61	1:00:	Flight Leader	Anju
Mar 20	62	1:20	Flight Leader	Wunan

1951	MISSION	DURATION	POSITION	TARGET
Mar 21	63	2:00	Flight Leader	Yangdok
Mar 22	64	1:30	Flight Leader	Uijong-bu
Mar 23	65	1:30	Flight Leader	Sangu-ri
Mar 23	66	1:40	Flight Leader	Munsan-ni
Mar 24	67	2:00	Flight Leader	Kang-dong
Mar 26	68	1:30	Flight Leader	Chunchon
Mar 26	69	1:55	Flight Leader	Sariwon
Mar 28	70	1:40	Flight Leader	Pachon
Mar 30	71	1:20	Flight Leader	Kasin-ne
Mar 30	72	2:00	Flight Leader	Chong-ju
Apr 5	73	2:00	Flight Leader	Chong-ju
Apr 7	74	2:10	Flight Leader	Pyongyang
Apr 8	75	1:15	Flight Leader	Pyongyang
Apr 10	76	2:25	Flight Leader	Kanggye
Apr 12	77	1:50	Flight Leader	Pyongyang
Apr 15	78	1:15	Flight Leader	Sariwon
Apr 16	79	1:40	Flight Leader	Pyongyang
Apr 17	80	1:50	Flight Leader	Chinnampo
Apr 18	81	1:35	Flight Leader	Pyongyang
Apr 20	82	1:50	Flight Leader	Otan-ni
Apr 21	83	1:20	Flight Leader	Pyongyang
Apr 22	84	1:45	Flight Leader	Pyongyang
Apr 23	85	1:30	Flight Leader	Chorwon
Apr 23	86	1:25	Flight Leader	Munsan
Apr 24	87	2:15	Flight Leader	Chorwon
Apr 25	88	1:25	Flight Leader	Namsan
Apr 26	89	2:10	Flight Leader	Sonchon
Apr 29	90	1:45	Flight Leader	Uijong-bu
Apr 30	91	1:50	Flight Leader	Sunchon
May 1	92	1:50	Flight Leader	Singgye
May 2	93	1:55	Flight Leader	Sunan
May 4	94	1:00	Flight Leader	Haeju
May 6	95	2:00	Flight Leader	Inje
May 7	96	2:00	Flight Leader	Munsan
May 9	97	2:30	Group Leader	Sinuiju
May 10	98	1:45	Flight Leader	Chjunghan
May 28		:40	Squadron Leader	To Tsuiki Air Base Japan
May 29	99	2:15	Flight Leader	Chorwon
Jun 2		:40	Squadron Leader	To Tsuiki Air Base Japan
Jun 2	100	2:15	Flight Leader	Hwach'on
Jun 6		:40	Squadron Leader	To Tsuiki Air Base Japan
Jun 6	101	2:15	Flight Leader	Chorwon

1951	MISSION	DURATION	POSITION	TARGET
Jun 9		:40	Squadron Leader	To Tsuiki Air Base Japan
Jun 9	102	2:15	Flight Leader	Kaesong
Jun 12		:40	Squadron Leader	To Tsuiki Air Base Japan
Jun 13	103	2:10	Flight Leader	Suoju
Jun 17	104	1:55	Flight Leader	Kumsong
Jun 22	105	2:05	Flight Leader	Pukohang-ni
Jun 26	106	1:40	Squadron Leader	Sukchon

Sources

Appleton, Roy E. *South to the Naktong, North to the Yalu*. Washington, DC: Center of
   Military History, 1961.
Fifth Air Force Unit History, 1950 and 1951. Maxwell Air Force Base, AL: Air Force Histor-
   ical Research Agency.
49th Fighter-Bomber Group Unit History, 1951. Maxwell Air Force Base, AL: Air Force
   Historical Research Agency.
Futrell, Robert F. *The United States Air Force in Korea, 1950–1953*. Washington, DC:
   Office of the Chief of Air Force History, 1983.
Mossman, Billy C. *Ebb And Flow, November 1950–July 1951*. Washington, DC: Center of
   Military History, 1990.
9th Fighter-Bomber Squadron Unit History, 1951. Maxwell Air Force Base, AL: Air Force
   Historical Research Agency.
Ridgway, Matthew B. *The Korean War*. Garden City, NY: Doubleday & Company, 1967.

Acknowledgments

The archivists at the Air Force Historical Research Agency and Army War College Library were unfailingly helpful in uncovering much of the basic information needed to write this book. I thank them for responding to all of my requests in a timely fashion.

The dramatic artwork that adorns the book's cover and depicts the F-80 I flew on many missions is the work of my friend David J. Ails. I am most grateful to him for his splendid contribution to my book.

Early during my writing, I set out to locate the 9th Fighter-Bomber Squadron pilots with whom I flew during the Korean War. I asked what they remembered about their combat experiences, what stood out as the most interesting, the most exciting. I wanted to include those memories in my manuscript to make it more than just my story. All of them responded in helpful ways, providing detailed accounts of memorable missions they had flown and incidents they remembered, as well as commentary on a variety of related subjects. Here is a listing with their wartime ranks: 1st Lt. Walter L. "Jack" Doerty, who generously provided extensive material on his prisoner-of-war experiences; 1st Lt. Marvin E. Brantley, who provided diary entries describing two challenging missions; 1st Lt. Nervin "Bud" Evans, who responded promptly with an intensely interesting account of the first 9th Fighter-Bomber Squadron mission of the war; 1st Lt. Richard G. Immig, who furnished a vivid description of a MiG encounter as well as interesting accounts of bombing missions; 2nd Lt. Carl E. Overstreet, who sent summaries of some of his most exciting missions; Capt. Ray O. Roberts, who provided answers to a long list of questions and sent a detailed description of a MiG encounter; and 2nd Lt. Donald I. VanDerKarr, who sent a copy of his entire diary, which contained descriptions of many missions and incidents that would otherwise have been overlooked. I thank all of them for their generous support.